The Tough Kid® Book

Book

GINGER RHODE, PH.D.

WILLIAM R. JENSON, PH.D.

H. KENTON REAVIS, ED.D.

SECOND EDITION
Published in the United States by
Pacific Northwest Publishing
21 W. 6th St.
Eugene, Oregon 97401

ISBN 978-1-59909-042-9

Pacific
Northwest
Publishing

Eugene, Oregon | www.pacificnwpublish.com

Table of Contents

About the Authors

Ginger Rhode, Ph.D.

Dr. Rhode is the Deputy Superintendent for Academic Achievement in the Canyons School District in Sandy, Utah. Previous assignments in other school districts have included Director of Special Education, Director of Federal and State Programs, elementary school principal, junior high school vice principal, and teacher in elementary and secondary classrooms for severe behavior disordered/emotionally disturbed students. Dr. Rhode is an adjunct faculty member at the University of Utah in the Educational Psychology Department. She has taught numerous university classes and has published many books, journal articles, book chapters, and professional papers. Her main areas of interest and expertise include classroom and schoolwide management, social skills training, generalization and maintenance of behavior, legal issues affecting students with disabilities, and providing a rigorous academic environment for all students.

William R. Jenson, Ph.D.

Dr. William R. Jenson is a professor and past chair of the Department of Educational Psychology at the University of Utah. He received his Ph.D. in School Psychology/Applied Behavior Analysis from Utah State University in 1975. He directed the Adolescent Residential Unit in Las Vegas, Nevada, and the Children's Behavior Therapy Unit (CBTU) for Salt Lake Mental Health. CBTU is a day hospital program for severely emotionally disturbed and autistic children. Dr. Jenson's interests include behavior management for severe behavior problems, behavioral assessment, school-based interventions, parent training, applied technology, and meta-analytic research. He has authored and coauthored more than one hundred articles, chapters, and books, including *The Tough Kid Book*, *Tough Kid Tool Box*, *Tough Kid Parent Book*, *Tough Kid New Teacher Book*, *Tough Kid Principal's Briefcase*, *Understanding Childhood Behavior Disorders*, *Structured Teaching*, *Best Practices: Behavioral and Educational Strategies*, *Teaching Behaviorally Disordered Students: Preferred Practices*, *School-Based Interventions for Students with Behavior Problems*, *Functional Assessment and Intervention Program*, *Get 'Em on Task* computer program, and several others.

H. Kenton Reavis, Ed.D.

Dr. Ken Reavis, our honored colleague, was Coordinator of the Comprehensive System of Personnel Development and Specialist for Behavior Disorders and Discipline in the Services for the At Risk Section of the Utah State Office of Education. Dr. Reavis's extensive educational experience in the field as classroom teacher, university professor, and administrator was reflected in his research, writing, and presentations. Dr. Reavis's career focused on student management, discipline, school climate, noncompliance, school assistance teams, and prereferral strategies. Dr. Reavis's work continues to benefit teachers, administrators, resource personnel, and parents. Dr. Reavis passed away in 2001.

··

What This Book Will Do For You

Major reasons that teachers leave teaching are the problems they encounter with difficult students and loss of control in their classrooms. Aggression, arguing, tantrums, and poor academic progress, coupled with difficult interactions with parents, make teachers feel like failures. These problems are compounded by excessive time demands imposed by difficult students. A teacher can spend from 20 to 30% of her time trying to manage these students. This time drain leaves many teachers with a sense of powerlessness and little time to actually teach. Loss of classroom control, not enough time to instruct, and problematic students with severe classroom behaviors have a dramatic impact on teachers' job satisfaction and confidence.

This book will help teachers manage the **Tough Kid**. A Tough Kid is a student who is generally not covered in most college courses in education. It is estimated that approximately 2 to 5% of all students meet our definition of a Tough Kid. This is enough to ensure that all classrooms will have at least one or two tough students every year. Often the number is greater.

We would like to note that this book is part of the Tough Kid Series, which includes:

- *The Tough Kid Tool Box*
- *The Tough Kid Social Skills Book*
- *The Tough Kid New Teacher Book*
- *The Tough Kid Bully Blocker Book*
- *The Tough Kid Bully Blocker Shorts DVD*
- *The Tough Kid Parent Book*
- *The Tough Kid Principal's Briefcase*
- *Social Skills for the Tough Kid: Tips and Tools for Parents*

All of the books build on the basic information covered in this book and expand it specifically for parents, school principals, and new teachers. The techniques and interventions included in this book, like other books in the *Tough Kid Series*, are based on research-proven, evidence-based practices. The term *evidence-based practice* (EBP) means that the techniques or interventions have been evaluated for their effectiveness through a rigorous research process. This validation process includes using acceptable research designs and appropriate data analysis techniques to demonstrate effectiveness. The results are generally published in peer-reviewed journals and presented at national professional conferences. A list of studies and presentations that demonstrate the effectiveness of suggested Tough Kid techniques and related techniques appears on the CD included with this book.

The Tough Kid Book is intended for use by regular education teachers, special education teachers, and any educators who want effective and positively focused classrooms. The purpose of this book is to provide practical techniques for managing difficult students—techniques that can be implemented without great cost in materials, time, or money. However, nothing is free. You should view the time required to implement the suggested techniques as a wise investment. Though some initial teacher time and planning are needed, in the long run the techniques will provide educational dividends that clearly outweigh the initial investments.

In This Book

To achieve these goals, this book is divided into five basic chapters. Each chapter contains practical information about managing Tough Kids in classrooms and schools.

The first chapter is a *getting started* chapter, **What Does a Tough Kid Look Like?** This chapter defines the Tough Kid and helps you understand why behavior problems occur. It also covers the realistic assessment of difficult students and proactive ways to set up a classroom.

The second chapter, called **Unique Positive Procedures**, focuses on interventions you can use to reward students for coming to school, following classroom procedures, and performing academically. It is critical that *positive* procedures are used with Tough Kids before reductive procedures (those that stop behaviors) are used because:

- The majority of Tough Kids have a long history of punishment to which they have grown immune.
- They have a high risk for school dropout (estimated to be 65%) and will not stay in environments that are not positive.
- In the long run, lasting behavior changes are maintained only by positive procedures.

If punishment-oriented reductive techniques are the most frequently used techniques in a classroom, Tough Kids will act out even more or simply stop coming to school. This book, however, does not espouse a totally reward-based approach.

The third chapter of the book, **Practical Reductive Techniques for the Classroom**, reviews realistic techniques that you can use to stop problem behaviors. The authors recognize that some reductive techniques are needed to quickly manage such behaviors as aggression, noncompliance, arguing, and tantrums. Behavior-reducing techniques are important in stopping the "pain control" that is frequently used by Tough Kids. If these techniques are not examined, however, they are likely to be improperly or excessively used by untrained classroom staff.

The fourth chapter is titled **Advanced Systems for Tough Kids** because these techniques are more complex in nature. Techniques covered as advanced procedures include social skills training, instructional techniques, programs to improve on-task behavior, parent training information, and more. The more advanced techniques are viewed as finishing procedures that allow you to develop skills beyond the basic procedures presented in the first three sections of the book.

The fifth chapter is called **Getting Tough Kids Back to General Education Settings**. Tough Kids have great difficulty returning to the regular classroom because of their past behaviors and inability to cope with the academic and social challenges of an inclusive environment. If Tough Kids are returned to regular school settings without adequate preparation, many of them will revert to their old behavioral excesses of aggression and noncompliance. They do this to escape an inclusive environment in which they are not successful and which they find punishing. This chapter offers several approaches to the inclusion of Tough Kids into regular school settings. These approaches include:

- Teaching self-management strategies
- Encouraging development of social skills through the Tough Kid Teacher Pleaser Social Skills Program

- Addressing the classroom behavior expectations of the Tough Kid's future general education teacher
- Assessing common classroom stimuli in the regular school environment
- Using *Lucky Charms* as a generalization strategy

Each chapter contains Boxes, Figures, Pointer Boxes, and How-To Boxes. No single book can cover *all* the techniques and information teachers need. The **Pointer Boxes** are designed to point out additional resources if you are interested in pursuing a topic in more detail or want specific classroom materials. Similar to the Pointer Boxes are the **How-To Boxes**. These boxes are designed to give specific examples and step-by-step instructions for designing and implementing a particular technique (e.g., how to design a school-home note or implement a program such as "Sure I Will").

Each chapter also includes filled-out examples of Reproducibles that are available on the companion CD. Permission is given to educators who purchase the book to reproduce any form labeled "Reproducible" solely for their own use. Further reproduction of the forms is prohibited. This is similar to buying software that is licensed for use with only one computer. Each book and CD should be used for only one classroom or by one professional in his or her work.

The reproducible forms on the CD are provided in PDF format. They can be printed and filled out by hand. Where appropriate, they are also enabled so they can be filled out on your computer and saved electronically when you open them in Adobe Reader version 6 or above. See the "Using the CD" file on the CD for more detailed instructions on how to fill out forms using Adobe Reader.

The PBS Picture

It is important to conceptualize how *The Tough Kid Book* fits with the current emphasis on the Positive Behavior Supports (PBS) model in many public schools. The Tough Kid techniques and interventions fit into the PBS model in several ways. The PBS approach emphasizes a triangular model, with 80% of a school's student body fitting into the base of the triangle. These students are generally managed very well by a school's

---

POINTER BOX I-1

THE TOUGH KID TOOL BOX

Many of the examples shown in this book are taken from *The Tough Kid Tool Box*, a companion volume that features ready-to-use materials for implementing behavior management strategies with Tough Kids. This book and its accompanying CD contain reproducible tools in both English and Spanish, along with detailed directions for using them. *The Tough Kid Tool Box* provides everything you need to implement Mystery Motivators, Spinners, Lotteries/Raffles, and more. The book is available from Pacific Northwest Publishing, www.pacificnwpublish.com.

basic discipline and management procedures and pose few problems. The second, middle part of the PBS triangle represents "at-risk" students, who make up approximately 15% of a school's student body. These students have had several office discipline referrals (ODRs) for problematic behavior and are viewed as on the verge of being a serious discipline problem. The very top part of the triangle includes the 3 to 7% of the student body who have been identified as students with severe problem behaviors. These students have had multiple discipline referrals and are generally failing both academically and socially. They are the tip of the triangle, and they are the school's Tough Kids (see Figure I-1).

Many of the strategies presented in this book can be used directly with the top-of-the-triangle problem students. Like many PBS models, the Tough Kid approach emphasizes positive and preventive strategies for behavior management. An emphasis is placed on positive intervention strategies, such as Mystery Motivators, Dots for Motivation, and Reward Spinners, to reward Tough Kids and keep them motivated both academically and socially. Emphasis is placed on positive classroom and school rules that represent clear and objective behavioral expectations. In addition, many of the techniques presented in this book can be used with the 15% at-risk students to help them adjust, be successful, and

Figure I-1 • Student Intervention Needs Triangle

perform academically. The "Sure I Will" social skills intervention presented in **Chapter 3** is an excellent intervention for at-risk students. Also covered are techniques that can be used with a whole classroom—for example, the Teacher's 100 Club, a whole class positive discipline program presented in **Chapter 4**. This program has been shown to reduce classroom behavior problems and significantly reduce office disciplinary referrals.

The Tough Kid techniques and interventions also work very well with existing Positive Behavior Interventions and Supports (PBIS) programs such as those developed by the University of Oregon and several other universities and schools (Sailor, Dunlap, Sugai, & Horner, 2009). Similarly, the Tough Kid approach fits and works with well-established classroom management programs such as *Safe & Civil Schools'* CHAMPS program (Sprick, 2009) and all-school discipline programs such as the Foundations program (Sprick & Garrison, 2002). A major benefit of using the Tough Kid

approach with existing PBS and behavior management programs is that it focuses on the most difficult students in a school. These top-of-the-triangle Tough Kids are often the most difficult and challenging students for schools that follow a PBS model. When techniques from the PBS model prove ineffective, the Tough Kid approach offers a wealth of additional strategies and techniques for the toughest students.

References

Sailor, W., Dunlap, G., Sugai, G., & Horner, R. (Eds.). (2009). *Handbook of positive behavior supports*. New York, NY: Springer Publications.

Sprick, R. (2009). *CHAMPS: A positive and proactive approach to classroom management* (2nd ed.). Eugene, OR: Pacific Northwest Publishing.

Sprick, R., & Garrison, M. (2002). *Foundations: Establishing positive discipline policies*. Eugene, OR: Pacific Northwest Publishing.

A Note of Caution

Teachers should recognize that they cannot immediately implement all of the techniques presented in this book. Such a task is overwhelming. Selecting those techniques that best fit your classroom is an effective strategy. However, it is very important not to skip or halfheartedly implement the suggested positive classroom techniques. A positive classroom is the foundation for all other techniques recommended in this book. Basic classroom interventions, pointers to additional material, and how to instructions are all important. But a common understanding and definition of a Tough Kid is fundamental. If we do not have a common definition, it is difficult to come to consensus on how to manage and educate these students.

The Tough Kid® Book

CHAPTER 1

What Does a Tough Kid Look Like?

Most of us believe we can recognize tough or difficult students. To have one in your classroom is to recognize one. They can make our teaching lives miserable and single-handedly disrupt a classroom. They hurt others. They are disruptive. They do not learn easily. They are not well liked.

Tough Kids come with a plethora of labels such as behavior disordered, seriously emotionally disturbed, at risk, conduct disordered, oppositional disordered, antisocial, bipolar disordered, and attention-deficit disordered, to name a few. Though the labels may be different, these students have common traits and behaviors that are easy for us to identify. Let's look at these traits to arrive at a definition that incorporates them and also allows us to design educational procedures to help Tough Kids.

Excesses

First, Tough Kids stand out and are referred for special services because of particular excessive types of behavior. They argue with teachers. They are often defiant when given requests by adults or peers. If pressed, they commonly increase the ante and become aggressive, or tantrum and throw fits.

The central characteristic of Tough Kids is the frequency, or degree, of behavioral excesses. They frequently will not follow adult requests. Or they habitually break classroom and school rules. To some extent, average students also argue, tantrum, don't comply, and occasionally fight. But the key to this description is the word *degree*. Tough Kids have a high degree, or frequency, of these behavioral excesses (noncompliance, arguing, tantrum throwing, rule breaking, etc.). They show too much of these behaviors.

Noncompliance and Coercion

A *kingpin* is something that is central or holds something together. Tough Kids have a kingpin behavior that is central to their behavioral excesses. This kingpin or hub around which other behavioral excesses revolve is noncompliance. We define *noncompliance* as not following a direction within a reasonable amount of time. Most of a Tough Kid's arguing, tantrums, fighting,

High degree of excessive behaviors

and rule breaking is secondary to avoiding requests or required tasks. When you ask a Tough Kid to do a simple task (e.g., the assigned work), he may argue or tantrum to get you to withdraw the request. When you withdraw or reduce the request, the arguing or tantrum throwing is rewarded. This process has been called *pain control* or *coercion* because painful behavior (that is, arguing, whining, excuse making, delays, tantrums, aggression, and property destruction) is used to force a teacher to withdraw a request (Patterson, 1982; Patterson, Reid, & Dishion, 1992). This coercive process between a student and teacher is outlined in the "How To Understand Coercive Pain Control" box and is fundamental to understanding Tough Kids' problems.

When a student's compliance with an adult's requests falls below 40%, the noncompliance is excessive enough to disable a student. At this point, the student stands out in the teacher's mind as difficult and tough. Most students comply with about 80% of a teacher's requests. Tough Kids comply with 40% or fewer of a teacher's requests. A simple way to test compliance rates is to keep track of a series of everyday requests made of students in your classroom. If

you give an average of ten requests and a student responds to four or fewer of them the first time asked and within a reasonable amount of time, the student meets our definition of *tough*. This simple approach to assessing compliance is covered in more detail later in this chapter.

Behavioral Deficits

An insidious by-product of coercive behavior is that the student typically does not learn or develop like other students in the classroom. When the student uses the pain control behaviors of arguing, aggression, excuse making, and tantrum throwing to avoid compliance, basic skill development in other areas is arrested. Teachers ask students to do academic assignments to develop basic academic skills. If a Tough Kid uses coercion with her teacher, she develops an academic deficit. Similarly, students interact in give-and-take social exchanges. If a student uses coercive behaviors to always get her way with peers, social skills do not develop. If a student expects each demand to be immediately met or engages in coercive behaviors, the student develops a deficit in learning to delay gratification and abide by rules. In other words, the Tough Kid develops a deficit in self-management skills or rule-following behavior. *socially + academically*

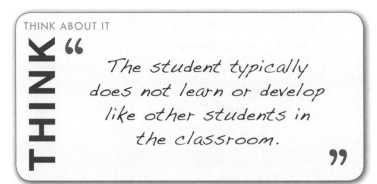

THINK ABOUT IT

THINK

"The student typically does not learn or develop like other students in the classroom."

How to . . .

UNDERSTAND COERCIVE PAIN CONTROL (OR, HOW TO MAKE IT WORSE)

Problems with compliance occur only after a request is made and the student is expected to obey. Read the steps below and follow along with the requests made in Figure 1-1. Imaging a teacher trying to get a student to do his in-seat mathematics assignment.

Step 1. The teacher asks, "Bubba, **wouldn't you like to** hurry and get this assignment finished?" Bubba ignores the question-request. If you think about it, this is not too smart of a question.

Step 2. The teacher then tries to cajole Bubba into working with: "**Come on, please**, I will help you with the first problem." Bubba now **delays** and says, "Wait just a minute. I'll finish it when I'm done drawing my picture."

Step 3. After several minutes of Bubba doing nothing but doodling, the teacher now **yells, "Now you better** do it! I'm not going to ask again." Bubba now **argues**: "You always pick on me. You have never liked me." Or he **makes an excuse**: "Can't you see I am having a tough day?"

Step 4. Bubba is still noncompliant, and the teacher is upset and ready to do something. She overdoes it and yells, "**Now you have had it!** Get to the principal's office. If you are not going to work, you can't be in my class." Bubba explodes. He **becomes aggressive and tantrums.**

Step 5. The teacher is so upset that she feels it is not worth pushing Bubba. She thinks, "He is too tough. I don't care if he doesn't learn." The teacher withdraws her request by simply walking away and doing nothing. When this happens:

- Bubba is reinforced for all his disruptive behavior (ignoring, delaying, arguing, and throwing a tantrum).

- Bubba stops throwing his tantrum, and so the teacher is reinforced for withdrawing her request.

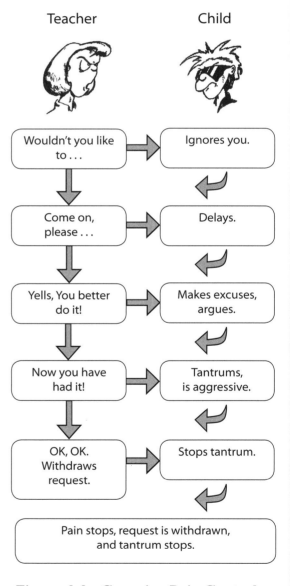

Figure 1-1 • Coercive Pain Control

* *Both student and teacher are reinforced!*

THINK ABOUT IT

THINK

"
Most of the real work comes in identifying and remediating the behavioral deficits.

"

It is easy to identify students' behavioral excesses. These are the behaviors that commonly get Tough Kids referred for special services. However, most of the real work comes in identifying and remediating the behavioral deficits of these students. The longer a student successfully engages in coercive pain control to avoid requests, the more profound her behavioral deficits will be. Even if coercion is eventually stopped, few students can be successful in school with significant deficits in basic academics, social skills, and self-management.

Academic Deficits

Among the best predictors of long-term adjustment for Tough Kids are basic academic skills, particularly reading. If students have not learned to read, they are not likely to be successfully employed in our technology-oriented society. Reading is a critical skill. If they cannot find work because they have difficulty reading, many students will fall back on old excessive behavioral strategies. They are more likely to be arrested as adolescents and adults for assault or theft (Walker, Ramsey, & Gresham, 2004). They frequently lash out, argue with and manipulate others, and refuse to do what is requested in their jobs. The basic academic skills of reading, mathematics, writing, and spelling are essential, and coercion cannot be allowed to stop their development. **Chapter 4, Advanced Systems for Tough Kids**, presents a number of strategies and curricula in the context of a Response to Intervention (RTI) model that can be used successfully with Tough Kids. An effective RTI model provides the supports they require to learn. Because academic deficits are so common in Tough Kids, they must be a central focus of any plan to improve Tough Kid behavior in the long term.

Basic on-task behavior and increased academic engagement time are also critical to the development of academic skills (Rathvon, 2008). Academic learning time will be covered in more detail in the Assessment section of this chapter. However, many coercive Tough Kids are frequently off task. These students simply do not pay attention to the teacher during lectures or to their written work. They frequently talk to other students, daydream, doodle, make noises, and play with objects.

Average students in a classroom are on task approximately 85% of the time. During this time, they actively attend to the teacher and to their assigned work. The Tough Kid's average on-task behavior is only about 50% or less during teacher-directed instruction and in-seat work activities. This 35% or more difference between Tough Kids and their peers in time spent on-task has a dramatic impact on academic skill development. When Tough Kids remain off task, they fall further and further behind other students. Their on-task rate must be increased to at least an 85% level. Several techniques and commercial programs for improving on-task behaviors are recommended in **Chapter 4**.

Social Skills

Primary social skills are defined simply as the basic skills needed to successfully interact with adults and peers. These skills include foundation skills such as:

- Starting a conversation
- Entering games
- Cooperating
- Giving appropriate positive feedback to others
- Grooming

Intermediate to advanced socials skills build on the foundation skills and include the more complicated skills of:

- Asserting oneself appropriately
- Accepting negative feedback
- Learning to say "No" appropriately
- Resisting peer pressure
- Dealing with teasing
- Managing anger

All students must have and use appropriate social skills if they are to be successful in *any* situation and setting. However, if they have not developed these skills naturally over time, the skills must be specifically and directly taught just like any other basic skill, including academics.

Tough Kids who use coercive pain control to manage peers generally have not developed the basic foundation and intermediate social skills they need. They are often described as bullies, socially immature, pushy, uncooperative, or needing to always be in control. Tough Kids frequently go through a series of friendships that do not last. Rapid turnover in friends occurs because other students do not like their dominating and unpleasant interactions.

When pain control coercion retards social skills development, Tough Kids often choose younger friends or interact with other students who have similar behavior problems. Tough Kids pick these friends because they are easily dominated and their social skills are on a par with them.

Tough Kids' social skills generally *do not* develop appropriately on their own. Even if their behavioral excesses and coercion are stopped, there is still a deficit in their basic social skills. If they are not taught appropriate social skills to take the place of their dysfunctional ones, they will revert back to their old coercive strategies when they interact with peers.

We would like to note here that pull-out group social skills training *alone* does not work with Tough Kids. The pull-out approach, without a specific generalization component, simply places Tough Kids in a group with other Tough Kids to teach them a social skills curriculum. In social skills groups, Tough Kids learn to model the skills, role-play the skills, and verbalize occasions when the skills are needed. If the pull-out group is the extent of the training, however, they do not use the skills when they are outside the group. In the absence of a specific and systematic generalization component, Tough Kids will not use their newly learned social skills when needed (Jenson, Clark, & Burrow-Sanchez, 2009).

Has to be more than 1 pullout group

Tough Kids need social skills training with a generalization component throughout the day, with error correction procedures and incentives for using the skills, not just pull-out group training. Several evidence-based social skills programs are listed in **Chapter 4,** along with guidelines for teaching the skills. In addition, social skills assessment is covered later in this chapter.

Rule Following, Impulsivity, and Self-Management

The final characteristic of Tough Kids is lack of rule following and self-management skills. Most teachers and parents would like Tough Kids to internalize a set of values and behave on their own like other students do. A common complaint by teachers is, "Why can't he behave like other students?"

The problem is that Tough Kids do not internalize commonly accepted values. They operate on immediate gratification. Guilt questions that involve values, such as "What would your parents think?" or "Can't you see how that hurts others?" or "Imagine how that makes him feel," simply do not work. We can wait forever for the magical inculcation of appropriate values from family, teachers, peers, and community, but for Tough Kids it simply will not happen.

THINK ABOUT IT

THINK

"

Tough Kids operate on immediate gratification.

"

Expecting Tough Kids to internalize values is a common mistake in their education. It is too easy to blame students or their families for this failure to internalize values. To do so helps nothing and only makes things worse. A more functional concept is to recognize that coercive pain control leads to demands for immediate gratification. This is why Tough Kids are frequently described as impulsive, demanding, uncooperative, and attention getting. When the coercive process is allowed to take place, the basic skills of learning to wait for gratification and abiding by rules are stunted. This may actually be less a problem of internalization of values and more a problem of not learning basic self-management skills.

Compounding the problem of impulsivity for most Tough Kids is the fact that their behavior is *contingency governed* as opposed to *rule governed*. What we mean by this is the next thing that catches Tough Kids' attention will impulsively

govern or control their behavior. This is especially the case when Tough Kids are unsupervised or in transition situations. Most other students use internalized rules to govern their behaviors during unsupervised times. For Tough Kids, whatever jumps out and catches their attention impulsively controls what they do.

Impulsive behaviors !

Self-management skills are skills learned in order to put off immediate gratification for a long-term benefit. In other words, students learn to practically manage their immediate wants and impulses for a later benefit. Rules (from society, schools, classrooms, and families) are often shorthand guides for self-managing behavior. If a rule is broken, there is a consequence. When guidelines or rules become habits, we often refer to them as internalized. That is, the student is rule governed. The basic steps for the development of

self-management or rule-governed behavior are (Skinner, 1953):

Step 1. Learning to comply with requests
Step 2. Learning self-control
Step 3. Learning problem-solving skills

With Tough Kids, consistent and immediate consequences for either following or breaking rules are essential. When teachers are consistent in applying consequences to rules, students learn consistency as a habit. When teachers are inconsistent, students learn inconsistency as a habit and will continue with coercion. Advanced self-management skills are taught in some social skills training programs. The programs that do so are reviewed in **Chapter 4**.

....

Tough Kid Defined

Our overall definition of a Tough Kid is a student who has behavioral excesses and deficits. The excesses that make the student stand out include noncompliance, arguing, making excuses, throwing tantrums, and aggression. The equally important but often overlooked deficits include deficiencies in basic academic, social, rule-following, and self-management skills (see Box 1-1 on the next page).

Not all students fit this model definition of a Tough Kid exactly. Some Tough Kids may be socially skilled or have academic ability; however, they are exceptions to the general rule. Most Tough Kids will display one or more of these characteristics. Thus, when working with Tough Kids, it becomes important to know how to conduct practical assessments of excesses and deficits.

BOX 1-1

Practical Definition of a *Tough Kid*

BEHAVIORAL EXCESSES:
TOO MUCH
OF A BEHAVIOR

NONCOMPLIANCE
- Does not do what is requested
- Breaks rules
- Argues
- Makes excuses
- Delays
- Does the opposite of what is asked

AGGRESSION
- Tantrums
- Fights
- Destroys property
- Vandalizes
- Sets fires
- Teases
- Verbally abuses
- Is revengeful
- Is cruel to others

BEHAVIORAL DEFICITS:
INABILITY TO ADEQUATELY
PERFORM A BEHAVIOR

SELF-MANAGEMENT SKILLS
- Cannot delay rewards
- Acts before thinking—impulsive
- Shows little remorse or guilt
- Will not follow rules
- Cannot foresee consequences

SOCIAL SKILLS
- Has few friends
- Goes through friends fast
- Noncooperative—bossy
- Does not know how to reward others
- Lacks in showing affection
- Has few problem-solving skills
- Constantly seeks attention

ACADEMIC SKILLS
- Generally behind in academics, particularly reading
- Off-task
- Fails to finish work
- Truant or frequently tardy
- Forgets acquired information

PRACTICAL ASSESSMENT OF TOUGH KIDS

A teacher might ask why assessment is necessary for Tough Kids. To have one in your class is to know one. However, assessment is important for the following reasons:

- To accurately identify a Tough Kid, particularly if requests or referrals for additional help are made
- To determine the specific problem behavior or behaviors that require change
- To understand the *function* of the behavior, or the *purpose* the behavior serves for the student

- To use a standard measurement approach to determine whether progress has been made after a behavior change plan has been initiated

Assessment is merely structured information gathering. The information gathered is generally worthless unless it can be used to design and/or adapt an intervention to help the student. However, there can be problems even with assessment techniques that are designed for program interventions. No assessment method is perfect—all assessment procedures have error associated with them. To reduce error and improve decisions, it is important to use multiple assessment measures and assessment techniques that are standardized.

Using multiple measures simply means two or more assessment methods or raters (assessors) are used to measure the problem behavior in question. When you use multiple valid measures, the errors in each tend to cancel out and so a much more accurate result is obtained. It is good practice to use a variety of assessment measures, such as behavior checklists, functional behavior assessments, social skills checklists, curriculum probes, and in-class observations for difficult students. It is also wise to use more than one rater. For example, two teachers are better than one. Or parents can be used as raters, or even the students themselves.

Standardization usually means that the measure is administered and scored in a consistent way to ensure good reliability and validity. *Reliability* is a direct measure of consistency. If the measure is given twice to the same student, we should get similar results (test-retest reliability). Similarly, when two different people use the measure on the same student, the results should be similar

> THINK ABOUT IT
>
> **THINK**
>
> " What one teacher thinks is exceptional or aberrant may seem average to another. "

(inter-rater reliability). Reliability measures how consistent an assessment result will be either across time or across raters.

Validity is an indicator of the accuracy of a measure or test. A valid assessment method truly measures what it purports to measure. If a behavioral checklist claims to identify attention deficit hyperactivity disordered (ADHD) students but systematically omits several ADHD students, it has poor validity. Teachers should be conscientious consumers and ask about the reliability and validity of assessment measures they give. Reliability of .80 or greater is generally considered good for most assessment methods. Good assessment measures also describe validity studies in their instruction manuals. Ask to see them.

Standardization also allows the determination of whether a student is truly disabled and different from his average peers. This is important because what one teacher thinks is exceptional or aberrant may seem average to another. Most good assessment measures are based on standardization groups of hundreds of students. When the measures were first developed, average scores, or *means*, for typical nondisabled students were established. These scores were determined for cognitive abilities, classroom behaviors, social skills, and academic abilities. They can be especially useful when identifying and working with Tough Kids. For example, we know the scores are distributed on a normal bell-shaped curve, with the mean score located right in the middle of the curve (where the "X" is on the curve, as shown in Figure 1-2 below).

Standard deviation is a measure of variability that can help define deviant or abnormal scores. A score two standard deviations higher than the mean score is a very different score and helps define Tough Kids. It signifies that only 2% of students in the original standardization group had scores this high and different. Picture a group of 100 students lined up against a wall (Figure 1-2). Each student represents an increasingly different score from the first student in line. Only the last two students in the line of 100 students would have scores different enough to be two standard deviations above the mean score (or above the 98th percentile).

The two-standard-deviation method gives us an objective way to determine whether a student is truly tough. If several teachers or aides (multiple measure raters) fill out behavior checklists on a student and the scores fall two standard deviations from the mean, that student meets our definition of tough. Two common ways for behavior checklists and other tests to express this standard deviation difference are T and Z standard scores. The mean T score is always 50, and a score that is two standard deviations from the mean is always 70 or higher. A mean Z score is always zero (0), and a score of 2 is two standard deviations from the mean. For example, an Aggression score of T-70 or above on the *Child Behavior Checklist* (Achenbach & Rescorla, 2001) puts a student two standard deviations from the mean, or above the 98th percentile—a truly tough student.

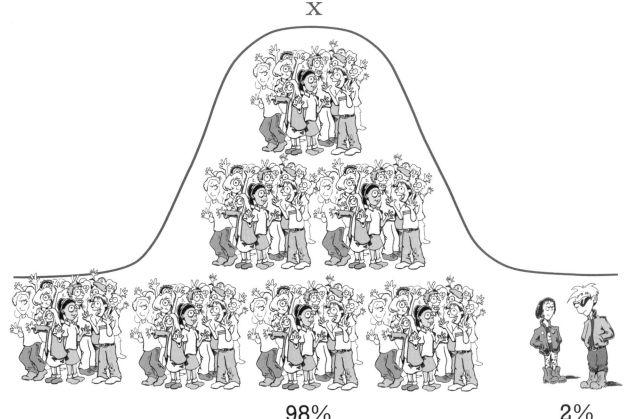

X

98%   2%

Figure 1-2 • Normal Curve With Tough Kids

Checklists

Basic standardized checklists can be very useful in identifying Tough Kids and their problem behavior. Checklists are generally easy to use, standardized, and economical. They have good reliability and validity. Problem behavior checklists frequently list behaviors with definitions. Teachers are asked to rate each behavior along a scale with ratings such as very true, sometimes true, or not true. See the example in Figure 1-3 below from the *Child Behavior Checklist*.

Checklists do not require actual observation of the student—you are asked to recall the behavior and make a judgment as to its severity. Good behavior checklists are standardized and

allow the two-standard-deviation comparisons described earlier.

In addition, some behavior checklists come with a variety of parallel forms that allow several raters to fill out the checklists (multiple measures). For example, the *Child Behavior Checklist* (Achenbach & Rescorla, 2001) has parallel forms for the teacher, parent, and even the student. A source list of standardized checklists appears in Pointer Box 1-1 on the next page.

Social skills checklists are similar to problem behavior checklists. They identify social skills deficits rather than problem behaviors. These checklists are rated on similar dimensions (see

	Very True	Sometimes True	Not True
3. Argues a lot	2	1	0

Figure 1-3 • Example of Behavior Checklist Item

POINTER BOX 1-1

SOURCES FOR STANDARDIZED PROBLEM BEHAVIOR CHECKLISTS

Behavior Assessment System for Children (2nd ed., 2004)
by C. R. Reynolds and R. W. Kamphaus
Pearson: www.pearsonassessments.com

Behavioral and Emotional Rating Scale (2nd ed., 2004)
by M. H. Epstein
PRO-ED: www.proedinc.com

Manual for ASEBA School-Age Forms & Profiles (2001)
by T. M. Achenbach and L. A. Rescorla
University of Vermont, Research Center for Children, Youth & Families: www.aseba.org/

the example in Figure 1-4 from the *Social Skills Rating System*, Gresham & Elliot, 1990) and allow standard deviation comparisons to determine whether a problem genuinely exists.

Some social skills checklists provide multiple parallel forms for the teacher, parent, and student. Pointer Box 1-2 lists some good social skills checklists.

Both behavior and social skills checklists help teachers pinpoint behavioral excesses and deficits in Tough Kids. They can also indicate the severity of a problem if the standard deviation method of comparison is used. However, they do not give a direct practical measure of problem behaviors or why they occur. To get this information, we need to use functional behavior assessments, compliance probes, and direct classroom observations.

Functional Behavior Assessment: The Purpose and Why of Behavior

Standardized behavior and social skills checklists are good at identifying problem behaviors, but they do not tell the purpose of behaviors. Functional behavior assessment (FBA) gives an insight into why a behavior occurs. The off-task

5. Politely refuses unreasonable requests from others—rate as:	*HOW OFTEN*			*HOW IMPORTANT*		
	Never	Sometimes	Very Often	Not Important	Important	Critical
	1	2	3	1	2	3

Figure 1-4 • Example of Social Skills Checklist Item

POINTER BOX 1-2

SOURCES FOR SOCIAL SKILLS CHECKLISTS

School Social Behavior Scale (1993)
by K. W. Merrell
Pro-Ed: www.proedinc.com

Social Skills Rating System (1990)
by F. M. Gresham and S. N. Elliot
Pearson: www.pearsonassessments.com

The Walker-McConnell Scale Of Social Competence And School Adjustment (1995)
Elementary and Secondary versions
by H. M. Walker and S. R. McConnell
Thompson Learning: www.thomson learning.com

behavior of two students in the classroom may look exactly the same, but the reasons they occur may be completely different. For example, one student may go off task because peers in the classroom distract him. The second student may be off task because the work is too complex and beyond his ability. The behaviors look the same but occur for different reasons. Different reasons for the off-task behaviors call for selecting different interventions to remediate them. Functional behavior assessment gives insight into why a behavior occurs and allows the design of a more effective intervention that takes this "why" into account.

Teachers should also realize that functional behavior assessments are not always optional. Under certain circumstances, federal law requires them for Tough Kids who are also in special education and have an Individual Education Plan (IEP). However, using a functional behavior assessment in designing interventions and understanding problem behaviors is good practice for all Tough Kids.

Functional behavior assessments follow a specific ABC model. In this model, the "B" stands for the problematic behavior (noncompliance, arguing,

aggression, etc.), the "A" stands for the behavior's antecedents, and the "C" stands for any consequences following the behavior that may motivate it. Antecedents can be any stimulus that "sets the occasion" or comes just before the behavior. They are like little signs that you see while traveling down a road—they indicate or warn that the problem behavior is about to occur. They can include anything that seems to trigger a behavior, such as specific people, places, times, and activities. Antecedents are important because sometimes we can change the antecedents and see the behavior improve. This is especially true for noncompliance, the "kingpin" behavior for Tough Kids. Altering the antecedents that come just before noncompliance can help reduce it. This will be covered in detail in **Chapter 3**.

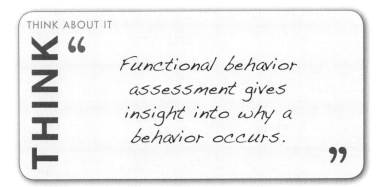

THINK ABOUT IT

THINK

"
Functional behavior assessment gives insight into why a behavior occurs.
"

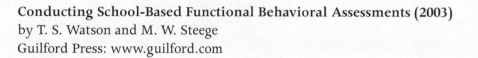

POINTER BOX 1-3

PUBLISHED FUNCTIONAL BEHAVIOR ASSESSMENT SYSTEMS

Conducting School-Based Functional Behavioral Assessments (2003)
by T. S. Watson and M. W. Steege
Guilford Press: www.guilford.com

**Functional Assessment and Intervention Program (FAIP)—A Computerized
    Functional Behavior Assessment System (1999)**
by W. R. Jenson, B. Althouse, D. Morgan, and M. Likins
Sopris West: www.soprislearning.com

**Functional Assessment and Program Development for Problem Behavior: A Practical
    Handbook (2nd ed., 1997)**
by R. E. O'Neil, R. H. Horner, R. W. Albin, J. R. Sprague, K. Storey, and J. S. Newton
Brooks/Cole: www.cengage.com/brookscole

**Functional Behavior Assessment: A Step-By-Step Guide to Solving Academic and
    Behavior Problems (2000)**
by J. C. Witt, E. M. Daly, and G. Noell
Sopris West: www.soprislearning.com

The "C," or consequences, in the ABC functional assessment model are generally one of three types of motivators. The first type of consequence is a *positively reinforcing stimulus*, which is defined as any stimulus that increases or maintains a behavior. It is important to recognize that any stimulus can be a positive reinforcer. For example, if a teacher yells at a Tough Kid and the problem behavior increases, by definition yelling is a positive reinforcer for the Tough Kid. Likewise, the same stimulus may be a positive reinforcer for one student (the behavior increases) and have no effect on a second student (behavior stays the same).

The second type of consequence is a *punisher*. A punishing stimulus is any stimulus that causes a decrease in a behavior. If the behavior goes down after the stimulus is applied, it is a punisher by definition. If a Tough Kid stops or decreases a behavior after a teacher yells at him, for example, yelling is a punisher.

The third type of consequence is a *negative reinforcer*. It is the most difficult to understand but also the most important to understand. Negative reinforcement motivates a lot of misbehavior for Tough Kids—for example, in the coercive pain control cycle diagrammed in Figure 1-1. Negative reinforcement is defined as any stimulus that increases or maintains a behavior to escape or avoid that stimulus. Negative reinforcers work by ending an unpleasant stimulus. Back to our yelling teacher example. If the teacher yells at a Tough Kid and he increases his misbehavior so aversively that the teacher stops her yelling (escape), the misbehavior is negatively reinforced. Both positive and negative reinforcement increase or maintain a behavior. However, for positive reinforcement, the purpose of the behavior is to gain access to the stimulus. For negative reinforcement, it is to escape or avoid the stimulus. People often confuse punishment and negative reinforcement. It is assumed that the word *negative* implies punishment. Not so. With negative reinforcement the behavior goes up, and with punishment the behavior goes down.

There are several ways to collect information and do a functional behavior assessment. These include interviews, reviews of the student's files and records, observations, and formal published systems. Pointer Box 1-3 lists several good published functional behavior assessment programs. When deciding to do a functional behavior assessment, you must balance efficiency and the time it takes to do one (some require more than 12 hours) with the need to obtain results that give an understanding of the purpose of the behavior and lead to an effective intervention. For teachers who are pressed for time, using ABC functional behavior assessment tracking sheets is an effective and realistic approach for designing an intervention for a Tough Kid. If a more thorough functional behavior assessment is needed, select a program from Pointer Box 1-3.

Reproducible 1-1, the ABC Functional Behavior Assessment Tracking Sheet, is provided on the CD. Print out about 10 copies and have them ready for use. When the Tough Kid engages in the inappropriate behavior of interest, such as temper tantruming, the teacher quickly fills out a tracking sheet, noting any antecedents that occur and the outcomes or consequences that follow the behavior.

Reproducible 1-1 • ABC Functional Behavior Assessment Tracking Sheet

For example, the Tough Kid tantrums during recess when the classroom aide tells him to go into class. "Recess" and "aide" are antecedents. As a result of the tantrum, the aide withdraws the command, and the Tough Kid runs back onto the playground for an additional 10 minutes of play time. Each time the Tough Kid has a tantrum, the teacher fills out an ABC FBA Tracking Sheet. When approximately 10 have been filled out, she spreads them on her desk and looks for commonalities. It becomes obvious from the tracking sheets that the Tough Kid frequently disobeys the aide, especially during recess (antecedents). As a result, the aide grows frustrated and withdraws his command (negative reinforcement), allowing the Tough Kid extra time on the playground (positive reinforcement). In this situation, the interventions are clear. The aide has to be taught how to give effective commands and follow through with consequences, and the Tough Kid cannot be allowed to gain extra time on the playground by tantruming and being noncompliant.

ABC FBA Tracking Sheets are especially useful for understanding complex behaviors. Filling out multiple tracking sheets, spreading them out on a table, and looking for common antecedents and consequences is like putting together a behavior jigsaw puzzle. You might even want to create a chart or spreadsheet to track and analyze the data you collect using the ABC Functional Behavior Assessment Tracking Sheet.

SETTING EVENTS AND REPLACEMENT BEHAVIORS

Sometimes a Tough Kid's home life or experiences outside of school also influence his behavior. Family conflicts, not getting to bed at a reasonable time, or being teased while walking to school may affect a Tough Kid's behavior in the classroom. These are setting events. An event in one environment sets up or influences a behavior in another environment. There is a space on the ABC FBA Tracking Sheet for tracking setting events.

If the student engages in a problem behavior and it's difficult to discern obvious antecedents or consequences, it is good practice to talk with the Tough Kid and observe his appearance or state.

If he cannot stay on task in the morning and looks tired and worn out, he may not be getting enough sleep. If he is frustrated the moment he walks into the classroom, this may be a carryover from an outside event such as a family conflict, having a fight on the way to school, or being teased on the bus.

The ABC FBA Tracking Sheet also includes a line for listing potential replacement behaviors. If a problem behavior occurs for a purpose that leads to a goal or consequence, it may make sense to teach an appropriate replacement behavior that leads to the same goal. In a sense, teaching an appropriate replacement behavior displaces or interferes with the problem behavior. A good example of an appropriate replacement behavior for noncompliance in a Tough Kid is the "Sure I Will" program presented in **Chapter 4**. Teaching Tough Kids replacement behaviors is good practice, but it may not be possible in every circumstance.

FUNCTIONAL BEHAVIOR ANALYSIS—A SPECIAL CASE

Functional behavior analysis is a special case of the more general functional behavior assessment. With functional behavior analysis, instead of interviewing and collecting information with an ABC model or filling out an ABC Functional Behavior Assessment Tracking Sheet, the Tough Kid is actually probed with an antecedent or consequence to see if the behavior follows. A functional behavior analysis is like a little experiment in which probes are actively used and the results are observed.

The Teacher Compliance Probe (Reproducible 1-2) is a good example of using a teacher's common classroom commands to probe Tough Kids and assess noncompliance. A blank version of Reproducible 1-2 appears on the CD that accompanies this book.

Teacher Compliance Probes

Compliance is simply defined as starting a requested behavior within a reasonably short period of time. Most students will respond to a request from a teacher within ten seconds. However, Tough Kids delay, make excuses, and argue when given a request. They comply only about 40% or less of the time with teacher requests, while the average student complies 80% of the time.

A simple way to probe and measure compliance is to systematically give a student a series (approximately ten requests) of common classroom tasks or behaviors over a week's period of time.

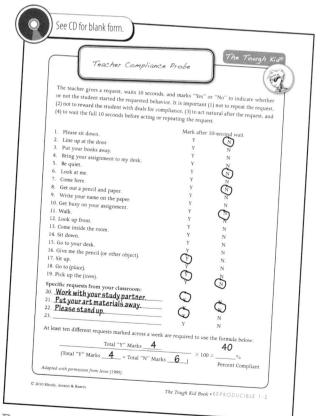

Reproducible 1-2 • Teacher Compliance Probe

The Teacher Compliance Probe (Reproducible 1-2) lists some common classroom requests. To conduct a probe, select requests and ask the student to do them. After each request, wait ten seconds for compliance. It is important not to interact with the student or repeat the request during this 10-second interval. Similarly, it is important to act naturally when giving the request and not offer rewards for compliance or scolding and lectures for noncompliance. Mark down on the sheet whether the student complies or does not comply with the request.

Give at least 10 (and as many as 20) requests during the week and keep track of them on the request sheet. At the end of the week, calculate the percentage of requests with which the student complied. If the percentage is 40% or less, the student meets our definition of a Tough Kid. Some students may be above 40% but well below the 80% for average students. These are generally easier students who should respond faster to the suggested procedures in this book.

Behavioral Observations as Part of an FBA

Behavioral observation of a student is possibly one of the most accurate and valid of all the suggested assessment measures and adds a great deal of information to a functional behavior assessment. In effect, behavioral observation collects a sample of the problem behavior in the setting in which it occurs. It requires no recall from memory or judgment as to severity. If the behavior occurs, it is simply recorded. However, difficulties with a behavioral observation occur when observation systems are complicated and time consuming. In addition, few classroom observation systems have been standardized on groups of children to allow normative comparisons between students, such as the two-standard-deviation method comparison described previously.

One simple behavioral observation approach that does allow normative comparisons is the *response discrepancy observation method*. The system is called response discrepancy because it allows a behavior discrepancy (difference) comparison between a target student (suspected Tough Kid) and classroom peers. We suggest a teacher use Reproducible 1-3, the Behavior Observation Form. A blank version is provided on the CD.

This observation form is used to record the on- and off-task behavior of a referred target student. The observer should be familiar with the on-task and off-task behavior codes listed at the bottom of the form. The basic class activity for a particular observation should be checked (e.g., teacher-directed whole class, teacher-directed small group, independent seatwork), and any additional information should be filled in on the form.

Actual observations are based on 10-second intervals. Each box in the center of the form represents 10 seconds. Ninety of these intervals are included in the 15-minute observation period on which this form is based. The top interval box is for the referred target student, and the bottom interval box is for a randomly selected same-sex peer. For each 10-second interval, the target student and a peer are both observed. If the target student is on task for the entire 10-second interval, an on-task code (i.e., a dot) is recorded. However, if the target student is off task, the appropriate off-task code is recorded in the interval box. Only one off-task behavior is recorded for

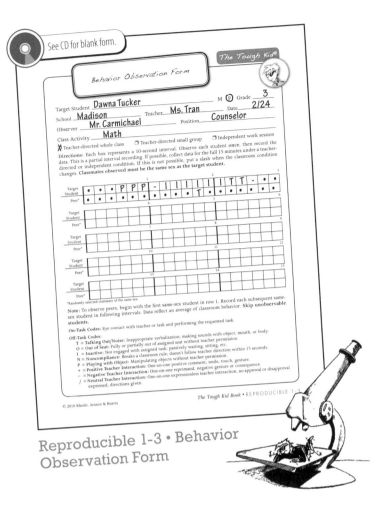

Reproducible 1-3 • Behavior Observation Form

each 10-second box. If more off-task behaviors occur, they are ignored until the next 10-second interval. The same recording process occurs for another same-sex peer during the same 10-second interval for each box.

At the end of a 15-minute observation sample, you have collected a record of on- and off-task behavior for the referred target student. You can easily calculate the actual on-task percentage for the 15-minute observation sample using the following equation: divide the number of on-task intervals by the total number of on- and off-task intervals, then multiply by one hundred. This equals the actual on-task percentage. In addition, a *micro-norm,* or sample, for on- and off-task behavior by same-sex peers in the classroom has been simultaneously collected and can be similarly calculated. This allows a comparison between the suspected Tough Kid and his or her peers. If the target student is on task 60% or less of the time and the on-task average for the student's peers is 85% or more of the time, you know you have a distractible student. However, if both the suspected Tough Kid percentage and the peer average for on-task behavior are below 60%, the problem may be a more general classroom management problem.

For functional behavior assessments, on-task behavior is a good index for other classroom problem behaviors that occur at a much lower frequency. Aggression, temper tantrums, and fighting are high-profile behaviors that Tough Kids may engage in infrequently. But when they do occur, they have a high impact on the classroom and school. Off-task behavior occurs much more frequently and is linked or correlated with these low-frequency, high-impact behaviors. If the Tough Kid is frequently off task, these high-profile behaviors are also likely to occur sooner or later.

ASSESSING WHOLE SCHOOLS

Just as you assess Tough Kids, whole schools can be assessed to identify the most problematic students. Whole-school assessment also pinpoints the most frequently occurring problem behaviors as well as where they are occurring. The whole-school assessment systems we recommend

(see Pointer Box 1-4) consist of computerized databases that generate detailed reports. For example, when a significant discipline problem occurs, the student's name, the specific behavior, and where it occurred are entered into the computer program's database. Over time, the database grows until a complete picture of a school's discipline problems is developed. The students with the most problematic behaviors are identified. Effective interventions for them and for the school as a whole can be developed and implemented based on these data. These types of data systems are essential for whole-school Positive Behavior Supports (PBS) systems.

Academic Assessment

Most teachers are familiar with standard academic achievement tests such as the Stanford Achievement Test and the Peabody Individual Achievement Test–Revised. These are good tests for obtaining a global academic measure of how well a student is performing by grade level or by chronological age at a particular time such as the end of a school year. Such assessment is referred to as *summative*. However, tests such as those mentioned above are not meant for indicating general basic skill success or for measuring improvements in basic skills on an ongoing, or *formative*, basis over time.

POINTER BOX 1-4

WHOLE-SCHOOL ASSESSMENT SYSTEMS

Two good examples of these whole-school computerized assessment systems are the Schoolwide Information System (SWIS) developed at the University of Oregon (www.swis.org) and Discipline Tracker (www.manskersoftware.com).

POINTER BOX 1-5

WHERE TO FIND GOOD CBM SYSTEMS

AIMSweb provides standard CBM measurement for early literacy, reading, writing, spelling, and math for grades K-8. Free probes are available online, and a comprehensive data management system may be purchased.

> Pearson
> www.aimsweb.com

Dynamic Indicators of Basic Early Literacy Skills (DIBELS) is another standard CBM system for assessing reading and early literacy. DIBELS also offers probes at no cost, with a data management system available for a reasonable fee.

> Dynamic Indicators of Basic Early Literacy Skills
> Institute for the Development of Educational Achievement
> https://dibels.uoregon.edu/

Free curriculum-based probes for reading, mathematics, and spelling are available online at www.interventioncentral.org.

CURRICULUM-BASED MEASUREMENT

Curriculum-based measurement (CBM) was originally designed to assess student growth and progress in actual classroom curricula. Many teachers developed their own CBM probes based on their own curricula and used the information they gained to examine student rates of progress. They then used this information to make changes in their instruction.

When teachers used their own curricula in this way, the positive effects of the testing were offset by a lack of standard information about student progress. Differences among schools, teachers, changing curricula, and the like made accurate decisions about student progress very difficult. For many teachers, creating their own assess-ments was time consuming, and assessment practices varied.

Over time, research indicated that it was not necessary to have a perfect match between students' specific curricula and what was assessed with CBM. The same information about students' reading skill levels and progress could be obtained accurately by using standard test materials such as those listed in Pointer Box 1-5. Appropriate standards of development and growth across varied schools, school districts, and teachers could also be accurately determined using standardized measures.

In summary, this body of research concluded that achievement could be improved by assessing students *using standard, valid*

Pointer Box 1-6

RESOURCES FOR CURRICULUM-BASED MEASUREMENT

BOOKS

Advanced Applications of Curriculum-Based Measurement (1998)
by M. R. Shinn
Guilford Press: www.guilford.com

Using Curriculum-Based Measurement in a Problem Solving Model (2002)
by M. R. Shinn, S. L. Deno, and L. S. Fuchs
Guilford Press: www.guilford.com

BOOK CHAPTERS

"Best Practices in Evaluating Psychoeducational Services Based on Student Outcome Data"
by K. A. Gibbons and M. M. Shinn
"Best Practices in Curriculum-based Measurement"
by M. R. Shinn
in **Best Practices in School Psychology IV (2001)**, A. Thomas and J. Grimes (Eds.)
NASP: www.nasponline.org

"Using Curriculum-Based Measurement in General Education Classrooms to Promote
    Reading Success"
by M. R. Shinn, M. M. Shinn, C. Hamilton, and B. Clark
in **Interventions for Achievement and Behavior Problems II: Preventive and Remedial
    Approaches (2002)**, M. R. Shinn, H. M. Walker, and G. Stoner (Eds.)
NASP: www.nasponline.org

assessments that measured something important over time on tasks of about equal difficulty tied to general curriculum. The value of this assessment model is that it informs the instructional process on an ongoing basis by identifying at-risk students early, both those who are not making adequate progress and those who are learning (Shinn, Hamilton, & Clark, 2002). See Pointer Box 1-6 for resources that provide additional information about CBM.

Target Behaviors

Assessment information is valuable in identifying and determining the severity of problem behaviors in Tough Kids. However, the most important function of assessment information is to select and define behaviors that require intervention. Too often, assessment information that has been gathered is ignored when behaviors are selected for change. The most severe behavior excesses and deficits identified from behavior checklists, observations, and probes should become priority target behaviors for change.

A good target behavior is one that is:

- **Observable**. The behavior can actually be seen. It is not something that is underlying and *assumed* to be occurring.
- **Measurable**. The behavior can actually be measured (it leaves a permanent product, like solutions to a math problem) or rated on a behavior checklist or similar tool.
- **Well defined.** The behavior is defined objectively and simply so two or more people can agree when the behavior occurs.

Poor target behaviors for change include:

- A bad attitude
- Poor sense of responsibility
- No internalized controls
- Damaged self-esteem

These target behaviors all fail the tests of observability, measurability, and an objective definition. Workable target behaviors that parallel our definition of a Tough Kid are listed in Box 1-2.

PROACTIVE INTERVENTION STRATEGIES

The first line of classroom intervention for Tough Kids should be preventive or *proactive* strategies. Proactive means that the preplanned strategy stops or interferes with most problem behaviors *before* they even occur. The key to proactive or preventive strategies is to anticipate problem behaviors before they occur. It is much more

BOX 1-2

Target Behaviors for *Tough Kids*

THE TOUGH KID WILL:
(NONCOMPLIANCE)
- Follow a teacher's request within 10 seconds
- Follow posted classroom rules
- Not argue
- Not make excuses

(AGGRESSION)
- Not fight
- Not be verbally abusive
- Not destroy property
- Not tantrum (scream, make threats, etc.)

(SELF-MANAGEMENT SKILLS)
- Follow directions
- Exhibit problem-solving skills (after training)
- Explain the consequences of behaviors
- Follow rules
- Accept "No" for an answer

(SOCIAL SKILLS)
- Learn to reward others
- Explain and demonstrate cooperative behavior (after training)
- Enter conversations appropriately
- Demonstrate the skills of accepting negative feedback

(ACADEMIC SKILLS)
- Finish assignments with 80% accuracy
- Be on task 85% of the time
- Be on time to class
- Attend school every day
- Hand in completed homework
- Engage in peer tutoring
- Be part of a cooperative learning team

difficult to remediate the problems caused by a Tough Kid than to prevent them. Once a teacher has lost the management tempo in a classroom and things are out of control, it is difficult to re-establish control. Numerous strategies are available to teachers, and these strategies should be preplanned before school starts. These suggested strategies work for Tough Kids, and they also work for average students to help enhance the overall quality of a classroom.

Classroom Rules: Don't Leave Home Without Them

Good classroom rules are the backbone of any proactive strategy to reduce problem behaviors. Rules should form the nucleus of the behavior a teacher expects from all the students in a classroom. They should also describe minimum expectations for behavior for every student in the classroom. *All* students should be expected to follow the rules—gifted and average students as well as Tough Kids. Once rule exceptions are made for special students, a double standard exists in a classroom and rules become worthless. "How To Develop Good Proactive Rules" on the next page lists eight characteristics of good rules.

Do not make separate rules !

Make certain that students understand the resulting consequences (both positive and privilege loss) of the classroom rules. At the start of each day during the first two weeks of school, randomly select students to:

- Read a posted rule.
- Discuss and/or role-play why the rule is important.
- Explain what will happen if the rule is followed.

- Explain what will happen if the rule is not followed.

Teachers should select and post the classroom rules before the first day of school. (See Reproducible 1-4 for a sample format. A blank fillable version of Reproducible 1-4 appears on the CD.)

We believe students should not select their own rules for several reasons:

- When students self-select rules, they tend to be overly punitive.
- Students often generate too many rules or nonspecific rules.
- Some Tough Kids feel they do not have to follow rules selected by other students.
- Teachers must have classroom rules that allow them to teach.

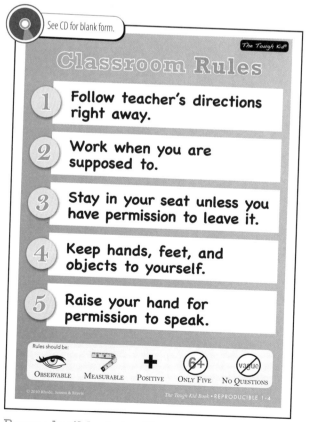

Reproducible 1-4 • Classroom Rules

How to . . .

DEVELOP GOOD PROACTIVE RULES

- Keep the number of rules to a minimum—about five rules for each classroom.

- Keep the wording of rules simple—pictures or icons that depict the rules help younger students understand them.

- Have the rules logically represent your basic expectations for a student's behavior in your classroom.

- Keep the wording positive when possible. Most rules can be stated in a positive manner; some rules cannot. However, the majority of classroom rules should be positive.

- Make your rules specific. The more ambiguous (i.e., open to several different interpretations) the rules are, the more difficult they are to understand. Tough Kids can take advantage of nonspecific loopholes in poorly stated rules.

- Make your rules describe behavior that is observable. The behavior must be observable so that you can make an unequivocal decision about whether or not the rule has been followed.

- Make your rules describe behavior that is measurable. That means you must be able to count or quantify the behavior in some way for monitoring purposes.

- Publicly post the rules in a prominent place in your classroom, such as in the front of the classroom near the door. The lettering should be large and in block print.

- We have found no empirical evidence indicating that rules formulated with student participation result in better outcomes than do teacher-selected rules.

The fine-tuning of preselected rules takes place in conjunction with the rule discussion during the first two weeks of school. It is appropriate for students to question a rule's fairness or why it exists during a discussion and review of the rules. However, the teacher should make the final decision about the acceptability of a rule. It should not be a democratic decision by student vote.

If a rule is overly stringent or unreasonable, you can change it or construct a new rule during the discussion time. However, students should not question rules at other times during the

day, particularly when a rule has been broken. The beginning of the day is the time for rule discussion.

Observe, review as necessary

After the first two weeks, watch for indications that the rules need to be reviewed again. It is also good practice to periodically review the classroom rules after holiday breaks, when new students come into the classroom, and when there are extended periods of problem behaviors in the classroom. Box 1-3 gives several examples of inappropriate and appropriate rules.

Problematic rules on the inappropriate rules list include several that are frequently used in classrooms and schools. These include the words *respect*, *responsible*, and *safe*. When it comes to rules that contain these words, Tough Kids in particular tend to fail the Flash Test. What we mean by the Flash Test is that a teacher should be able to ask any student in the class the definition of a specific rule. If the student cannot tell the teacher in a flash—without hesitation—what the rule means, the rule is probably unclear. If the rule is unclear, compliance with the teacher's expectation will be minimized.

Tough Kids are the most at risk for problem behaviors when they do not understand classroom rules. Even in the instances where they do understand ambiguous rules, they may *choose* to interpret them differently to avoid following them. If ambiguous rules are to be used at all, they need to be broken down into more specific sub-rules.

Following are examples of ambiguous rules broken down into more specific sub-rules:

BOX 1-3

Examples of Classroom *Rules*

INAPPROPRIATE RULES
- Be responsible.
- Be a good citizen.
- Pay attention.
- Be ready to learn.
- Demonstrate respect for others.
- Respect others' rights.
- Respect authority.
- Treat school property appropriately.
- Do your best.
- Take care of your materials.
- Maintain appropriate behavior in the classroom.
- Be kind to others.
- Be polite.

PREFERRED RULE EXAMPLES
- Turn in completed assignments on time.
- Bring paper, pencil, and books to class.
- Sit in your seat unless you have permission to leave it.
- Do what your teacher asks right away.
- Raise your hand and wait for permission to speak.
- Unless you have permission to speak, talk only about your work.
- Work when you are supposed to.
- Do not bother or hurt others.
- Walk, don't run, when moving around the classroom.
- Keep hands, feet, and objects to yourself.
- Bring books, notebooks, pens, and pencils to class.
- Be in your seat when the bell rings.
- Be in the classroom when the bell rings.

BE RESPONSIBLE

- Follow directions.
- Be on time.
- Be prepared.

BE RESPECTFUL

- Raise hand and ask for permission to speak.
- No put-downs.
- Listen to others.

BE SAFE

- Follow directions.
- Keep hands and feet to yourself.
- Walk, and no rough-housing.

When ambiguous rules are broken into more specific sub-parts, there is less room for misinterpretation and confusion. The result is that the Tough Kid is less likely to get into trouble.

Your Classroom Schedule— Downtime Causes Problems

Time not scheduled in a classroom is an open invitation to disruptive behavior. Scheduled academic learning time is critical to the academic success and appropriate classroom behavior of a Tough Kid. It is one of the basic proactive variables under a teacher's control. Academic learning time has three basic components:

Do not have downtime!

1. Percentage of the day scheduled for academics (70% of the day)
2. On-task time of the student (85% on-task)
3. Success of the student once he is academically engaged (80% correct)

The total amount of time allocated in an instructional day is 100% (i.e., 6.5 hours in a typical

How to . . .

ALLOCATE ACADEMIC TIME (CLASSROOM SCHEDULE EXAMPLE)

A.M.

9:00–9:10	Attendance, lunch payments, announcements
9:10–10:45	Whole class reading instruction/ guided practice/independent practice/differentiation
10:45–11:00	Recess
11:00–12:00	Whole class math instruction/ guided practice/independent practice/differentiation

P.M.

12:00–12:40	Lunch
12:40–1:20	Science
1:20–2:00	P.E. (M,W,F); art (T, Th)
2:00–2:15	Recess
2:15–2:55	Social Studies
2:55–3:25	Social Skills (M,W,F); Music (T,TH)
3:25–3:30	Clean up and prepare for dismissal

100% Scheduled

classroom). The amount of allocated time that should be scheduled for academic activities is approximately 70%, or 4.5 hours of the instructional day. When daily academic time, including transition times, recess, and lunch, is less than this amount, disruptive behavior is much more likely to occur.

To test her schedule, a teacher can simply multiply the total hours students are in school (allocated time) by 70%. The result is the amount of time that should be scheduled for academic activity (see the sample schedule in "How To Allocate Academic Time").

Many teachers feel overwhelmed at the thought of successfully engaging students academically for 70% of the day. However, strategies such as peer tutoring and cooperative learning approaches make this a realistic goal. These strategies will be reviewed in **Chapter 4**.

Structuring Your Classroom Space

Two simple rules apply to Tough Kids when planning classroom space:

1. Move them close to you.
2. Do not let Tough Kids sit together.

These rules seem like common sense; however, they are constantly violated.

Many teachers seem to feel uncomfortable about having an argumentative, disruptive, noncompliant student sit near them. These students are often placed in the back of the classroom (the out-of-sight, out-of-mind approach) or on

the periphery of the classroom. This type of placement invites trouble. Tough Kids should be placed in the *front* of the classroom near the teacher. We'll note here that the reason for placing Tough Kids close to you is not just so you can keep an eye on them. If they are close, they are more easily reinforced. When Tough Kids are just an arm's length away, it is convenient to socially reward them in front of their peers and to ask them to help with basic classroom tasks (e.g., handing out papers).

Having Tough Kids sit together is like disruptive behavior ability grouping. Separate Tough Kids no matter what they promise or offer. When two or more Tough Kids sit together, they frequently reward each other for disruptive behavior. Some of this inappropriate encouragement is so subtle it is difficult for a teacher to detect. If there is a group of Tough Kids in a classroom, have the

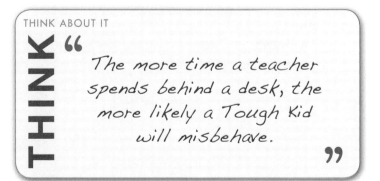

THINK ABOUT IT

THINK

"
The more time a teacher spends behind a desk, the more likely a Tough Kid will misbehave.
"

most difficult sit up front and separate them by placing students who usually behave appropriately near them.

Get Up and Move !

One of the most effective and easy proactive strategies for teachers to use is simply to move around the classroom. The more time a teacher spends behind a desk, the more likely a Tough Kid will misbehave. Spend the time while students are working at their desks walking around the class. Meet them at the door when they enter the classroom. A random walking approach, particularly where Tough Kids sit, is the most effective. Teachers who walk around and move are more able to anticipate problems and manage them before they get out of hand. It also allows teachers to subtly reinforce students. For example, touching a student's shoulder, bending down and looking at a student's work, or pointing at a student's work and saying "Good job" are all easily done while walking around but difficult to do from behind a desk.

Conduct a couple of simple tests. Keep track of the amount of time you actually spend behind your desk. For one week, we ask that you cut this desk time in half and instead wander the classroom making positive comments. Then look at your desk. Is it piled with material to occupy your time (e.g., books, objects, pictures, papers to grade)? We suggest you clean it off and walk. You will be amazed at the effect on classroom behavior!

Do not sit behind your desk!

Influence Techniques for Tough Kids

Some of the most effective approaches to working with Tough Kids are proactive influence strategies. A great deal of research has been done on how businesses, religions, and social organizations influence our everyday behavior. One of the best summaries of this research is the book *Influence: Science and Practice* by Robert Cialdini (2008). In this book, Cialdini presents research on the many ways we are influenced by fixed-action patterns, which he calls *click, whirr responses*. These are regular, mechanical patterns of action that occur automatically in response to a specific trigger. They explain why we say "Yes" when we generally would say "No."

Cialdini cites a study by psychologist Ellen Langer, who studies mindlessness, and colleagues (Langer, Blank, & Chanowitz, 1978). They tested several different requests at a library copy machine. One person asked the others waiting in line: "Excuse me. I have five pages. May I use the Xerox machine?" Only 60% of those waiting let the person cut in.

The next request was: "Excuse me. I have five pages. May I use the Xerox machine because I'm in a rush?" With this addition, 94% of those waiting gave a "Yes" answer. Giving a rationale (a *because*) would appear to explain the dramatic jump in compliance.

The final request was: "Excuse me. I have five pages. May I use the Xerox machine because I have to make some copies?" Again, nearly all (93%) of those waiting agreed to let the requester go ahead, even though the reason given after *because* wasn't much of a reason.

A lame reason works just as well as a good reason. The word *because* is a *click, whirr* stimuli that can produce an automatic "Yes" response regardless of the rationale that follows it.

We generally try to motivate Tough Kids and increase their compliance to adult requests. Proactive influence techniques can help accomplish both these goals. Box 1-4 lists the six influence principles from Cialdini's book. We will discuss how to apply them in proactive ways with Tough Kids.

BEHAVIOR RECIPROCATION

Have you ever received an unexpected Christmas present from someone and immediately felt the need to get her a gift, although you were not planning on buying her one? Similarly, have you ever gone to dinner at someone's house and while driving home thought to yourself, "I need to have him over for dinner sometime"? This is the *principle of reciprocation*. If you receive something positive from another

Principle of *Behavior Reciprocation*

The behaviors you give out are the ones you are likely to get back (and in the same form).

person, you automatically feel obligated to give something positive back in return and in the same form as what you received. The opposite can also happen. That is, if you give out a negative behavior, you can expect to get a negative behavior in return. For example, if someone criticizes you, you typically want to criticize him back. If you do, he is likely to criticize you even more, and then you criticize him even more than that. This is how human beings often inadvertently escalate behavior, both negative and positive.

Behavior reciprocation is one of the best arguments for making positive praise statements to Tough Kids, especially for compliance and following directions. The more positives a teacher gives, the more she will get positive compliance in return. This is an important point to make, because when a Tough Kid follows a teacher's directions, he is *not* likely to receive a positive praise statement in return. In fact, unless a teacher has been specifically trained to do so, a Tough Kid will receive positive praise for following directions only about 15% of the time (Jenson, Olympia, Farley, & Clark, 2004). A simple "You really help me when you follow through" or "I really appreciate your following my directions—it makes things easy" will result in more positive compliance from Tough Kids.

BOX 1-4

Six *Influence Principles* for Use With Tough Kids

- Behavior Reciprocation
- Commitment and Consistency
- Social Proof
- Liking
- Authority
- Scarcity

> ## THINK ABOUT IT
>
> " *In an escalating situation, follow John Wayne's advice to talk low, talk slow, and don't say too much.* "

He cites an example (Sherman, 1980) where people were asked in a telephone survey if they would theoretically volunteer to collect money for the American Cancer Society. Not wanting to sound uncharitable on the phone, most people said they would be willing to do so. When they were asked to volunteer in reality a few days later, there was a 700% increase in actual volunteers.

It is also easy to fall into the negative reciprocity trap with Tough Kids. For example, if a Tough Kid loses control and escalates his behavior by swearing, throwing his papers on the ground, and yelling, it is easy to become negative yourself by yelling or threatening him. This is where it pays to be cool, calm, collected, and professional. You need to stand your ground, but in a firm and calm manner. Follow John Wayne's advice to "talk low, talk slow, and don't say too much." If you continue to interact with the student with this demeanor, the Tough Kid is more likely to begin to give out behavior similar to what you are giving out. At the first instance of cessation or de-escalation of problem behavior as the Tough Kid becomes more compliant, you should socially reinforce him. To be mad or hold grudges results only in a reciprocal mad and grudge-holding Tough Kid. In other words, the teacher must control her own behavior in order to control the Tough Kid's.

Do not let emotions get in the way

COMMITMENT AND CONSISTENCY

An important part of being a good teacher is to commit to consistency in following through with Tough Kids. Tough Kids themselves can also be influenced to commit to positive behaviors and then consistently exhibit them. In his book, Cialdini notes that when people make a formal commitment, even a small one, they are more likely to follow through with the commitment.

Commitment and consistency can and should be used with Tough Kids. A behavior contract, whereby Tough Kids are asked to set positive goals, engage in specific appropriate behaviors, and sign the contract, is an effective strategy. In our *Tough Kid Bully Blockers Book*, students in classrooms are asked to state the Bully Blocker Pledge out loud, talk about how they will help stop bullying in their school, and sign the Bully Blocker Pledge Poster. This is an anti-bullying commitment and consistency strategy. *Click, whirr* to stop bullying.

SOCIAL PROOF

We are likely to do what we see and hear others do. Seeing someone else do something is social proof that it is appropriate to engage in that behavior, too. Cialdini cites the example of canned laughter in television programs. Most people say they hate canned laughter in television shows. But even a great TV comedy show like *Seinfeld* used canned laughter. Why? Because research invariably shows that when we hear others laugh (even if it is canned), we laugh harder and longer than if we don't hear it. Interestingly, research also shows canned laughter helps get the biggest laughs for the worst jokes.

Social proof also works for Tough Kids. Seeing another student misbehave gives them permission to misbehave, too. In addition, peers often reward each other for inappropriate behaviors.

In these cases, social proof for the classroom becomes one of misbehavior. This is one reason we emphasize group contingencies in **Chapter 3**. With group contingencies, the whole group is rewarded when the individuals in that group follow the rules and behave appropriately. Reinforced appropriate behavior for the group becomes the classroom social proof norm.

We also give another example in the last chapter of this book. In **Chapter 5**, teachers are encouraged to teach Tough Kids to comment positively on the appropriate behavior of other Tough Kids (e.g., give Put-Ups). The positive comments are almost like canned laughter. When the students are directly rewarded for giving other students Put-Ups for appropriate behavior, the social proof phenomenon improves the overall social climate in a classroom.

Influences of positive comments !

LIKING

Liking is one of the most important influence principles when working with Tough Kids. You are more likely to get a "Yes" and compliance from a Tough Kid when she likes you than when she actively dislikes you. Cialdini gives us a fascinating example in his book. Interrogating a suspect for information using a Bad Cop/Good Cop approach is a common tactic in police work. When first interrogated by the negative Bad Cop, the suspect often shuts down and will not cooperate. (This isn't much different from Tough Kids shutting down in school when negative approaches are used.) The Bad Cop then leaves, and the Good Cop comes in, uses the suspect's name, points out positive aspects of the case if the suspect cooperates, offers the suspect coffee, asks about the suspect's family, expresses concern, and even uses humor. In this scenario, the Good Cop gets all sorts of cooperation and information.

> # The *Liking* Principle
>
> People are more likely to say "Yes" to someone they know and like. People trust and consequently are influenced by those they like.

Interestingly, the most successful interrogator of the mastermind of the 9/11 attacks never used harsh techniques. When asked how he obtained such valuable information and cooperation from the terrorist, he simply said, "I got him to like me."

We do not expect you to play Bad Cop/Good Cop or interrogate Tough Kids as terrorists. They have had enough negatives in their lives. Rather, consider some of the major characteristics of people we like, including:

- They are similar to us (not perfect beings).
- They have a sense of humor that makes us laugh.
- They tell us they like us.
- They give us compliments.

A sense of positive humor (no negative or belittling humor) is critical in working with Tough Kids. We once asked approximately 200 high school students what they liked most in teachers, and sense of humor topped the list. It's a fact. Make someone laugh and he will like you. Consider starting the school day off with a "Dumb" joke of the day. Tough Kids will laugh. *Click, whirr.*

A compliment, according to Cialdini, is one of the most powerful influence techniques. The power of compliments adds up over time.

Teachers must find something to like about Tough Kids and go out of their way to socially reinforce and compliment them. We suggest you keep a small private tally of the positive compliments you give out each day in your classroom. Then try to beat your best compliment average each day.

AUTHORITY

By authority, we do not mean someone who is an authoritarian despot. What we mean is someone who looks organized and gives off an aura of knowing what to do and how to do it. In his book, Cialdini points to the research on compliance with authority figures. If a request is given by an authority figure such as a doctor or professor, people are far more likely to comply. If you look the part of someone with authority and knowledge, you are far more likely to get someone to say "Yes" and comply.

Know your curriculum!

You are the authority in your classroom. When you have a proactive program in place the first day of school, good classroom rules, and a structured schedule, and you consistently follow your own positive program, you will give Tough Kids the sense that you are the authority and have things under control. Tough

Adults who are not in charge of themselves should not be in charge of students who are not in charge of themselves.

—Unknown

Kids like and want consistency and positive structure. If you change your program without good reason, bend the rules, look the other way, act disorganized, and are not consistent, you lose the sense of confidence and authority. Being a positive authority figure means that you have a planned, structured program and that you confidently and consistently implement it.

SCARCITY More value

We value things that are scarce, available for only a short period of time, or available to only a few people. Cialdini gives an example of a cookie study by Stephen Worchel and colleagues (Worchel, Lee, & Adewole, 1975) in which people were asked to rate the quality of a cookie they took from a jar. For half the participants, the jar held only two cookies; for the rest, the jar held 10 cookies. People almost always rated the cookie from the jar with two cookies (scarce) as more desirable and appealing than the cookie from the jar with 10 cookies.

Tough Kids are no different. The scarcity influence principle can be easily and effectively used to motivate Tough Kids. Mystery Motivators, described in **Chapter 2**, should be presented as rare and mysterious. Reinforcement Spinners, which we describe in the same chapter, operate on the principle of scarcity. The Spinner is a circle with wedges of different sizes and an arrow that can be spun by a Tough Kid when she earns the privilege. Whatever the arrow lands on when the Tough Kid spins it is what she gets. The big wedges represent the more common reinforcers. The narrow or skinny wedges represent something more scarce and rare. The level system described in **Chapter 5** provides a similar example related to motivation and the scarcity

> ## BOX 1-5
>
> ## Proactive *Strategies* for Teachers
>
> **CLASSROOM RULES**
>   Don't leave home without them.
>
> **YOUR CLASSROOM SCHEDULE**
>   Downtime causes problems.
>
> **STRUCTURING YOUR CLASSROOM SPACE**
>   Put Tough Kids near you.
>
> **GET UP AND MOVE**
>   Be a wandering reinforcer.
>
> **INFLUENCE PRINCIPLES**
>   - Behavior reciprocation
>   - Commitment and consistency
>   - Social proof
>   - Liking
>   - Authority
>   - Scarcity

Ideas

principle. With level systems, a Tough Kid earns his way up the levels by demonstrating appropriate behaviors and skills. On the lower levels, he accesses more common everyday rewards and privileges. More valued, scarce, and rare rewards and privileges are available at the top levels, motivating the Tough Kid to work hard to move up to higher levels. If you want to motivate a Tough Kid, have him earn something scarce, rare, and mysterious. *Click, whirr.*

Box 1-5 summarizes the proactive strategies teachers can employ to reduce problem behavior.

In a nutshell

All teachers have Tough Kids in their classroom sooner or later. The average is at least one or two of these students per year, and this average is not likely to go down. Tough Kids need not demoralize teachers or disrupt classrooms. It is important to remember that the behavioral excesses that cause teachers to perceive these students as difficult are present in all students. The only difference is that the frequency and intensity of aggression, noncompliance, arguing, and tantrum throwing is higher with Tough Kids. It is also critical to remember that noncompliance is the kingpin behavior around which these other behavioral excesses revolve. Reduce coercion and noncompliance in Tough Kids, and much of the arguing, aggression, and tantrum throwing will also be reduced.

Reducing noncompliance is only half of the battle with Tough Kids, however. The vast majority of them have substantial behavioral deficits that interfere with adjustment. Tough Kids have significant deficits in basic academic, social, and self-management skills. Reducing coercion and noncompliance is only a temporary gain. If they do not have their basic deficits remediated, they will revert back to their excessive strategies to manage their environments. We cannot expect Tough Kids to do well in spite of feeling stupid, being rejected by their peers, or lacking the basic skills to manage their own behaviors.

Three last points are critical if we hope to educate Tough Kids and enjoy the process. First, we cannot drop our expectations for them. We must have the same high standards for academic and school behavior for them that we have for average students. When we drop our expectations because these students come from poor backgrounds and are so deficient, research indicates they will fail. High expectations are one of the critical factors of effective schools.

Second, we must recognize that many Tough Kids will not be "cured" during the time they are in our classrooms. The Tough Kid is managed. Accurate identification, proactive strategies, and classroom interventions—these all make the educational environment work for the Tough Kid. It is not education's business to cure them. No one, at this time, can do that. The business of education is to teach Tough Kids as many adaptive, academic, social, and self-management skills as possible. If we do that, we immensely improve their chances for successful outcomes.

(Continued)

In a nutshell *(Continued)*

Third, Tough Kids must be educated in positive classroom environments. It is all too easy to use only punitive procedures with Tough Kids and then blame them for failing. Some reductive techniques may be necessary. However, unless basic positive approaches are used, and used to a much greater extent than are punitive procedures, we will lose the majority of these students. They will simply drop out of school, with an enormous cost to us as educators and to society as a whole. The next chapter outlines the basic positive procedures that are the backbone of classrooms that educate Tough Kids.

References

Achenbach, T. M., & Rescorla, L. A. (2001). *Manual for the ASEBA school-age forms and profiles.* Burlington, VT: University of Vermont, Department of Psychiatry.

Cialdini, R. (2008) *Influence: Science and Practice* (5th ed.), New York: Allyn and Bacon.

Gresham, F., & Elliot, S. (1990). *Social skills rating system.* Circle Pines, MN: American Guidance Services.

Jenson, W. R., Clark, E., & Burrows-Sanchez, J. (2009). Practical strategies in working with difficult students. In A. Akin-Little, S. G. Little, M.A. Bray, & T. J. Keble (Eds.), *Behavior interventions in the schools: Evidence based positive strategies* (pp. 247–264). Washington, D.C.: American Psychological Association.

Jesse, V. (1989). *Compliance training and generalization effects using a compliance matrix and spinner system.* Unpublished doctoral dissertation, University of Utah, Salt Lake City, UT.

Patterson, G. R. (1982). *Coercive family process.* Eugene, OR: Castalia Publishing.

Patterson, G. R., Reid, J. B., & Dishion, T. J. (1992). *Antisocial boys.* Eugene, OR: Castalia Publishing.

Rathvon, N. (2008). *Effective school interventions* (2nd ed.). New York: Guilford Press.

Shinn, M. R., Shinn, M. M., Hamilton, C., & Clark, B. (2002). Using curriculum-based measurement in general education classrooms to promote reading success. In M. R. Shinn, H. M. Walker, and G. Stoner (Eds.). *Interventions for achievement and behavior problems II: Preventive and remedial approaches.* Bethesda, MD: National Association of School Psychologists.

Skinner, B. F. (1953). *Science and human behavior.* New York: Macmillan.

Walker, H. M., Ramsey, E., & Gresham, F. (2004). *Antisocial behavior in school: Evidence-based practices* (2nd ed.). Belmont, CA: Wadsworth.

CHAPTER 2

Unique Positive Procedures

"I tried that positive reinforcement stuff, but it didn't work!" So say many teachers of Tough Kids. However, it is an indisputable fact that supported and recognized behaviors are the ones that will increase. The trick is for the teacher to positively support and recognize Tough Kids' appropriate behavior in ways that are meaningful to the Tough Kids.

If more teacher attention is given for inappropriate student behavior than for appropriate behavior, the inappropriate behavior will increase. With Tough Kids' teachers, this attention very often takes the form of excessive prompting, reminding, threatening, reprimanding, and verbal abuse, because these reactions seem to come naturally when teachers attempt "pain control" of their own.

Unfortunately, in many, if not most, classrooms where teachers rely on their natural tendencies for management, this pattern of teacher behavior can actually cause the students' problem behaviors to increase rather than decrease. In these cases, arbitrary and capricious teacher attention focused on inappropriate behaviors is responsible for the maintenance and increase of undesired student behavior during the school year! When teachers refer to their students as having *spring fever* during the final months of the school year, this is typically what has occurred.

Thus, once teachers have established classroom rules at the beginning of the school year, the major driving force behind their classroom management *must* be the way they motivate and recognize students. Only when Tough Kids view the classroom as a positive place will they want to be in the classroom and have no need to practice their "pain control" behaviors.

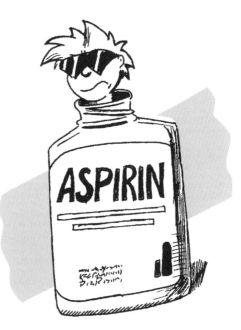

Tough Kids' teachers must find unique and interesting ways to consistently provide motivation and recognition to their students for exhibiting the behaviors they desire to increase. Not only will teachers be able to effect behavior changes in the students, but the classroom will be a more positive place for them to be as well. If adequate motivation and recognition are not in place, *no* classroom management plan will ever be effective.

POSITIVE STRATEGIES

Positive Reinforcement

Let's start with a word about positive reinforcement. Positive reinforcement involves the contingent presentation of something valued or desired by the student. Mind you, this may not be the same thing the teacher thinks the student values or desires or should value or desire. This "something" the student values is provided immediately after the desired behavior and results in an increase in the behavior.

Some everyday examples include the following:

- Every day that Emily finishes her reading assignment on time, Mrs. Ruedas allows her to take sports equipment out at recess. If Emily enjoys using the equipment at recess, she is likely to continue finishing her assignments on time.
- When Isaiah raises his hand before speaking in class, Mr. Armstrong awards a point to the class toward a class party. Because Isaiah's peers now encourage him to raise his hand and because he enjoys parties, Isaiah is likely to raise his hand in Mr. Armstrong's class.

While the above examples demonstrate the appropriate use of positive reinforcement for increasing desired student behavior, Tough Kids' teachers often inadvertently provide positive reinforcement for behaviors they do not wish to see increase. Some examples include:

- Every time Amber is out of her seat, Mrs. Flores tells her to sit down. Mrs. Flores cannot understand why it seems that Amber is out of her seat more than ever.

- Mr. Stoddard sends Ronnie out in the hall to sit on a chair because of disruptive behavior in the classroom. Ronnie talks to other students and adults who pass by him, in addition to helping himself to candy he finds in the pocket of another student's coat. Mr. Stoddard finds Ronnie is disruptive again soon after he is permitted to return to the classroom.

In both of these situations, students receive attention from others as a result of their inappropriate behavior. Many students, like Amber, find even negative attention from the teacher

BOX 2-1

A *Review* of Positive Reinforcement, Negative Reinforcement, and Punishment

Many educators confuse *positive reinforcement, negative reinforcement*, and *punishment*. **Both** positive and negative reinforcement *increase* behavior, while punishment *decreases* it.

Positive reinforcement is said to occur when something a student desires is presented *after* appropriate behavior has been exhibited.

- Example: *Calvin can earn up to ten points for completing his reading assignment correctly. The points can be exchanged for dinosaur stickers. Because Calvin enjoys the stickers he can earn, the accuracy of his reading assignments has increased.*

Negative reinforcement is said to occur when students engage in particular behavior to *avoid* or *escape* something they dislike.

- Example: *Madalyn's truant behavior increases to avoid an English class in which she is unable to successfully do the work.*

- Example: *A.J. hurries to finish his math assignment so he will not be kept in from recess to complete it.*

Punishment is said to occur when something the student does not like or wishes to avoid is applied after the behavior has occurred, resulting in a *decrease* in the behavior.

- Example: *Every time Beth skips school, she is required to make up the missed time in an after-school detention. Because she dislikes after-school detention so much, the skipping stops.*

reinforcing, particularly in classrooms where their appropriate behavior is not recognized or rewarded. By definition, if a Tough Kid's behavior increases, it has been reinforced. This is true even if the teacher thought the student was being punished (see Box 2-1).

Teacher interactions should consist of no fewer than *four* positive ones to every negative one, and ideally *eight* or *ten* positives to each negative one for the toughest Tough Kids. The rule of thumb is: The more difficult the problem behavior of the student, the *higher* the ratio of

positives to negatives must be. This is tough to carry out, especially when it seems that a student is not engaging in much appropriate behavior that deserves positive recognition. If a teacher succumbs to her human tendencies for managing behavior, she naturally focuses on the negative, or what the student *is not* doing correctly. Ironically, recognizing the negatives serves to increase those behaviors, not decrease them.

Thus, if the teacher wishes to increase the Tough Kid's appropriate behavior and provides what she believes to be positive reinforcement after the desired behavior has been exhibited, the results of her action must be examined. If the behavior increases, reinforcement has occurred. If it does not, what the teacher provided was not reinforcing to the Tough Kid.

In order to determine whether desired behavior has actually increased, a simple monitoring system must be established. If the behavior is not monitored, it is almost impossible to tell whether or not appropriate behavior is increasing. If it is not, the teacher will want to know soon so that neither the teacher's nor the Tough Kid's time and effort are wasted with an ineffective strategy.

Arguments Against Positive Reinforcement

Some teachers think that it is wrong to use positive reinforcement. They believe that Tough Kids should exhibit appropriate behavior just because it is the responsible thing to do. They may view reinforcement as a crutch or bribe. It is true that many regular education students exhibit appropriate behavior because it is the responsible and "right" thing to do. Even so, the authors believe these students should still receive periodic positive reinforcement for displaying it. The authors have heard four basic arguments against using positive reinforcement in the form of incentives,

THINK ABOUT IT

THINK

" *Appropriately administered positive reinforcement is not a bribe.* "

rewards, and praise. We believe that *none* of these arguments are supported by research findings and, in fact, result in poor practice in the behavior management of any student.

THE BRIBERY ARGUMENT

Some believe that rewards are just another form of bribery. As far as the bribery issue goes, we agree that teachers should not use bribery with any student. However, appropriately administered positive reinforcement is not a bribe. We define bribery as an inducement for an illegal or unethical act. Behaving well in a classroom and performing well academically are not illegal or illicit. However, there is a form of extortionary bribery in which a student will misbehave on purpose if he does not receive a reward. In this situation, a student should never receive a reward. If he is given a reward in this case, he has just been reinforced for making a threat.

Similarly, the giving of a reward to an individual to stop misbehavior is inappropriate. Examples of this can be seen every day in grocery stores and restaurants when a parent gives her child a cookie if the child stops crying or throwing a tantrum. This use of a reward is *never* appropriate for any individual. Proper positive reinforcement is given *only after* an appropriate behavior to increase or maintain that behavior.

THE FAIRNESS ARGUMENT

Some teachers believe that if they provide an incentive for good behavior to a Tough Kid, to be fair they must provide every student in the classroom with exactly the same incentive. This is a false way to define fairness. A better definition of fairness is to provide each student with what she needs to have an equal chance for success. Wheelchairs are provided to students who have mobility problems so they can successfully access an education at school. It would be illogical to give all students in the school wheelchairs regardless of whether they need one. If a Tough Kid is highly unmotivated because of years of academic failure, he will need an external incentive system to keep him motivated as he acquires necessary academic skills.

THE KILLS INTERNAL MOTIVATION ARGUMENT

Some teachers believe that if students are given external rewards, their internal motivation will be reduced. This argument has been promoted by Alfie Kohn in his book *Punished by Rewards: The Trouble with Gold Stars, Incentive Plans, A's, Praise, and Other Bribes* (1999). The authors believe this approach offers a very limited review of the research literature on external rewards. Other scholars, such as Eisenberger and Cameron (1996), have conducted research reviews and meta-analyses that show rewards reduce internal motivation only "under limited conditions that are easily avoided" (p. 1164). If external rewards are given for performance that is positively improving, meaningful, and successful, external rewards enhance both external and internal motivation.

For example, we believe that not very many Tough Kids' teachers would continue to work if they did not receive paychecks and that paying teachers for their work is the right thing to do. Similarly, most teachers (and other adults) like to be recognized for their accomplishments. These can be things as simple as a note from the principal in the teacher's school mailbox expressing appreciation for filling in for an ill colleague who had been assigned lunch supervision duty. It might be a positive statement from a supervisor, in front of colleagues, recognizing what an effective and professional job the teacher did

> THINK
>
> THINK ABOUT IT
>
> " All students (and adults) need legitimate and appropriate reinforcement. "

in managing a conference with an extremely difficult parent. Because behavior is reciprocal, people are likely to behave positively toward those who interact positively with them.

For us, the bottom line is that all students (and adults) need legitimate and appropriate reinforcement. Positive reinforcement is no more a crutch for students than money, credit cards, and public recognition are crutches for adults. On the other hand, if rewards are given for "busy work," non-meaningful progress, or only for tasks that are too difficult and frustrating, internal motivation will be decreased.

We are reinforced throughout our lives!

THE HOOKED ON PRAISE ARGUMENT

Students who receive verbal praise for their performance or behavior will become "hooked" on praise. This is another argument made by Alfie Kohn in the book cited above. There is very little research evidence that students become overly dependent on praise. However, there is evidence, reviewed by Jenson, Olympia, Farley, and Clark (2004), that teachers underutilize praise with Tough Kids. Teacher praise is a very potent motivating force for students when used correctly. When asked to rate rewards, students select verbal praise as one of the most motivating incentives they can receive.

In addition to these arguments, some teachers believe that giving positive reinforcement takes too much time or is not sincere and genuine. A feeling of spontaneity and genuineness comes only with practice. The teacher who believes that giving routine reinforcement to students takes too much time or detracts from more important tasks is on the wrong track. With this attitude, classroom management will never be effective, especially with Tough Kids, and the teacher can count on spending a great deal of time and effort dealing with increased student misbehavior. Nothing is more important than positively reinforcing students for appropriate behavior! This is even more critical with Tough Kids than with other students.

ANTECEDENT STRATEGIES

An antecedent strategy is one that comes before a behavior and increases or maintains it. Antecedent strategies increase Tough Kids' motivation and encourage them to exhibit desired behavior. Use of antecedent strategies may be viewed as setting the stage for appropriate behavior to occur. When it is possible to use antecedent strategies, it is desirable to do so, rather than just waiting for the appropriate behavior to occur and then reinforcing it.

The effectiveness of antecedent strategies is not limited to education and has gained widespread attention in the business world over the past twenty years. Ways to help workers work more effectively is a hot topic in many arenas. Top-performing businesses around the world recognize and reward employees with performance incentives. The logic in creating incentive and recognition programs for employees is inescapable. Both formal and informal research demonstrates that people who feel appreciated hustle more, treat customers better, and in general provide a higher level of service that, in turn, brings customers back (Hequet, 1990).

In the business world, effective motivators can include merchandise, time off with pay, recognition banquets, training to enhance skills or build new ones, company picnics, tickets to ball games, travel, and money. Box 2-2 lists examples of positive antecedent strategies for classroom use.

Motivation and Encouragement

Motivating and encouraging desired performance is much the same in the classroom as it is in the business world. The steps are simple:

Step 1. Tell students what you want them to do (and make certain they understand it).

Step 2. Tell them what will happen if they do what you want them to do.

Step 3. When students do what you want them to do, give them immediate positive feedback in ways that are direct and meaningful to them.

The key word in Step 3 is *immediate*. If recognition is delayed until the end of the month, term, or school year, it might as well not be given at all. For most students (and employees), a long delay translates into ineffective or essentially meaningless recognition. Recognition systems should be ongoing in the classroom all of the time. In essence, recognition should consist of the teacher's ongoing dialogue with the students

BOX 2-2

Positive Antecedent *Strategies*

STRUCTURING INCENTIVES

- "Students who are in their seats when the bell rings can choose where they sit tomorrow."

- "When the class has accumulated five days with no tardies, we'll have an extra 20-minute recess in the afternoon."

- "Students who have not been sent to the office or had a phone call home for inappropriate behavior all week will be eligible for our class raffle drawing."

- "For every day you turn in your homework on time, you can use the magic pen to color in the Mystery Motivator box on your chart for that day."

HYPE

- "Don't forget—we'll be having a raffle drawing on Friday for everyone who has earned it. The prizes are way cool! You're definitely going to want to be there. You've got a great chance of winning something. Just remember to follow the class rules."

- "This afternoon I'm having a Teacher's Blue Light Special right before you go home. Everyone who has no more than one class rule infraction today can participate. You know the Blue Light Specials are always fun! Remind yourself and each other to stick to the rules. You will be glad you did!"

RELATING ACADEMIC ACCOMPLISHMENTS TO OUTCOMES

- "Students who beat their own scores on the math fluency check can skip our study session and take an extra 15-minute recess."

- "Students who are caught up with all of their work are eligible to work as peer tutors in the second grade classrooms."

- "All students who reach mastery on their reading goals for the month will receive an award at the Parents' Night Assembly."

ENCOURAGEMENT

- "Give it a try!"

- "Let's see if you can do it as well as you did it yesterday."

- "I know you can do this."

- "Keep going. You're on the right track."

and orchestration of the classroom climate for learning and good behavior. For many students, recognition of desired performance can be more powerful than a tangible reward.

The proactive strategies detailed in **Chapter 1** are also considered antecedent strategies. Classroom desk arrangement, specification of expectations and rules, a set daily schedule, appropriate and motivating curriculum, appropriate pacing of instruction, and adequate supervision all help to prevent behavior problems from occurring in the first place. You should always assess whether you have adequately addressed antecedent strategies before proceeding with more intrusive interventions for Tough Kids.

EFFECTIVE USE OF POSITIVE REINFORCEMENT

A critical element in effective classroom management with Tough Kids is determining the positive reinforcement that will be made available to them contingent upon their appropriate behavior. Careful selection and use of positive reinforcement is essential because the teacher will rely heavily on positive reinforcement to increase appropriate behavior. Cautions to keep in mind when selecting and using positive reinforcement are listed in "How To Select and Use Positive Reinforcement."

Two categories of positive reinforcement must be examined:

1. Natural reinforcement that is readily available within the classroom or school or that can be made available as an ongoing part of the school program

2. Other reinforcement to which the teacher has access and can make available

In identifying either type of positive reinforcement, creativity is critical!

Natural and Novel Positive Reinforcement

Many forms of natural positive reinforcement are available in school settings if you only look for them. By *natural,* we simply mean activities or things that students already find rewarding. Many times teachers have become so used to allowing students noncontingent access to available natural positive reinforcement that they forget it is there—and available for use as powerful contingent reinforcement *based* on appropriate behavior. Box 2-3 on p. 52 gives examples of potential natural positive reinforcement that teachers may want to use.

Example

A teacher dealing with Tough Kids must consider all natural reinforcements she can think of that are already available within the classroom or school. For example, one teacher of Tough Kids we know was befriended by the elderly Italian school custodian, who reaped mountains of produce from his large vegetable garden each fall. Nearly every day, in his attempts to be helpful, he would bring her armloads of giant zucchinis

> THINK ABOUT IT
>
> **THINK**
> " Many forms of natural positive reinforcement are available in school settings if you only look for them. "

How to . . .

SELECT AND USE POSITIVE REINFORCEMENT

- Select age-appropriate reinforcement.

- Use natural reinforcement whenever it is effective.

- Use reinforcement appropriate to the student's level of functioning. (For example, don't send a student for unsupervised free time in the library when she usually gets in trouble in the library even when she is directly supervised.)

- Make certain you have parental and administrative support for the reinforcement you plan to use.

- Avoid partial praise statements, such as "I'm glad you finished your work—finally!"

- Always make the most of opportunities to reinforce appropriate behavior.

- Be genuinely polite and courteous to Tough Kids at all times and demonstrate concern and interest toward them. Always stay calm.

- Do not confuse positive reinforcement or privileges with a student's basic rights. (For example, depriving a student of lunch, reasonable access to the bathroom or clothing, or a telephone call home is probably illegal. It is also not appropriate to deprive students of their rights and then have them earn them back under the guise of reinforcement.)

for the class. She began by planning cooking projects using zucchinis as rewards for the class. Once zucchini cookies, bread, and dip had been exhausted, she went on to use them in art projects, even having students create decorative centerpieces and bookends from the seemingly neverending supply of the green vegetable. One day when the custodian proudly rolled a large cart containing at least two dozen gargantuan zucchinis into her classroom, she was at her wit's end. On the spur of the moment and with a great deal of fanfare, she announced to the class that anyone who earned 90 or more out of a possible 100 behavior points for the day would receive two zucchinis to take home, and those with at least 80 points would receive one! Throughout the day, students were encouraged to work hard

to earn zucchinis (e.g., "Think how surprised your mom will be!"). As points were tallied at the end of the day, the teacher had each student come forward to accept the earned zucchinis as the class applauded. Afterwards, she had a good laugh with her colleagues over the use of her novel reinforcement and the probable comments in the homes of her students that evening as they explained how they had earned their zucchinis with good behavior.

Being familiar with the students, of course, is very helpful in determining what is likely to be positively reinforcing to them. The teacher who knows her students fairly well has had opportunities to observe them to see what they like to do and what they are willing to work for,

BOX 2-3

Suggestions for Natural and Novel
Positive Reinforcement

- Access to lunchroom snack machines (student supplies money)
- Play with can of "slime" for five minutes
- Earn tickets to play a game on the class Wii (e.g., Dance Revolution and Guitar Hero)
- String of novel holiday lights (e.g., flamingos) in front of class that are lit when students are working. Change lights to maintain interest.
- Be first in line (to anything)
- Throw a "sticky eyeball" at the wall for three minutes (www.orientaltrading.com)
- Chew bubble gum at desk for 15 minutes
- Attend school dances (during the day)
- Positive note home
- Positive phone call home
- Attend school assemblies
- Care for class pets (e.g., give the hermit crab a bath with a spray bottle)
- Choose activity or game for class
- Go on class field trips
- Decorate the classroom
- Eat lunch with a favorite adult
- Extra P.E., recess, or break time
- Free time to use specific equipment or supplies
- Place to display student's work
- Use a school locker
- Help custodian
- Serve as class or office messenger or aide
- Work at teacher's desk for a specified period of time
- Sit by a friend
- Positive visit to the principal (prearranged)
- Visit the school library (individual or group)
- Water class plants
- Work as lunchroom server
- Skip an assignment
- Pass out paper or other supplies
- Run DVD player for class
- Spend time with a favorite adult or peer
- Tutor in class or with younger students
- Use playground or P.E. equipment
- Use class MP3 player
- Use markers and/or art supplies

and to ask them what they like. Parents, former teachers, and experiences with similar students are sources for a list with which to begin. You can make changes as appropriate later on.

use your sources!

For those Tough Kids whose appropriate behavior is extremely limited, natural positive reinforcement may not be powerful enough initially to increase desired behavior. More importantly, the teacher may be unable to use much of the available natural reinforcement if the student's behavior is too unstable or inappropriate to allow him access to the environment where it can be delivered.

For example, a physically and verbally abusive student cannot be sent to serve as a lunchroom worker or deliver office messages. For these students, the teacher needs to identify other powerful reinforcers that can be made available in the classroom and that the teacher is willing to provide until the student's behavior is under control enough to allow access to more natural reinforcement. Other reinforcement may take several forms.

Edible Reinforcement

Edible reinforcement refers to providing foods students like to eat. Generally, it is equally effective with both elementary and secondary populations. Some common forms of edible reinforcement are candy, ice cream, pop, pizza, french fries, pretzels, chips, and juice. Interestingly, research has shown that five- to twelve-year-old Tough Kids rate french fries as the most highly desirable edible reinforcer. Secondary Tough Kids prefer pizza.

We should note that some students with severe disabilities like to eat nonnutritive substances such as cigarette butts, buttons, rocks, dirt, and chalk. It would be erroneous to assume that these items do not serve as reinforcement for the students who eat them. If the substance that a student eats increases or maintains a behavior, it serves as positive reinforcement. (And no, we are not suggesting you provide rocks, dirt, and cigarette butts to students who find them reinforcing.) However, for most Tough Kids it is not difficult to identify appropriate edible reinforcement.

The same teacher who convinced her junior high class that it was great to earn zucchinis as a reward also had them believing that earning a Wally's donut was sheer ecstasy. When she planned to make Wally's donuts available as reinforcement, she began ahead of time by announcing the day she would be bringing them and what was needed to earn one. She would describe them in juicy detail until the students were virtually drooling. On the day she brought the donuts, she would display them on her desk

TECHNIQUE TIP

Observe your students and other kids to see what they like to do, what they are willing to work for, and what items are currently popular with that age group. Keep a list of possible reinforcers and update it regularly to reflect what works and what doesn't. We'll discuss this process in greater detail later in the chapter.

at the front of the room and again remind students just how fabulous they were. This teacher's students would do almost anything to earn a Wally's donut by the time she was finished with her "marketing" plan.

There are, of course, arguments against edible reinforcement. In fact, some educators are against them on general principle. They may believe that providing edible reinforcement is babyish or that all edible reinforcement is unhealthy. The fact is we know a high school AP Calculus teacher who provides donuts for his students who receive "A" grades on their tests. One of the authors asked a student in this teacher's AP class, "Don't you think that's kind of babyish?" The student quickly and emphatically answered, "Heck no, I think it's really cool!" (*Note:* In this case, the teacher knew that all students in the class were capable of achieving an "A" grade on tests.)

As for the unhealthy claim, edible reinforcement does not have to be in the form of sweets. Students are often found to be willing to work for cubes of cheese, popcorn, fruit, and raw veggie pieces. Obviously, *common sense* needs

to weigh in here! A teacher would never give sweets or other prohibited foods or beverages to a diabetic student. She also should not provide calorie-laden foods to one who is overweight. Particularly for the very toughest Tough Kids, edible reinforcement may be the most powerful kind to jump-start them in the initial stages of their educational programs. If this is the case, once good progress has been made, the teacher will want to begin to fade out the edible reinforcement and substitute other types of reinforcement.

Material Reinforcement

Earning material items can be highly reinforcing for Tough Kids. Material reinforcement involves the delivery of some type of tangible item that increases or maintains behavior. Five- to twelve-year-old Tough Kids have frequently rated stickers as their most preferred nonedible reinforcers. Box 2-4 lists some tangible items that Tough Kids' teachers have effectively used for reinforcement. Pointer Box 2-1 on p. 56 lists suggestions of places to find novel reinforcers.

Generally, edible and material reinforcement are more useful than natural reinforcement for Tough Kids, who *initially* require reinforcement that is immediate, more frequent, and deliverable in small amounts at a time. For example, a

THINK ABOUT IT

> Once good progress has been made, the teacher will want to fade out the edible reinforcement.

BOX 2-4

Suggestions for Material *Reinforcement*

- Wax lips or teeth
- Toiletries (e.g., shampoo or lotion) collected at hotel stays
- Slinkies
- DVD movie/game rental coupons
- Sports cards
- Pokémon cards
- Yo-yos
- Temporary tattoos
- Grab bag or treasure box (toys, treats, decals)
- Modeling clay
- Address books
- Plastic wrist bands
- Balls
- Art supplies
- Jacks
- Marbles

- Jump ropes
- Jewelry
- New pencils
- Puzzles
- Surprise treats or rewards (random)
- Key chains
- School supplies
- Stickers
- Miniature cars
- Coloring books
- Posters to be colored with markers
- Bubble-blowing kits
- Play money
- Footbag (hackey-sack)
- Bean bags
- Crayons
- Markers

Tough Kid may be required to work appropriately for a 10-minute block of time to earn two minutes' use of a handheld video game. The specific Tough Kids the teacher is working with will determine the reinforcement form, amount, and frequency with which it must be delivered to be effective. In addition to the types of reinforcement already explained, there is one more that is probably the most important form of reinforcement for all human beings. We discuss it next.

Social Reinforcement

A smile, a comment on a job well done, and a compliment are all examples of social reinforcement. Social reinforcement is any social behavior by the teacher that increases or maintains student behavior. Because many Tough Kids are socially unskilled and have difficulty interacting with others, they may be starved for social reinforcement. Many of the annoying and aggravating behaviors of Tough Kids are also linked to this social reinforcement deprivation.

POINTER BOX 2-1

WHERE TO FIND NOVEL REINFORCERS

Interesting and unique reinforcers may be found in a variety of places. Some of the more popular places with examples of what they offer are listed below:

ONLINE SOURCES

- www.orientaltrading.com
- www.amazon.com
- www.ebay.com

COSTUME SHOPS

- Costume accessories
- Makeup
- Masks
- Wigs
- Goofy glasses

FLEA MARKETS AND TEACHERS' ATTICS/BASEMENTS

- "White elephants" donated by colleagues and friends
- Old clothes for "dress up"
- Sports equipment
- Toys, books, comic books, games

MAGIC OR TRICK SHOP

- "Mind bender" puzzles and games
- Simple magic tricks

NOVELTY STORES

- Artificial scars
- Broken-glass decals
- Disappearing ink
- Fake melted ice cream bars
- Fake broken eggs
- Flavored toothpicks
- Hand buzzers
- Plastic ants
- Plastic ice cube with fly in it
- Rubber vomit

OTHERS

- Dollar stores
- Garage sales

Attention, even negative attention, from another person can serve as extremely powerful reinforcement. Tough Kids have often learned over time that if they can't get noticed for something good, they will get noticed for something bad. There are also those Tough Kids who have progressed to the point where they don't even find what is normally socially reinforcing for other students to be reinforcing for them. In these cases, at least in the beginning, what is normally socially reinforcing (e.g., specific praise) must be *paired* with something else the Tough Kid already finds reinforcing. Over time, the social reinforcement takes on the reinforcing qualities of the paired reinforcement.

The teacher then begins to fade the paired reinforcement and continues to deliver the social reinforcement. In this way, Tough Kids can be taught to find the social reinforcement *reinforcing.* Unfortunately, many teachers who work with Tough Kids do not deliver anywhere near the level of social reinforcement that effective classroom management requires for these students. Box 2-5 lists a variety of sample praise statements.

ASSESSING AND SELECTING REINFORCEMENT

It is a mistake to assume that you automatically know what will serve as reinforcement for Tough Kids. The rule of thumb for teachers is to try the *potential* reinforcer with the student. If the behavior increases, then reinforcement has occurred. Many teachers assume that if they like something, or if similar students like something, a particular Tough Kid will also find (or should find) that something reinforcing. It is not unusual to hear a teacher say, "I tried positive reinforcement, but it didn't work!" Remember, if the behavior did not actually increase, there was no positive reinforcement. Several practical steps help in assessing potential reinforcement for Tough Kids:

STEP 1 First, *observe* or *watch.* By watching Tough Kids, you can determine what they like to do. The activities that students engage in are generally reinforcing. A student can be observed during free time, transition times, leisure time, and even class time. The activities the student voluntarily engages in are likely to be reinforcing.

STEP 2 *Asking* is also an important step in assessing reinforcers. While in some cases students may have a hard time thinking of things they would like to earn,

BOX 2-5

Sample *Praise* Statements

- Atta boy/girl!
- What terrific work!
- Class "A" work!
- Do you believe it?
- Excellent!
- Fantastic!
- Great paying attention!
- You really outdid yourself this time!
- Incredible job!
- Keep it up!
- Like, wow!
- I'm really impressed!
- Nice work!
- Performance plus!
- Quintessential perfection!
- Radical work!
- Superb finishing your assignment!
- Terrific!
- Very good work completion!
- Way to go!
- You've knocked the socks off that assignment!

others will be able to give the teacher ideas. It is certainly worth your time to simply ask students what they would like to earn. Also keep track of what students *ask for* and use those activities or items as reinforcement. In other words, make those things contingent based on good performance rather than simply making them available. Above all, a Tough Kid's teacher must learn to think like a Tough Kid in order to select effective reinforcement!

STEP 3 *Reinforcer checklists* are another way to determine effective reinforcement for individual students. The checklists contain lists of potential reinforcers, which are generally listed according to categories such as edible, material, social, etc. A reinforcer checklist may be made by the teacher or purchased commercially (see www.interventioncentral.org for suggestions). Students are simply asked to check items they would like to earn. For students who cannot read, the teacher can interview the students and read the lists to them, marking the selections.

A variation of a reinforcer checklist is a reinforcer menu (see Figure 2-1). This approach may be particularly useful with students who have difficulty communicating their needs and wants. A menu is simply a list of pictures of known reinforcers the student likes. You might cut pictures from magazines, draw them, or generate them electronically. To select a reinforcer, the student has only to point to the item of choice. The items can be changed or updated periodically. Mystery choices or surprise items denoted by a question mark (?) may also be included on the menu.

STEP 4 *Reinforcement sampling* is another assessment technique to determine effective reinforcers. In fact, the authors love to engage in reinforcement sampling themselves at Sam's Club or Costco. On sample days, vendors of different food products have arranged for samples of their products to be handed out to passing shoppers. The vendors have found that shoppers will often buy their products after tasting free samples. The idea is the same with reinforcement sampling for Tough

Kids. A number of potential reinforcers are displayed for a limited period of time, such as an hour or a day, so students can see, access, and try them. The teacher simply observes the types of reinforcers students sample (e.g., food, toys, activities) during this time and writes them down. Selected reinforcers can then be included on a reinforcement menu.

One mistake that teachers of Tough Kids sometimes make is to give students the reinforcer first, after extracting a promise that the students will do what they have been asked to do. For example, Connor's teacher may tell him he may go on the class field trip if he promises to not get in any fights the rest of the week. Ava's teacher may tell her she can take out playground equipment at recess if she promises she will share better.

Grandma's Law, also known as the *Premack Principle*, is a rule about reinforcement that grandmothers seem to have known about and used since the beginning of time (Premack, 1959). According to this principle, the reinforcer is always given *after* the desired behavior, *never before*. For example:

- Grandma tells Fiona, "Eat your liver and onions first, and then you may have cookies and ice cream." Grandma *never* says, "You may have cookies and ice cream first if you promise to then eat your liver and onions."
- Levi's teacher, Ms. Villar, says, "After you finish your work, you may go out to recess." Ms. Villar *never* says, "You may go out to recess now if you promise to finish your work when you come in."

Grandma's Law is common sense. Do this, and then I will give you what you want. Teachers frequently turn the principle around, however,

Figure 2-1 • Reinforcer Menu

rendering what they consider to be reinforcement ineffective. Providing the reinforcement first is a common mistake. When this happens, the desired behaviors (e.g., chores, school work) usually do not occur.

"But Doctor, Nothing Reinforces My Student!"

While it is more difficult to find effective reinforcers for some students than others, there is always something that will reinforce a student. The only time this is not true is if the student is dead! There is always some edible, natural, material, or social reinforcer that will work—the trick is to find it (see Box 2-6).

Once reinforcers have been selected, you may have to improve the effectiveness of the reinforcers to make them work. As we have mentioned previously, think like a Tough Kid and not like an adult.

VARIABLES THAT MAKE REINFORCEMENT EFFECTIVE

Following a simple set of rules can make reinforcers more effective. These rules are called IFEED-AV strategies. Each letter in the name stands for a strategy that makes a reinforcer more effective. The IFEED-AV rules are described in "How To Use IFEED-AV" on the next page.

Taking a chance or not being able to predict the reinforcement that will be earned is exciting for a student, particularly if there is a chance of receiving a bigger reinforcer. Stores frequently capitalize on this strategy in their promotional campaigns to get people to patronize their businesses. For example, a fast-food restaurant may offer a chance for a trip to Hawaii along with lots of chances to win a small soft drink or an order of french fries when a customer buys a meal. A similar strategy may be used very effectively with Tough Kids through the use of Spinners

BOX 2-6

The _Golden Rule_ for Selecting Reinforcement

There is a **Golden Rule** for selecting reinforcers. If it is not followed, the reinforcers generally do not work. The Golden Rule states that any selected reinforcers should not cost a lot of **money**, should not take a lot of staff **time**, and should be **natural**, whenever possible.

Anyone can think of expensive, highly artificial, or time-consuming reinforcers. The problem is that the reinforcers will not be used consistently or frequently under these circumstances. There are thousands of reinforcers that are not too costly in terms of time and money and many that are also natural. Selecting reinforcers is a great time for Tough Kids' teachers to exercise creativity!

How to . . .

USE IFEED-AV

IMMEDIATELY. The **I** stands for reinforcing the student *immediately*. The longer the teacher waits to reinforce a student, the *less effective* the reinforcer will be. This is particularly true with younger students or students with severe disabilities. For example, reinforcer effectiveness will be limited if the student has to wait until the end of the week to receive it.

FREQUENTLY. The **F** stands for *frequently* reinforcing a student. It is especially important to frequently reinforce when a student is learning a new behavior or skill. If reinforcers are not delivered frequently enough, the student may not produce enough of a new behavior for it to become well established. The standard rule is a *minimum* of four positive reinforcers for every one negative consequence, including negative verbal comments, the teacher delivers. In the beginning, when there is a great deal of inappropriate behavior to which the teacher must attend, positive reinforcement and recognition of appropriate behavior must be increased accordingly to maintain the minimum of four positives to each negative. The reinforcer can be a simple social reinforcer, such as "Good job. You finished your math assignment."

ENTHUSIASM. The first **E** stands for *enthusiasm* in the delivery of the reinforcer. It is easy to simply hand an edible reinforcer to a student; it takes more effort to pair it with an enthusiastic comment. Modulation in the voice and excitement with a congratulatory air conveys that the student has done something important. For most teachers, this seems artificial at first. However, with practice, enthusiasm makes the difference between a drab, uninteresting delivery and one that indicates something important has taken place.

EYE CONTACT. It is also important for the teacher to look the student in the eyes when giving a reinforcer, even if the student is not looking at her. Like enthusiasm, *eye contact* suggests that a student is special and has the teacher's undivided attention. Over time, eye contact may become reinforcing in and of itself.

DESCRIBE the behavior. **D** stands for *describing* the behavior that is being reinforced. The younger the student or the more severely disabled, the more important it is to specifically describe the appropriate behavior that is being reinforced. Teachers often assume that students know what they did right that resulted in the delivery of reinforcement. However, this is often not the case. The student may not know why reinforcement is being delivered or may think it is being delivered for some behavior other than what the teacher intends to reinforce. Even if the student does know what behavior is being reinforced, describing it is important for two key reasons:

- Describing the behavior highlights and emphasizes the behavior the teacher wishes to reinforce.

- If the behavior has several steps, describing it helps to review the specific expectations for the student. An example is, "Wow, you got yourself dressed—look at you! You have your socks on, your shoes are laced, your pants are on with a belt, and your shirt has all the buttons fastened and is tucked in." This is much more effective than saying, "Good dressing."

ANTICIPATION. Building excitement and *anticipation* for the earning of a reinforcer can motivate students to do their very best. The more hype the teacher uses, the more excited students become to earn the reinforcer. Presenting the potential reinforcer in a mysterious way will also build anticipation.

VARIETY. Just like adults, students, particularly Tough Kids, get tired of the same things. A certain reinforcer may be highly desired, but after repeated exposure, it loses its effectiveness. It is easy to get caught up in giving students the same old reinforcers time and time again. However, variety is the spice of life. Generally, when teachers are asked why they do not vary their reinforcers, they indicate that the ones they use have worked very well. It is necessary to change reinforcers frequently to *keep* reinforcement effective.

and Grab Bags. These strategies will be described in detail later in this chapter.

In addition to the IFEED-AV rules, other guidelines should be kept in mind for enhancing reinforcer effectiveness. First, deprivation makes students want a reinforcer more. In other words, if they have not just had access to the reinforcer, it is much more likely to be effective. Hunger is a good example of this. If someone has not eaten for several hours, food will serve as a more powerful reinforcer than it would right after a large meal. However, it is important to remember that students must never be deprived of the essentials to which they have a right (e.g., food, water, bathroom).

The magnitude of the reinforcer is another variable that affects its potency. Tough Kids are more likely to work for a larger reward than for a smaller one. However, this is true only up to a point. If the reinforcer is too large, the student will quickly tire of it. If it is too small, the student may become frustrated and stop performing. It is very important to select just the right amount of reinforcer, whether it is food, money, activities, or praise, to keep the Tough Kid motivated.

The delivery schedule of a reinforcer is another important effectiveness variable. By schedule, we mean the amount of the desired behavior that is required before the reinforcer is given. When a student is first learning a new behavior, continuous reinforcement is best. This means that after every correct response, a reinforcer is given. Likewise, when a student is first learning a complex task, it is important to reinforce after every correct step. However, once the student has learned the correct behavior or steps, intermittent reinforcement is

preferable. For example, when using intermittent reinforcement, the teacher might reinforce after every third (or some other number) math problem completed correctly. This is called a *fixed* schedule of reinforcement because the teacher has fixed the requirement for reinforcement at three.

An advantage of this fixed schedule is that the student will not tire of the reinforcer as quickly as with a continuous reinforcement schedule. The disadvantage is that some students will stop working right after the reinforcement is given and won't start back to work immediately.

If this is a problem, it can be remedied by switching to what is called a *variable* schedule of reinforcement. With a variable schedule, for example, on the average every third response (or some other number) might be reinforced. However, the important difference here is the term *average*. Sometimes the teacher might reinforce the student after seven correct responses, then three responses, then four responses, then ten responses, then one response. The Tough Kid can never be sure he will not be reinforced immediately after he gives the next correct response because the response requirement is random and only the average is fixed. Because of this uncertainty, variable reinforcement is usually very effective when used with Tough Kids.

Fading

Some teachers criticize the use of positive reinforcement because they believe students will become too dependent on reinforcement and always expect to receive it for everything they do. They assume that all positive reinforcement is artificial and that students should behave appropriately because it is the responsible thing to do.

This reasoning has two basic flaws. First, our students are Tough Kids who may need extra inducements to get them to even begin to exhibit desired behavior. Without reinforcement, there is little motivation for these students to change their behavior. Second, it is erroneous to believe that most people work without some type of reinforcer. As we've already mentioned, few teachers (or other employees) would show up at work if paychecks were not distributed periodically.

Ideally, the teacher gets the Tough Kid started using potent and even artificial reinforcers, if necessary. She then reduces the amount of reinforcement over time, requiring more and more of the appropriate behavior and gradually shifting to more natural rewards. This reduction in reinforcers is called *fading*. "How To Fade Reinforcement" outlines the steps to use for fading.

Fading frequently fails when reinforcement is stopped too quickly or is not paired with social praise. Through this pairing, social praise will eventually assume the reinforcing qualities of the reinforcement with which it is paired. Gradually the reinforcement is reduced, leaving social praise as the major reinforcer of the appropriate behavior. It is never desirable to completely fade out social praise.

Ideally, a teacher's goal is to fade all students from more artificial forms of reinforcement. However,

How to . . .

FADE REINFORCEMENT

Step 1. Provide reinforcement to the student for desired performance. Continuous or frequent reinforcement is usually desirable when the student is learning a new skill or until the student is performing at an acceptable level.

Step 2. Always pair the delivery of the reinforcement with specific social reinforcement, such as "I was impressed by how you lined up without pushing or shoving."

Step 3. Gradually move from a continuous reinforcement schedule to a fixed or variable intermittent schedule.

Step 4. As reinforcement becomes more intermittent, gradually move from artificial reinforcement to more natural reinforcement.

Step 5. Continue to use social reinforcement generously. Social reinforcement is always appropriate.

many Tough Kids with longstanding histories of severe behavior problems may require some form of intermittent reinforcement program for a long period of time, perhaps even for years. The effort required for the teacher to maintain a reduced form of the original reinforcement, as opposed to that required to deal with the Tough Kid's initial levels of inappropriate behavior, is in most cases well worth the trouble.

UNIQUE DELIVERY SYSTEMS FOR POSITIVE REINFORCEMENT

Wandering Social Reinforcer

One of the most effective but underused delivery systems for positive reinforcement is the wandering teacher. The wandering teacher serves several useful purposes. First of all, by wandering randomly while students are working independently or in small groups, or even while presenting material, the teacher's proximity serves to help prevent problems from occurring in the first place. Because random wandering does not allow students to predict when the teacher will be in their location, some inappropriate behavior will simply be avoided altogether.

Wandering provides the teacher with the perfect opportunity to provide positive social reinforcement to students. A smile, wink, or nod can be delivered quickly and easily. Encouragement and quick checks of academic work (no more than 30 seconds per stop) can help students who are on task remain on task. Wandering teachers can provide positive, corrective feedback where needed.

disadvantage!

The teacher who parks at her desk and does not circulate is missing many prime opportunities for social reinforcement with students. Additionally, by requiring students to come to her desk for assistance or to have work checked, the teacher is contributing to the escalation of behavior problems. When students come to the teacher rather than the teacher to the students, students' proximity to each other is increased as they pass desks and wait in line for assistance. Pushing, shoving, and negative comments often result and can blow up into bigger problems.

We recommend that new teachers not be issued desks until they have been teaching for two years! In this way, they will become accustomed to moving around the room and will not establish the bad habit of sitting behind the desk to carry out classroom learning activities.

Chart Moves

Chart Moves make use of a teacher-constructed dot-to-dot picture that is posted so the student can track her own progress. The chart determines when reinforcement will be delivered. Figure 2-2 shows three examples of Chart Moves posters. These examples are taken from *The Tough Kid Tool Box*, which features blackline master versions of all examples shown in this book. See Pointer Box 2-2 on p. 66 for more details. You can also easily create your own Chart Moves sheets with pictures cut from magazines.

With Chart Moves, each time reinforcement is earned, the student is allowed to connect another dot on the chart. She then earns the prespecified reward each time a special reward dot is reached. The reward dots are colored or circled to indicate that the student will receive the reinforcement when she has earned enough chart moves to reach the special dot. In addition, the first or last chart move earned each day may be <u>dated</u> so that a student's daily progress is automatically recorded on the chart.

The distance (or number of chart moves) between the special reward dots will <u>vary</u> <u>depending on</u> <u>the frequency with which the teacher believes</u> <u>the student's behavior needs to be reinforced.</u> It is expected that a student will need fewer chart moves initially to reach the reward dot when she is first learning a new behavior. Reward dots are spaced further apart (requiring more chart moves) as the student's behavior improves. Thus, the Chart Moves reinforcer has built into it an effective means of gradually fading the positive reinforcement.

Variations on the use of Chart Moves include making the <u>dot-to-dot chart an actual picture of</u> <u>what the student wishes to earn.</u> For example, a drawing of an ice cream cone, an action figure, or a squirt gun might be used as the outline for the chart (Figure 2-2b). Likewise, the student might earn a puzzle piece each time she lands on a reward dot. When completed, the puzzle forms a picture of the earned item, and the student receives the item when the puzzle is complete. The student can also earn the privilege of coloring in blocks of a graphed tower (Figure 2-2c). When the student reaches a predetermined level of the tower, certain prespecified positive reinforcement is delivered.

The Chart Moves system is suited for use with many behaviors, including noncompliance, tantruming, and talk-outs. It can also be used to increase behavior such as positive peer interactions.

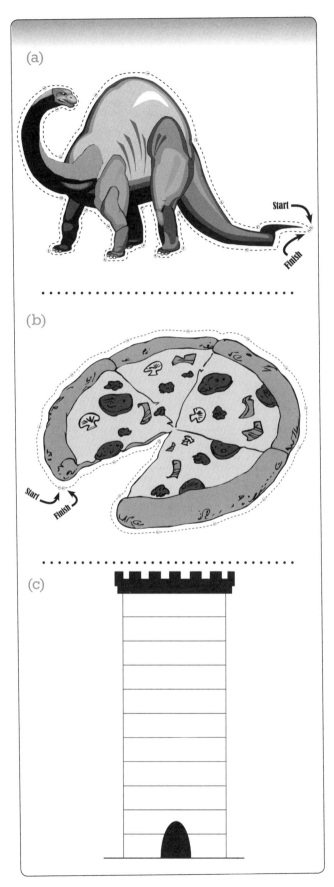

Figure 2-2 • Chart Moves Examples

POINTER BOX 2-2

READY-TO-USE TOUGH KID TOOLS

Many of the examples shown in this book are taken from *The Tough Kid Tool Box*, a companion volume of materials for implementing behavior management strategies with Tough Kids. The book and accompanying CD contain reproducible tools in both English and Spanish, along with detailed directions for using them. *The Tough Kid Tool Box* provides everything needed to implement Mystery Motivators, Spinners, Lotteries/Raffles, and more. The book is available from Pacific Northwest Publishing, www.PacificNWPublish.com.

Magic Pens

Another variation on the Chart Moves system is to combine it with the use of special markers and "decoding" pens, available at some office supply stores and online (see Pointer Box 2-3).

With this strategy, the reward dots are not circled or colored, but rather are marked with an invisible-ink marker. Each time the student earns a chart move, he touches the next dot with the decoding pen. If the dot has been marked with the invisible-ink marker, it turns a dark color to indicate that it is a reward dot. Thus, reinforcement is unpredictable and will usually result in high performance rates.

Spinners

A game-type Spinner like the one shown in Figure 2-3 may also be used to reinforce numerous behaviors. The Spinner is divided into five or more sections of various sizes. Each section of the Spinner represents a different positive reinforcer, such as being first in line to lunch, a new pencil or eraser, extra computer time, ten minutes of free time with a friend, or serving as an office aide for elementary students. Secondary students have been known to enjoy earning coupons that can be exchanged for gas for their cars, food from a fast-food restaurant, a parking space in front of the school for a day, or hairstyling services.

POINTER BOX 2-3

MAGIC DECODING PENS

Sets of markers and decoding pens are made by the Crayola Company and are available as Crayola Color Changeable Markers at www.CrayolaStore.com and office supply websites.

Jorge's Spinner Menu

1. Surprise Box of Things to Do
2. First in Line
3. 10 Minutes Choice of Game With Friend
4. Get to Pass Out Papers in Class
5. 20 Extra Bank Points
6. Sit Anywhere in Class
7. 15 Minutes Computer Time

From *The Tough Kid Tool Box*. See Pointer Box 2-2, p. 66.

Figure 2-3 • Spinner Example

Positive reinforcement that is represented on the Spinner should be planned and selected in conjunction with the student so that those positive reinforcers with higher value are given a smaller slice of the Spinner. In this way, higher value reinforcers represented on smaller slices of the Spinner will be delivered less often than lower value reinforcers represented on larger slices. When a Spinner is used in conjunction with the Chart Moves system, the student earns a spin when he reaches one of the colored reward dots. Care must be taken to periodically change the positive reinforcement represented on the Spinner so it retains its original effectiveness.

Vary to keep engaged!

Mystery Motivators

The first component of the Mystery Motivator is the motivator or reinforcer itself. The name of the reinforcer is written on a slip of paper, sealed inside an envelope, and displayed in a prominent position somewhere in the classroom, such as the middle of the chalkboard at the front of the room. The envelope should be marked with several large question marks (?), denoting mystery or the unknown. The second component is a weekly or monthly chart on which the teacher has randomly marked reinforcement days with a small colored "X." Each of the days has a self-sticking dot or small piece of masking tape on it. For those days with an "X" on them, the "X" is covered with the dot or tape (see the examples in

Mysterious

From *The Tough Kid Tool Box*. See Pointer Box 2-2, p. 66.

Figure 2-4 • Mystery Motivator
Chart Examples

TECHNIQUE TIP

Use a bonus square to provide additional incentive. Write a number up to five in the square at the beginning of the week and cover with a sticker or tape. At the end of the week, the student reveals the bonus number. If the student earned a Mystery Motivator on that many days or more during the week, the student earns an additional reward. In the top example in Figure 2-4, the student has removed the tape on three days, and the bonus number is three, so the student receives the bonus reward.

Figure 2-4). For each day that the student earns reinforcement, he is permitted to peel off the dot or piece of tape. If an "X" is under the dot or tape, the student is given the Mystery Motivator envelope to open. The reinforcement named on the piece of paper inside is then delivered. If there is no "X" under the dot or sticker, the student will have to wait until the next day to peel off the next dot. Randomly assigning the "X"s

under the dots creates high anticipation and provides a visual reminder each day of what the student must do to earn a chance at the Mystery Motivator.

Decoding pens can also be used effectively with Mystery Motivator charts (see Figure 2-5). With this strategy, the Mystery Motivator envelope is still posted. The teacher uses the invisible-ink pen ahead of time to mark the days the Mystery Motivator may be earned on the weekly or monthly chart. Until the student has met the criteria and earned the right to color in the box on the chart for that day (revealing the secret "X"), he won't know whether a Mystery Motivator will be delivered. Of course, if the student fails to meet criteria and is not permitted to color in the box, he will think that may have been a day when the Mystery Motivator would have been delivered.

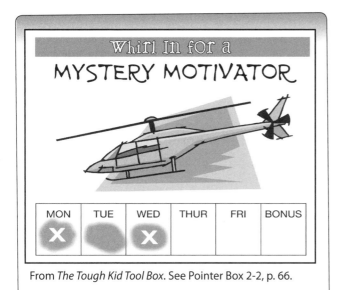

Whirl In for a
MYSTERY MOTIVATOR

MON	TUE	WED	THUR	FRI	BONUS
X		X			

From *The Tough Kid Tool Box*. See Pointer Box 2-2, p. 66.

Figure 2-5 • Mystery Motivator
Chart With Magic Pens Example

One critical component in making Mystery Motivators effective is the hype associated with presenting them to the class, reminders about the possibility of earning them, and what may or may not be in the envelope. The teacher must talk about the Mystery Motivators with excitement and anticipation, and make them as mysterious as possible. She may give hints, such as "It's not brown" or "You have liked it a lot in the past." If the teacher does a good job of marketing, Tough Kids will respond enthusiastically. Many variations of Mystery Motivators have been used successfully with both elementary and secondary students.

Mystery is fun!

Grab Bags

Grab Bags are based on essentially the same concept as the Mystery Motivator, except the reinforcer itself is placed in the bag and is earned when the student uncovers an "X" on her randomly marked chart. The Grab Bag may also be used in conjunction with a Spinner by making the Grab Bag the reward on one of the Spinner sections. In a variation of the Grab Bag, the bag contains a number of wrapped items of varying value. When the student has earned the right to the Grab Bag, she is allowed to select an item from the bag but can't unwrap it until after it has been selected.

Lottery/Raffle Tickets

Passing out Lottery or Raffle Tickets is one way the teacher can reinforce desired academic performance or behavior daily. "How To Use Lottery and Raffle Tickets" on the next page outlines guidelines for their use. Students write their names on earned tickets and deposit them in a designated container in the classroom. Figure 2-6 on p. 71 depicts some examples of Raffle Tickets used in different classrooms.

Depending on how frequently the teacher needs to reinforce the class, drawings for small prizes may be held once or twice each day, weekly, or monthly. The more reinforcement the class requires, the more frequently the teacher will hold the drawings and the more prizes she will award each time.

Prizes in raffle drawings may be small school items such as pencils or other supplies, food coupons, treats, puzzles, games, and other items donated by local businesses or the PTA. Drawings may also include prizes such as a positive note or phone call home to parents and classroom privileges such as using desirable sports or game equipment at recess, serving as classroom aide for a specified time of the day, taking a day off from homework in one subject, tutoring a younger student, and the like.

prize ideas

How to . . .

USE LOTTERY AND RAFFLE TICKETS

Step 1. Select the specific academic and/or social behaviors that need improvement.

Step 2. Design or select the tickets.

Step 3. Determine how often drawings must be held initially so students will stay motivated to work for tickets.

Step 4. Explain the program to the students. Define and describe the behaviors needed to earn the tickets. Give examples of the desired behaviors, and role-play if necessary to make certain students understand the expectations.

Step 5. Implement the program. Generously give out tickets for the targeted behaviors.

Step 6. When giving out each ticket, specifically describe and praise the behavior for which the ticket is being given (e.g., "Alicia, nice job of completing your reading assignment on time.").

Step 7. Make certain tickets are awarded to students who have not exhibited the targeted behaviors previously but who are exhibiting them now.

Step 8. Make certain tickets are awarded to students who have exhibited the target behaviors in the past and continue to exhibit them. Otherwise, students may get the idea that the only way they will receive reinforcement is if they first fail to behave appropriately.

Step 9. Within two weeks of implementing a daily raffle program or four weeks of implementing a weekly one, evaluate the effectiveness of the program. Make adjustments as needed in the target behaviors, the prizes that are awarded in the drawings, the frequency of the drawings, and the number of tickets available for students to earn each day.

For weekly or monthly drawings, all coupons earned for the week or the month, including those that have already been drawn for prizes, are placed in the container for a drawing. Thus, students know that they still have a chance to win a prize even if they weren't selected in a daily drawing. For the weekly or monthly drawing, we suggest that fewer names be drawn and that the prizes be somewhat bigger.

In implementing a daily, weekly, or monthly raffle program, the teacher also needs to build in a "cost" or "fine" system so that Tough Kids who have just recently exhibited inappropriate behavior are not rewarded by the system. We suggest a special rule that applies to any student whose inappropriate behavior has warranted being sent to the office, a phone call home to parents, or another classroom penalty for a severe behavior problem during that day (for a daily drawing) or during the week before a weekly or monthly drawing. Such students are disqualified from collecting a prize if their name is drawn in that particular drawing. To implement this rule,

Figure 2-6 • Lottery/Raffle Ticket Examples

the teacher will need to keep a list of students who will be disqualified if their names are drawn in the raffle. If a disqualified student's name is drawn, the teacher should *not* announce the name, but merely state that the name of someone who is disqualified has been drawn and that another name will be drawn. This procedure maximizes the "fine" system because all students who

TECHNIQUE TIP

As vice principal in a junior high, one of the authors learned the hard way the need for a special disqualification rule for raffle ticket drawings. The junior high held a raffle ticket drawing for reinforcement on a weekly and monthly basis throughout the year. The culminating raffle was held at year's end and included all weekly and monthly tickets for the year. The grand prize was a big one—a computer. The author was standing on the stage with the student body officers who selected the ticket out of a rotating drum under the vice principal's direction. The student selected to win the computer? None other than the student who had just been removed from the auditorium for highly disruptive behavior. No disqualification rule was in place. All of the student body officers saw the name on the ticket. If another ticket had been selected, the student body officers all knew whose name had really been selected, and word would probably have spread throughout the school. The prize was awarded in the student's absence, causing extreme duress to the vice principal. From then on, the school's disqualification rule was "must be present to win."

have been disqualified for the drawing will think they might have collected a prize had they not been disqualified.

Yes/No Program

The Yes/No Program is a variation of a lottery or raffle drawing. It is a simple ticket system that can be used for individual students or teams of students to improve academic or social behavior. For younger students, each ticket should have a smiley face, a frowny face, and a space for the student's name. For older students, each ticket should contain the words *Yes* and *No* as well as a space for the student's name (see examples in Figure 2-7). Create a master sheet of tickets and make multiple copies of it, then cut each sheet apart so each slip of paper constitutes one ticket. Steps for using the Yes/No Program follow:

From *The Tough Kid Tool Box*. See Pointer Box 2-2, p. 66.

Figure 2-7 • Yes/No Ticket Examples

STEP 1   Select a specific desired behavior to increase. This may include behaviors such as increasing compliance with adult requests, raising one's hand to talk, staying in one's seat, and making positive comments to others.

STEP 2   Select reinforcers to be earned by students who are participating in the Yes/No Program.

STEP 3   Explain the program to students who will be participating. Make certain they understand the specific behavior that will earn them a Yes or a smiley face and those behaviors that will earn them a No or frowny face.

STEP 4   When a student engages in the target behavior, mark the Yes or smiley face on a ticket, write the student's name on it, and deposit it into a container. If the student does not exhibit the target behavior when it is appropriate to do so, mark the No or frowny designation on a ticket, write the student's name on it, and deposit it in the container. Be sure to give the student specific feedback for each Yes or No earned. For example, if the target behavior is compliance with the teacher's request and the student complies, the teacher might say, "Miguel, you followed my directions right away. You just earned a Yes ticket." If the student does not comply, you might say, "Miguel, that's not following my directions. You just earned a No ticket."

STEP 5   At the end of the class or subject session, hold the Yes/No drawing. Select several tickets from the container and distribute rewards or privileges for students whose Yes or smiley face tickets are drawn.

 To maximize the effectiveness of the program and to avoid public embarrassment of students who earned Nos or frowny faces, when you select a No, simply say, "I'm sorry, but I've just drawn a ticket with a No on it. That person won't get the prize." By handling the Nos in this way, all students who have earned Nos will think it might be their ticket.

Once the targeted behavior is occurring regularly at acceptable levels, gradually fade the use of the program. For example, instead of awarding a Yes or smiley face every time a student exhibits the desired behavior, give one after an average of every second time, then every third time, and so on. Continue to award a No for each instance when the target behavior is not demonstrated when it should be. Try the Yes/No Program. You and your students will have fun with it!

eventually fade

Dots for Motivation

Dots for Motivation is a wonderful strategy to use with Tough Kids who seem unmotivated or students who, according to their teachers, "do nothing" (Doyle, Jenson, Clark, & Gates, 1999). The premise on which this strategy operates is that students who are unmotivated or *do nothing* are reinforced by *doing nothing* and will probably work *to do nothing*.

The "dots" used with this strategy are small colored dots that are sticky on one side, such as those used to mark file folders. There are usually 15 to 20 dots on a single sheet and several sheets of dots in each package. In preparation for using this system, cut the sheets apart so that each dot is separate. Then tape an empty envelope to the side of the desk of each student who will be using the system. Students will store the dots they earn in their envelopes.

Identify the subject or one of the subjects for which identified Tough Kids are unmotivated or *do nothing*. Let's say, for example, that one of the problem subjects is math. In this case, selected students are each given a dot when they are on task and working on their math. When they come to a problem they cannot or do not want to do, they can use one of the dots they have earned, sticking it next to the problem to indicate a "free" problem that they do not have to do.

> ## THINK
> THINK ABOUT IT
> " In essence, students work more in order to get out of work. "

Within a few weeks, many students on the Dots for Motivation system are completing more work than they have for a long time. In essence, they work more in order to get out of work. Over time, the teacher will need to cut the dots in half and finally into quarters so that students have to earn two halves or four quarters of a dot to earn a free problem or item.

fade!

Dots can also be used as a shaping procedure. Initially, students can earn them just for being on task and working. Then expand their use to cover the number of problems or items completed by the student. For the first week or two, for example, a student receives dots for being

TECHNIQUE TIP

ideas!

Here are several variations in using Dots for Motivation:

- Use different colored dots for different subjects.

- Require two dots to earn a free test question.

- Use the program in combination with a Mystery Motivator. Students can be required to earn a specific number of dots, say 25, in order to earn a Mystery Motivator.

on task and working. Once these behaviors are stable, the student earns a dot after completing a certain number of problems or items (e.g., after every five math problems completed). Gradually increase the number of completed items required—the student must complete seven problems, then ten problems, and so on to earn a dot.

Dots can be given to teams in cooperative learning situations. In this case, each team is assigned a different color and *each* student has to complete a prespecified number of problems before the team earns a dot. Dots can also be used on a larger scale. After completing a certain number of assignments, students can earn dots that get them out of future assignments or tests.

Some teachers worry that their Tough Kids are not completing every problem, item, or test when they are on the Dots for Motivation

system. The important thing to remember is these Tough Kids were essentially doing nothing previously. This system provides an effective way to jump-start a student, so to speak. The system will eventually be faded from use by cutting the dots into pieces and requiring more and more problems or items to earn each part of a dot. Try this strategy with some of your unmotivated students. In addition to effectively increasing student motivation, it can provide quiet amusement for the teacher!

Classroom Auctions

Consider holding classroom auctions periodically as an additional fun and interesting form of positive reinforcement. Tough Kids generally love the novelty they bring. The upside for the teacher is she can get rid of many unwanted items from her garage, basement, and even her classroom. It is usually difficult to collect enough items for a weekly classroom auction. Thus, we suggest holding a smaller one monthly or a larger one quarterly, or simply holding one whenever you are ready.

In addition to gathering your own unwanted items, you can collect free items from the following:

- Educational publishing companies
- Health insurance fairs
- Samples received in the mail at home
- Sales tables at stores
- Garage sales
- Dollar stores
- Donations from colleagues, friends, and relatives
- White elephants received in gift exchanges
- Anywhere else you can find them

BOX 2-7

Possible *Auction Items*

- Old ski equipment
- Old board games
- An old centerpiece
- Holiday decorations
- Used DVDs and CDs
- Stuffed animals
- The box of Girl Scout cookies your mother gave you that you are trying not to eat
- Old costume jewelry

- Old costumes, masks, and disguises
- Action figures
- Hot Wheels or other toy cars
- Pokémon cards
- Plastic dinosaurs and aliens
- Books
- Jigsaw puzzles
- Old souvenirs from trips
- That vase Aunt Marsha gave you six years ago (and you've never used)

Remember when you took that trip to Mexico and for some reason thought it a great idea to bring back an authentic sombrero? At least until you got back on the plane, that is. This is the time to recycle it. We also know a teacher who brought a scraped-up old ski (yes, one ski, not two) for her auction. A student in her class, Beverly, just had to have that ski. It may be because the teacher said things such as "Think how great this will look in your room leaning against the wall! Just look how this ski whispers quiet good taste! This looks like a treasure for a very cool person into new-age art!"

These kinds of items are a huge hit if you do your marketing campaign right. Think like a Tough Kid and market the items enthusiastically to increase their value in students' eyes.

Follow these steps to hold a classroom auction:

STEP 1 Gather enough items for students to have an interesting selection. Make certain there are enough items for all eligible students to obtain one or more. Box 2-7 provides ideas for possible auction items.

STEP 2 Determine what students will use for currency. Earned classroom points can be converted to "dollars," with one point worth one dollar. Classroom points can be banked for a week or more prior to the auction. Another suggestion is to use Yes/No tickets earned for several weeks prior to the auction for currency. Each Yes can be converted into five auction dollars for the student who earned it. General raffle tickets can also be earned by students for completing homework assignments, complimenting peers, appropriate recess or lunchroom behavior, following directions immediately, and other targeted behaviors. Raffle tickets can then be converted into dollars. The amount of "dollars" each student has to spend at the auction can be written with a marker on individual index cards students bring to the event. In this case, amounts are subtracted on the cards as items are "purchased," so each student knows how many dollars he has left to spend. Phony money can also be photocopied in denominations of ones, fives, tens, and twenties. Convert students' original currency (points, Yes/No or raffle tickets) into phony money, which students then bring to the auction to spend.

> ## THINK ABOUT IT
> **THINK** " Get students drooling over the selection of items, no matter how unlikely or even crazy it is. "

STEP 3 Beginning at least a week before the auction, or when you select an auction date and announce it to the class, start your marketing plan. Two or three times each day, remind students of the upcoming auction and tell them there will be some very "hot" or desirable items. Give hints (e.g., "One item is long and thin and brown"). A day or two before the event, put a few of the items on display at the front of the room and comment on them throughout the day. You might say things like:

- "Everyone will want this toy animal. I can't remember the last time I saw a stuffed gopher!"
- "Wow, a coonskin hat. Even Davy Crockett would be envious!"

- "Can you believe that gorgeous orange and green vase? Mother's Day is coming up, you know. This could be just the ticket!"

You get the idea. Get students drooling over the selection of items, no matter how unlikely or even crazy it is.

STEP 4 On auction day, explain these rules to the students:

- Raise your hand to bid. Wait to be called on.
- You will be called on again as long as you raise your hand again.
- If you yell out, you will be passed over for a turn to bid.
- Give your money to the teacher when you have a winning bid.
- All sales are final.
- Be polite to everyone.

Marketing plan for auctions to increase hype and motivation!

In a nutshell

It is human nature to react negatively to Tough Kids. If their teachers do what comes naturally, they will be far more negative than positive with their difficult students. Unfortunately, a negative teacher management style is more than ineffective—it will actually cause an increase in Tough Kids' inappropriate behavior over time!

Positive reinforcement and antecedent strategies must form the backbone of any educational program for Tough Kids. While negative consequences can temporarily stop or suppress inappropriate behavior, only positive strategies will help build or increase appropriate behavior. Thus, it is imperative that, with Tough Kids, teachers use at least four or more positive interactions at a minimum for every negative interaction. *4 or more:1 negative*

Finding things that Tough Kids consider reinforcing can require a great deal of ingenuity on the part of teachers. However, the effort will pay enormous dividends. Not only will students benefit from this approach, but you will find your classroom a much more positive environment in which to work. An emphasis on the strategies presented in this chapter in combination with the appropriate use of reductive strategies outlined in the following chapter will produce dramatic results!

References

Doyle, P., Jenson, W. R., Clark, E., & Gates, G. (1999). Free time and dots as negative reinforcement to improve academic completion and accuracy for mildly disabled students. *Proven Practice: Prevention, Remediation, Solutions for Schools, 2,* 10–15.

Eisenberger, R., & Cameron, J. (1996). Detrimental effects of reward: Reality or myth? *Journal of the American Psychological Association, 51,* 1153–1166.

Hequet, M. (1990). Non-sales incentive programs inspire service heroes. *Reward and Recognition, 8,* 3–17.

Jenson, W. R., Olympia, D., Farley, M., & Clark, E. (2004). Positive psychology and externalizing students in a sea of negativity. *Psychology in the Schools, 41,* 67–79.

Kohn, A. (1999). *Punished by rewards: The trouble with gold stars, incentive plans, A's, praise, and other bribes.* New York: Houghton Mifflin.

Premack, D. (1959). Toward empirical behavior laws: I. Positive reinforcement. *Psychological Review, 66,* 219–233.

CHAPTER 3

Practical Reductive Techniques for the Classroom

Many of the behaviors that characterize Tough Kids are the behaviors teachers want to stop. They are the behaviors that drive teachers crazy and make them want to give up teaching.

The behavioral excesses displayed by Tough Kids were detailed in **Chapter 1**. They include aggression, noncompliance, verbal abuse, arguing, tantrum throwing, excuse making, and more. Behavioral excesses interfere with learning for both the Tough Kid and other students in the classroom. This chapter focuses on practical classroom procedures that any teacher can use to reduce these problem behaviors. That is why we call these procedures *reductive*. A word of caution before proceeding: None of the techniques covered in this chapter will change behavior permanently. Teachers cannot implement a reductive technique and expect it to have lasting effects for two basic reasons:

1. These annoying behavioral excesses serve a purpose for Tough Kids. In a sense, they are functional and work for the Tough Kids. They may help a student avoid tasks, gain attention from peers, or obtain tangible rewards from the student's environment. If they are to be reduced permanently, these behavioral excesses must be replaced with appropriate behaviors that also meet the student's needs. Remember, our definition of a Tough Kid includes both behavioral excesses and deficits. For permanent change, functional abilities in the areas of social skills, academic performance, and self-management skills must replace behavioral excesses. These replacement behaviors must work as well as the behavioral excesses do for the Tough Kid.

2. The second reason reductive techniques are not permanent behavior change techniques is that Tough Kids are *immune* to punishment. They build up a resistance to shouts, threats, and even physical abuse, particularly from adults. It has been estimated that Tough Kids can take twice the amount of punishment as general education students and still not change their behavior (Patterson, 1976)! From second grade through junior high school, the average rate of teacher verbal reprimands in classrooms is one every two minutes (Jenson, Olympia,

Teachers can use the practical reductive techniques included in this book to stop behavioral excesses while they work on building appropriate replacement skills. The techniques are all proven effective by research (evidence-based). If a teacher uses nonvalid reductive techniques, she will be vulnerable to criticism, personnel action, and even legal difficulties if there are problems with the techniques. Only evidence-based techniques should be used with Tough Kids.

Farley, & Clark, 2004; Van Houten & Doleys, 1983). After second grade, the rate of teacher praise declines rapidly, with the rate of reprimands almost always exceeding praise rates. Tough Kids receive the majority of these reprimands, and they become immune to teachers' yelling, threats, and negative attention. The only way to make behavior change permanent is to use positive procedures to reward appropriate replacement behaviors. Reductive techniques can temporarily reduce behavioral excesses, but only positive procedures can build the social, academic, and self-management skills that are necessary to replace the excesses.

Sad starts

Exactly what are reductive techniques? When teachers think of reductive techniques, procedures like timeout, in-school suspension, names and checks on the board, expulsion, and others come to mind. Some reductive procedures are effective with Tough Kids, and some are not. The reductive techniques most frequently used by teachers include verbal reprimands (approximately 42%), parental contact (22%), revocation of privileges (17%), detention (10%), isolation of student from class (6%), sending student to principal's office (2%), and corporal punishment (used less than 1% of the time).

Common

What Are Reductive Techniques?

For our purposes, a reductive technique is any research-validated (sometimes referred to as evidence-based) technique that will temporarily stop or suppress a behavior. We prefer to call them reductive techniques rather than punishment for several reasons. Punishment is loaded with many emotions and is often tied to retribution (assumed deserved penalties). The term punishment can also be confusing for teachers.

Obviously, teacher reprimands are the most frequently used reductive technique. The problem with teacher reprimands is that they are overused and often not used effectively. The frequently used techniques we have mentioned are probably not even the most effective reductive techniques. It is important to use more positive, creative reductive techniques such as differential attention, timeout (e.g., Bumpy Bunny Timeout), Chance Jars, and the "Sure I Will" program. All of these techniques will be presented later in this chapter. However, before using any of them, it is important to be aware of the general variables that make them effective.

more positive

Effective Use of Reductive Techniques

Learning to use anything effectively means learning to use it with the least amount of *cost* for maximum results. If a technique takes too much time, effort, or classroom resources, a teacher will not continue to use it. Effective use also means that the technique is used sparingly, not wastefully. If a reductive technique is used too much, it becomes watered down and ineffective. As we mentioned earlier, Tough Kids become immune. Finally, teachers want to use reductive techniques to produce the largest behavior change possible. To get the most effective results with reductive techniques, five principles must be followed (see Box 3-1).

Oh No! Not From Someone I Like

Most people dislike it when reductive techniques are used with them, particularly when they are used by someone they like. It is much more difficult to receive a reprimand from a person who truly cares for them and for whom they care. Almost everyone is familiar with the characterization in movies (e.g., *The Breakfast*

BOX 3-1

Principles That Influence the Effectiveness of *Reductive Techniques*

- **Reward rates should be <u>high</u>.** The rate of reinforcement for appropriate behaviors should be high. It is much more effective for a student to receive a reductive technique from a person she likes and finds reinforcing.

- **Reward an appropriate behavior that interferes with the misbehavior.** Find a behavior that is incompatible with or an appropriate alternative to the misbehavior to reward so that it can replace the inappropriate behavior.

- **Do not adapt the student to the reductive technique.** Do not start off with a less intense form of the reductive technique and slowly work up. Use a form of the reductive technique that is <u>potent enough</u> to result in rapid behavior change so the student does not adapt to it.

- **Start early in a student's behavior chain of misbehavior.** Do not wait until the student is out of control. Identify the early "trigger" misbehaviors in a chain (e.g., ignoring, delaying, or arguing) and implement the reductive procedure early.

- **Manage peer attention to your advantage.** Use peer attention to reward appropriate behaviors through the use of group contingencies (detailed later in this chapter). Do not allow peers to reward inappropriate behaviors that make the Tough Kid more difficult.

Club) and on TV (*The Simpsons*) of the school disciplinarian whose sole job is to catch and punish misbehaving students. This person is frequently depicted as pathetic, inept, and disliked by students. He is often set up and made the brunt of jokes. There is a grain of truth in this characterization.

To achieve a liking effect, it is important for teachers to reinforce at higher rates than they punish (see "Liking Principle" in **Chapter 1**, p. 37). We have already pointed out that from third grade onward, the rate at which teachers reprimand exceeds their rate of praise. This is exactly the effect that is not wanted because it causes students to dislike teachers and the classroom in general. A teacher's praise and reinforcement rate must exceed her reductive technique rate to be effective. We suggest the simple formula of a minimum of three or four praise statements (using the IFEED-AV rules from **Chapter 2**, p. 61) for every negative statement (e.g., reprimand or criticism) or consequence you deliver. Under no circumstances should you give fewer than four praise statements per hour. More about this later.

Atleast 4 praises per hour!

You Can't Misbehave and Do That Too—It's Impossible!

This is an excellent technique to make reductive procedures more effective. It simply means if a teacher reinforces an appropriate behavior that actually interferes with the misbehavior, the misbehavior will be reduced naturally. For example, if a student is trichotillomanic (constantly pulls or plays with his hair) and a teacher rewards the student for keeping his hands in his pockets (the appropriate behavior), the hair pulling is naturally reduced. A student cannot pull hair and have his hands in his pockets at the same time.

This behavior interference principle is simple in theory but difficult in classroom practice. Teachers must be very creative and think of appropriate replacement behaviors that actually interfere with misbehaviors such as arguing, noncompliance, and aggression. The "Sure I Will" program presented later in this chapter is an excellent example of a technique that uses the behavior interference principle.

Swimming Pool Effect—Don't Let Them Get Used to the Water

We noted previously that most Tough Kids are immune to frequently used reductive techniques such as verbal reprimands. Teachers can make things worse by helping students adapt even more quickly to reductive techniques. Teachers often think they must use the least amount of a reductive technique, then gradually increase the amount if it is not effective. For instance, a teacher may want to use timeout in a chair, beginning with 30 seconds in the chair. When the technique fails, the teacher may then increase the time to 1 minute, then 3 minutes, then 5 minutes, then 15 minutes, then 30 minutes, and so on. In effect, the teacher gradually adapts the student to longer and longer periods in the timeout chair. It is similar to getting into a swimming pool with cold water. At first you may put only a toe in the water. When it no longer feels cold, you may ease more and more of your body in gradually as you adapt to the water.

A better way to use reductive techniques is to start with the amount of the technique the research literature suggests is most effective. For instance, about a minute for each year of the student's age is a good guideline for the use of several types of timeout. A seven-year-old student who behaves very inappropriately should sit in the timeout chair for approximately seven minutes. Using too little of a technique and slowly increasing is just as bad as using too much of a reductive technique. Teachers must be familiar enough with each technique to use the correct amount.

Use It Early—Don't Wait For the Explosion

Just like immediate reinforcement, using a reductive technique immediately is critically important, although it may be difficult to judge just how early. Should a teacher wait until the student actually exhibits aggressive behavior, or start earlier? Most Tough Kids' coercive behavior occurs in an escalating chain (see Figure 3-1). The student at first *ignores* (first link), then *delays* (second link), then *argues* (third link), and finally *tantrums* or is *aggressive* (fourth link).

If a teacher waits until the end of the chain to use reductive techniques, she will receive the most explosive and difficult behavior. It is much more effective to have a preplanned consequence ready when the first two behavior chain links take place. The teacher should:

- Not hold back or wait
- Anticipate problems by learning to identify the behavior chain links

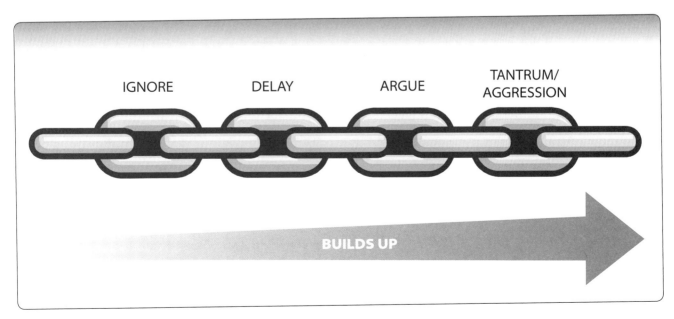

Figure 3-1 • Behavior Chain

- Have preplanned consequences
- Not try to make deals, negotiate with, or attempt to placate the Tough Kid once the coercive cycle begins. It will only make the behavior worse.

No negotiations!

Peer Attention—Use It to Your Own Advantage

Many of the inappropriate behaviors Tough Kids exhibit are directly rewarded by peer attention, especially when they are placed in groups with other Tough Kids (Dishion, McCord, & Poulin, 1999). Because so many Tough Kids have inadequate social skills, they use disruptive classroom behavior to appeal to their peers. Smiles, gestures, dares, and snickers are all subtle reinforcers from peers that encourage Tough Kids to misbehave.

Turning this peer attention to the teacher's advantage is one of the best ways to improve the effectiveness of reductive techniques. However, teachers are often reluctant to use peer attention to improve a Tough Kid's behavior. This does not make sense. If left to chance, peer attention will frequently reward inappropriate Tough Kid behavior and make the situation worse. Later in this chapter we will detail peer attention as a practical tool through the use of peer group contingencies.

THINK ABOUT IT

THINK

" *If left to chance, peer attention will frequently reward inappropriate Tough Kid behavior.* "

REDUCTIVE TECHNIQUES

Request and Reprimand Antecedents—First Line of Defense

As an educator, were you ever taught how to make an effective request or give an effective reprimand? Probably not. Yet teachers constantly have to ask students to do things in a classroom. Similarly, reprimands, as previously noted, are the reductive technique that teachers most frequently use in the classroom.

Requests and reprimands are closely related in several ways. First, most *Don't* requests are reprimands:

- "Don't pull her hair!"
- "Don't put that in your mouth!"
- "Don't talk out in my classroom!"

Second, requests always precede the behaviors that teachers are attempting to stop (such as arguing, noncompliance, tantrums). Because they always come before a behavior, they are called *antecedent* (coming just before the behavior). Reprimands generally follow the behavior (*consequence*). If request antecedents are used correctly, teachers will have fewer problems and less noncompliance (and therefore fewer reprimands). If they are used incorrectly, arguing, excuses, tantrums, aggression, and noncompliance will increase. It is easy to use request antecedents correctly. Following are some optimizing variables to remember when making a request or giving a reprimand.

1. **State the student's name.** Few things get people's attention faster than hearing their name. Start a reprimand or request using the student's name: "Bubba, I want you to take your seat now." Using a student's name personalizes the request immediately while getting his attention before you give the reprimand or request.

2. **Do not use a question format.** It is a mistake for teachers and parents to phrase a request in a question format:

   - "Isn't it time to get started?"
   - "Wouldn't you like to get your work done?"
   - "Don't you want to please your parents and follow the classroom rules?"

   All of these are foolish questions when the intention is not to give a choice. If a teacher can accept "No" for an answer from the student and live with it, it is reasonable to use a question format. If a teacher cannot live with a "No" answer, the question format should not be used. Better approaches are:

   - "It is time to get started."
   - "Please get your work done."
   - "I want you to follow the classroom rules because it will please me and your parents."

3. **Get up close.** It is interesting to note that many teachers make requests or give reprimands at relatively great distances (approximately 15–20 feet) from students. That is why so many teachers end up yelling or making pointing gestures. The greater the distance between a teacher and the student, the more a teacher yells and makes gestures.

Optimally, a request or reprimand should be made from approximately three feet, or arm's length. Some may question this distance and think it is too close. However, many social skills curricula suggest approximately three feet as an appropriate distance when engaging in a social interaction with another person. It is also much harder to ignore what a teacher is saying from three feet. If a teacher spends a great deal of time sitting behind her desk, it is impossible to take advantage of the optimal distance of three feet. Effective teachers spend as little time as possible behind their desks (see Figure 3-2). They randomly walk around their rooms and actually anticipate and avert problems before they occur.

4. **Use a quiet voice.** The more a teacher yells, the less effective she will be in the classroom. The purpose of yelling is usually to gain a student's attention and increase the emphasis on a request or reprimand. Yelling also often heightens the emotionality of the situation, making it worse. However, a quiet request made close to the student is much more effective than a yelled request from a

Figure 3-2 • Not Too Much Desk Time

distance. It also has the added advantage of not disturbing the rest of the class.

5. **Look 'em in the eyes.** Eye contact has an important impact in terms of both reinforcement and requests. If a teacher looks students in the eyes as she makes requests, she will get improved compliance. In one study, a teacher requested eye contact by saying, "Look me in the eyes," and then made a request such as "Now hang up your coat" or "Hand in your homework" (Hamlet, Axelrod, & Kuerschner, 1984). She knew it was really working when she got improved compliance overall and one of the students walked in the classroom one day and said, "You can stop this 'look at me' stuff. I've already hung up my coat, and here is my homework"!

One of the best ways to get eye contact is not to ask for it or grab a student's face. Simply get close and try a little experiment. Quietly walk up to a student who is engaged in a task and look at him. When you get within four to five feet of the student, he will automatically look up and into your eyes approximately 90% of the time. Proceed to within three feet of the student and give your request. You will get improvement in compliance even if the student breaks eye contact and looks away. One of the best ways to get eye contact is to get close.

6. **Give them time.** Once a request is made, a student needs a certain amount of time to begin the requested action. A teacher should wait at least 3 to 5 seconds after making a request. During this 3- to 5-second period, the teacher should not do or say anything. This compliance time window must not be interrupted. In one study (Forehand, 1977),

mothers interrupted during this window 40% of the time by either:

- Restating the request unnecessarily
- Making an entirely new request before the child had a chance to comply with the first request

Do not make these mistakes. Simply wait. You will increase compliance by being close to the student in terms of distance, by continuing to make eye contact, and by not talking.

7. **Ask only twice (the nagging effect).** The more *times* teachers make a request, the less likely they are to get compliance. Teachers and parents often say, "I have to ask her a hundred times before she will do anything." This trap is called the *nagging effect*, and it will greatly *reduce* compliance. The frequently asked student has trained adults to

> THINK ABOUT IT
>
> "The more times teachers make a request, the less likely they are to get compliance."

ask over and over again. It is not uncommon for a teacher to suspect hearing loss in Tough Kids with good hearing when they use this manipulative strategy with her. A teacher should make a request only *twice.* If the student does not comply either time, the teacher must follow through with a preplanned consequence for not complying with the request the first or second time asked. A hierarchy

8. **Don't give multiple requests.** It is easy to string a series of requests together in hopes of saving time. We refer to this as making *machine-gun* requests. However, multiple requests in a row reduce compliance, particularly with Tough Kids. Give one request, wait, follow through, and then issue the next request after the student has complied with the first one.

9. **Describe the request.** It is much better to give a detailed, specific request than a global one. Teachers often assume students know what they want them to do when the students truly do not understand. For example, saying, "Don't talk out in my class" is less effective than saying, "You need to raise your hand before you talk in my class." Instructional detail in a request helps focus a student and improve compliance.

10. **Be unemotional.** The more a teacher gets upset with a Tough Kid, the less compliance she will get. Yelling, threatening gestures, ugly faces, guilt-inducing statements, rough handling, and deprecating comments about the student or his family ("I've had problems with your whole family!") only reduce compliance. This type of teacher behavior also destroys the effects of the Liking Principle discussed previously.

11. **Make more start ("Do") requests than stop ("Don't") requests.** Teachers need to check themselves. If they make more *Don't* requests than *Do* requests, something is wrong. Possibly their classroom rules are not

well constructed or the other proactive strategies detailed in **Chapter 1** are not being implemented properly. A teacher whose *Don't* requests exceed her *Do* requests has a negative classroom. Interestingly, if teachers give too many *Don't* requests, they may actually experience a reduction in compliance with *Do* requests.

12. **Verbally reinforce compliance.** This seems self-evident, but it is not. First, it is easy for teachers to forget or not notice when students do comply with their requests, and they simply move on to the next task. Second, with some Tough Kids, teachers feel that if they verbally reinforce students for complying, they will stop the requested behavior (i.e., the "letting sleeping dogs lie" argument). This is completely wrong. If teachers want compliance in the future, they must reward it now. You might even shock Tough Kids by doing this because they so rarely get verbal reinforcement for compliance. Research (Jenson et al., 2004) has shown that in the general education classroom, verbal reinforcement for compliance for Tough Kids approximates zero. Box 3-2 on the next page summarizes the variables just detailed that affect compliance by students.

Precision Requests

A big problem in getting Tough Kids to stop their arguing and noncompliance is that each staff member has a different approach to making requests. It helps in managing a Tough Kid if all classroom staff use the same procedures. Some staff talk too much as they try to reason a student into compliance. Others may threaten, use guilt,

BOX 3-2

Variables That Affect _Compliance_

- **State the student's name.** Say the student's name before making a request. ("Shayna, please put your book away.") This helps to gain the student's attention just before the request is made.

- **Do not use a question format when making a request.** Do not use such statements as "Isn't it time to do your work?" or "Wouldn't you like to start to work?" Instead, make the request a polite one, such as "Please start your work."

- **Get close to the student when making a request.** The optimal distance for giving a command is approximately three feet. Do not make requests from great distances or from behind your desk.

- **Use a quiet voice, and do not yell.** When giving a command, give it in a quiet voice, up close, with eye contact.

- **Look students in the eyes.** Ask for eye contact when making a request of a student. For example, "John, look me in the eyes. Now I want you to . . ." Even if the student does not give you eye contact, continue to look him in the eyes. Do not try to force him to look at you.

- **Give the student time.** When making a request of a student, give him 3 to 5 seconds to begin to respond before (1) making the same request again or (2) making a new request.

- **Do not nag.** Make a request only twice. Then follow through with a preplanned consequence. The more times you make a request, the less likely you are to gain compliance.

- **Do not give multiple requests.** Make only one request at a time. Do not string requests together.

- **Describe the behavior you want.** Make specific and well-described requests rather than global requests.

- **Be unemotional.** Be calm, not emotional. Yelling, threatening gestures, ugly faces, guilt-inducing statements, rough handling, and deprecating comments about the student or his family only reduce compliance.

- **Make more start requests than stop requests.** Requests that start behaviors (_Do_ requests) are more desirable than requests that inhibit behaviors (_Don't_ requests). The majority of teacher requests should be _Do_ requests. If the majority of teacher requests are _Don't_ requests, it probably means the classroom rules or planned consequences are poorly designed or are not being implemented correctly.

- **Verbally reinforce compliance.** It is easy to forget to socially reward a student when she complies with your request. If you do not reward the student, compliance will decrease.

or yell at the student. It is better to synchronize request-making behavior for all classroom staff to achieve maximum compliance. A Precision Request takes all the compliance variables listed above and combines them into a standard approach (see Figure 3-3). The following are steps for making Precision Requests effectively.

STEP 1 Before you use the procedure, explain the Precision Request and its consequences to the whole class.

STEP 2 Make a quiet Precision Request that uses the student's name and the word *Please*—for example, "Maya, please get your materials out and start working." Make the request in a non-question format. Get up close to the student, use the student's first name, and make eye contact.

STEP 3 Wait three to five seconds after making the request, and do not interact further with the student during this time.

STEP 4 If the student starts to comply, verbally reinforce her using the IFEED-AV rules described in **Chapter 2**, p. 61.

STEP 5 If the student does not comply within 3–5 seconds, make the request a second time with the signal word *need*. ("Now I *need* you to get your materials out and start working.")

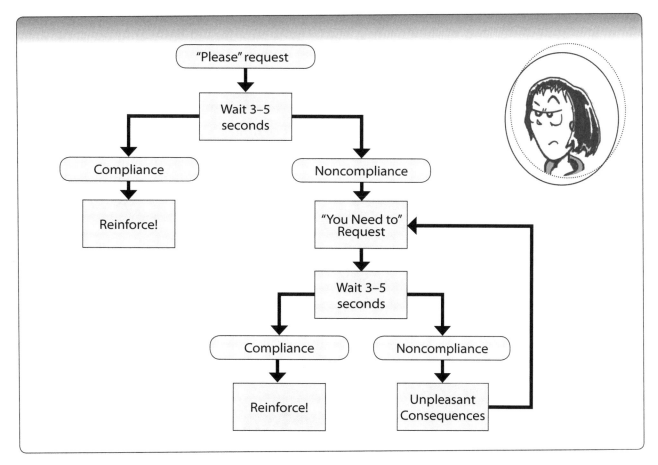

Figure 3-3 • Precision Request Sequence

STEP 6 If the student starts to comply, verbally reinforce her using the IFEED-AV rules.

STEP 7 If the student still does not comply within 3–5 seconds, follow through with a preplanned reductive consequence.

STEP 8 After delivering the reductive consequence, again repeat the request using the signal word *need*. If the student complies, reinforce her. If not, deliver the next preplanned consequence from the hierarchy.

There are several important components to a Precision Request. First, the signal word *need* is important because it signals the message: "You have only one more chance before I implement a reductive consequence." Second, once a student has experienced the reductive consequence, it is essential for the teacher to immediately repeat the original request. If the request is not repeated, a Tough Kid can escape the original request by simply receiving a consequence. The message must be that even if a student receives a reductive consequence, he will still be required to comply with the original request.

Frequently teachers ask, "What happens if the student still will not comply after he has experienced a consequence?" The answer is that a hierarchy of consequences must be preplanned and implemented. If one consequence does not work, move on to the next one. The trick is designing a hierarchy that includes effective, practical reductive consequences.

The *need* signal word used with Precision Requests warrants special discussion. First, the *need* word can be changed to any number of other words—for example, *want,* as in "I *want* you to . . ." We like the word *need* because it is less common and so a student easily recognizes it in a Precision Request sequence. However, it is not so unusual that it can't be used in public. Sometimes teachers wonder whether the Precision Request should be phrased "*I* need you to . . ." or "*You* need to . . ." An *I* or a *You* makes no difference. It is not the syntax or the specific word *need* that makes Precision Requests effective. It is the consistent relationship between the teacher using a Precision Request and following through with consequences (either positive or reductive) that makes it effective. The word *need* is just the last warning in the Precision Request sequence before a reductive consequence is implemented.

Designing a Hierarchy of Consequences

The worst time to select a reductive consequence is in the midst of the arguing, tantrum throwing, and yelling involved in a coercive episode. When a consequence is selected at that time, the temptation is to use an ultimate consequence ("Nuke 'em") because the teacher is upset. In this case, delivering a harsh consequence may feel good,

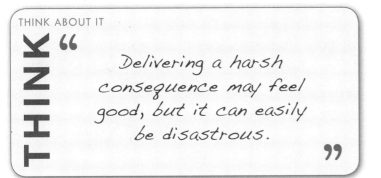

THINK

"*Delivering a harsh consequence may feel good, but it can easily be disastrous.*"

but it can easily be disastrous. An *ultimate* consequence is one that is too severe for the behavior. A teacher knows a consequence is an ultimate consequence as soon as the words leave her mouth; she knows it is overly harsh or impossible to carry out. Most ultimate consequences are poorly designed, unrealistic consequences that have open-ended time limits, are based on someone feeling good (generally the teacher) before they are stopped, or have unreasonable expectations.

Examples of consequences that are too severe for the misbehavior are statements such as:

- "You are out of my room for good—nobody does that in my classroom."
- "I absolutely will not have him back in my classroom." (open-ended time limit)
- "You have lost your recess privileges (or other privilege) for being irresponsible. I will tell you when I think you are ready to get them back." (an open-ended time limit and someone must feel good—the teacher)
- "Get down to the principal's office. You'll have to stay there until I say you can come back." (someone must feel good—the teacher)
- "You are expelled, and you can't come back until your parent comes in and guarantees you will behave." (unreasonable expectations—too harsh and unrealistic)

- "Give me all of your books and materials. If you play with things, then you can't have anything. Just sit until you can behave." (open-ended time limit)

A much better and safer approach to applying reductive consequences is a preplanned What If? Chart (see Figure 3-4). This chart lists reductive consequences (on the right side) along with how much or how long each consequence will be used. The reductive consequences increase in severity as they go down the hierarchy on the chart (see Box 3-3 on the next page for examples of reductive consequences).

It is important that reductive consequences be mild (but inconvenient to the student) and not take a lot of time to implement. If they are too severe or take too much time, the teacher will be

---

What If? Chart

Positive Consequences	Negative Consequences
Good job!	Verbal warning
Lottery ticket	Name in Consequence Book
Superstar List	5 minutes off recess
Classroom Helper	?? Mystery Consequence ??
Special Time	Not eligible for week's lottery
Seat Scramble	Lose computer reward time
Eligible for Home Note	Eat lunch in classroom
Spinner Surprise	Call to family

Serious Behavior Clause(s):

Out-of-class timeout
Visit to principal
Suspension

?
MYSTERY MOTIVATOR

Figure 3-4 • What If? Chart

BOX 3-3

Reductive Consequence *Examples* for the What If? Chart*

- Verbal warning from the teacher
- Teacher writes student's name in the Consequence Book
- Must remain in seat for 3 minutes after the class is dismissed
- Loss of 5 minutes of recess or free time (student must sit at his desk and work or wait)
- Loss of 10 minutes of recess or free time (student must sit at her desk and work or wait)
- Loss of rewarding activity (e.g., computer time, art activity)
- Required to eat lunch in the classroom
- Not allowed to use the school vending machines
- Must sit at the desk near the teacher for the day
- Must call her parent at home or work in the presence of the teacher and explain the problem behavior and what she will do to improve
- Must walk to the principal's office with the teacher and explain the problem behavior to the principal and what he will do to improve

* These consequences are not listed in hierarchical form. The teacher must decide on the hierarchy from least to most reductive.

---

reluctant to use them. See Pointer Box 3-1 for one of our favorites.

Reductive consequences are used <u>only</u> if:

- A student breaks preestablished classroom rules (see **Chapter 1**).
- A student does not comply with a Precision Request.

If a misbehavior that is not addressed in the rules occurs, the classroom rules should be reexamined. Most well-designed classroom rules will evolve Tand be refined over time. They should

handle the most difficult behaviors exhibited in a classroom.

In addition to less serious classroom misbehaviors, extreme or dangerous misbehaviors can occur. A What If? Chart hierarchy must include a preplanned set of consequences (serious behavior clauses) for crisis or out-of-control behaviors because these misbehaviors can be dangerous as well as greatly disruptive. Crisis misbehaviors include blatant or defiant noncompliance, a continuing physical fight, carrying a weapon, physical destruction of property (such as fire setting), or long-duration tantrums that involve yelling, swearing, or screaming. These behaviors are rare,

POINTER BOX 3-1

TIME WITH FRANK AND BARRY

One of our favorite mild reductive consequences is having a student stay after class or school or in any kind of detention with Frank and Barry. Who on earth are Frank and Barry? We're talking about Frank Sinatra and Barry Manilow.

To use this strategy, the teacher asks the student to sit quietly at his desk doing nothing during his assigned time (e.g., miss 5 or 10 minutes of recess). The teacher then plays Frank Sinatra or Barry Manilow music. The teacher uses the time how she wishes—perhaps grading papers or straightening her desk or the classroom. When the student's time is up, she excuses him. The trick is for the teacher to play music the student will probably not like but that she does. She may select opera or other artists from her collection as she chooses.

This strategy is particularly powerful with secondary students. One of the authors used this strategy in a junior high school and found ten minutes of time after school with Frank or Barry in most cases to be as effective as much longer in-school suspensions. In secondary settings, music undesired by students can also be played during lunch detentions and other reductive consequence times.

play music students don't like

but their crisis nature requires preplanned consequences that may temporarily remove the student from the classroom (see Box 3-4 on the next page for examples).

More serious

You may need extra help to implement the serious behavior clause. A two-way school intercom can be used to summon help, or another student can be sent to the principal's office or another teacher's classroom. The steps to request help should be predetermined in a faculty meeting by the faculty and principal before they are implemented.

All too often, only negative reductive consequences are listed on classroom What If? Chart hierarchies. The left side of the chart in Figure 3-4 lists positive consequences that students will receive if they follow the classroom rules. This approach offers a well-balanced approach

to classroom consequences. Box 3-5 on p. 95 lists several positive consequences that can be used with the whole class for following classroom rules. It is helpful to ask students what they would like on the positive side of the What If? Chart. Time can be set aside for a group activity in which you ask students what they would like to see on the positive menu. Students should be reminded when nominating possible positive consequences that the consequences cannot cost a lot of money or take a lot of time.

THINK ABOUT IT

THINK

" The steps to request help should be predetermined in a faculty meeting by the faculty and principal. "

BOX 3-4

Serious Behavior Clause *Examples* for the What If? Chart

- Student must go to another classroom for 20 minutes (e.g., Interclass Timeout).

- Student will be escorted to the principal's office and must sit there for 30 minutes. She must apologize and formulate a plan to improve her behavior in order to re-enter class.

- In-school suspension (see "How To Implement In-School Suspension Procedures," p. 109).

- Student's parent will be called at home or work to talk with her on the telephone about the behavior, or her parent will be required to come to school.

- Student will be suspended to home for one day for assault, possession of a weapon, or substantial property destruction. In addition, police will be called.

In addition, the What If? Chart has a Mystery Motivator envelope at the bottom to indicate an unknown reward for the class (see **Chapter 2**, pp. 67–69, for details). The Mystery Motivator can be used to enhance the positive consequences for following the rules. At the end of the day, all students who have earned positive consequences can be given a choice as a group. They can vote for one known item the whole group will receive from the positive consequences side of the menu. Or they can vote as a group to get the unknown positive consequence in the envelope. In our experience, students vote for the Mystery Motivator envelope for the group the majority of the time.

The blank box on the bottom of the What If? Chart is used for a special purpose. It contains a number the teacher may or may not actually write in the box. If students keep their rule breaking below this number for the day, they are the winning students who get to vote on which positive consequence (or Mystery Motivator) the group will receive. For example, when the teacher has

written a "2" in the box, all students in the classroom who keep their rule breaking to two rules or less are part of the group that will vote for the classroom positive consequence. In this case, students who break more than two rules do not get to vote and do not receive the positive consequence. These students work on a class assignment at the end of the day while the rest of the class receives the voted-upon reward. This technique is called an *independent group contingency* because students are *not* dependent on the behavior of other students to receive the reward. Rather, it is independent because students are dependent on only their behavior. We will discuss group contingencies in more detail later in this chapter.

There is one important aspect to this independent group contingency for not breaking classroom rules. The strategy is most effective when students do not know ahead of time the number of rules they can break in one day and still receive the positive consequence. If they know the number of rules that can be broken in any one day and they go above that number, they have

BOX 3-5

Positive Consequence _Examples_ for the Whole Class for the What If? Chart

- **Superstar List.** Names of student superstars will be written on a whiteboard in a conspicuous place. Students can be asked to come up to the board and write their own names. This list can include the whole class throughout the day.

- **Home Note.** A note will be sent home with three randomly selected students explaining what a good job they have done that day.

- **Bonus Book.** The teacher will read for an extra ten minutes from a high-interest adventure book.

- **Superstar Book.** Students will be selected to walk to the principal's office and sign their names in the School Superstars Book. This book is shown to parents during parent-teacher conferences. Make certain Tough Kids are sometimes selected for this reward.

- **Special Time.** Extra free time or a special activity is provided for the whole class.

- **Take the Teacher's Desk.** Randomly selected students are allowed to work at the teacher's desk.

- **Surprise Snack.** A snack is provided for the whole class (e.g., popcorn party).

- **Homework Free Pass.** One homework assignment is dropped for the day.

- **Special Lunch.** The whole class is allowed to eat lunch in a special place, such as the school lawn, in a park, or in class while listening to music.

- **DVD Treat.** The class is allowed to view 10 minutes of a high-interest DVD related to what they are learning.

- **Game Gains.** The class is allowed an extra 10 minutes of game time (e.g., compliance games—see "How To Use Behavioral Momentum" on p. 115).

- **Video Stars.** The teacher will videotape the class working and play it back to students at the next break.

- **Seat Scramble.** Students are allowed to sit where they want in the classroom for the day.

- **Menu Selection.** A student is allowed to select a classwide reinforcer from a reinforcement menu (see Chapter 2).

- **Spinner Surprise.** A student is allowed to spin a reinforcement Spinner for a class reward (see Chapter 2).

- **Classroom Helper.** A student is assigned a special job in the classroom for the week. Examples of jobs include office courier, line monitor, animal caretaker, and paper distributor.

little incentive not to break additional rules. This is why we suggest that you don't let students know how many rules they can break until the end of the day when the number is revealed. Only then will they know if they are in the winning group.

For practical purposes, the teacher can write a number in water-based ink in the box on the What If? Chart and tape a piece of paper over it until the end of the day. Or a Rules Grab Bag can be used. This is simply a bag that contains 20 or so slips of paper, each with a number written on it. For example, the bag might contain four pieces of paper with *0* written on them, eight pieces of paper with *1*, six with *2*, one with *3*, and one with *Wild Card* written on it.

At the end of the day, the teacher (or a student) reaches into the bag and randomly selects a piece of paper with the number of rules that can be broken that day. With the Wild Card, all students in the class get the positive consequence irrespective of how many rules they broke. This is suggested to keep even chronic rule breakers motivated. If they are having a bad day, they still get to join in to receive the positive consequence when the Wild Card is selected.

Mystery Consequence Box and Chronic Rule Breakers

We all like to know what is going to happen to us. The unknown can make even a mild consequence seem more serious. The Mystery Consequence Box is sort of a Mystery Motivator in reverse. It can be used as the fourth consequence on the What If? Chart. The Mystery Consequence Box contains 10 to 15 envelopes, each of which holds a slip of paper that has a

mild consequence written on it. Examples of mild consequences include:

- Sit near the teacher's desk for the day
- Three minutes and 13 seconds off the next recess
- Wait in seat 30 seconds after each bell rings for the rest of the day

If a student breaks four rules in any one day, he is required to randomly draw an envelope from the box to find out what is going to happen to him for the rest of the day. Or the teacher can draw an envelope out of the box and read it to the student. Not knowing what is in the envelope makes this consequence even more powerful.

If a student regularly breaks five or more rules in a day, he should be taken off the What If? Chart program and not allowed to participate until he earns his way back by following the rules. Move the student to a seat near the teacher's desk and tape a Monitoring Classroom Rules form to the student's desk. An example of this form is shown in **Chapter 4** (see Figure 4-5, p. 161), along with additional ways to use it. Several variations of the form are available in *The Tough Kid Tool Box* (see Pointer Box 2-2 on p. 66 for more details).

The student is required to self-monitor his rule following in the morning and afternoon and rate (on a scale from 1 to 4) how well he has followed the classroom rules. At the end of the morning and again at the end of the afternoon, he is asked to bring his self-monitoring form to the teacher, who also rates how well he has followed the rules. When the student has a good day (both morning and afternoon ratings of a 3 or a 4 and the teacher agrees), he is again permitted to sit at his original desk and be part of the What If? program.

PEER INFLUENCE: HOW TO USE IT ADVANTAGEOUSLY

A great many misbehaviors exhibited by Tough Kids are for the benefit of their peers. Because Tough Kids often lack in social skills, they frequently seek peer attention by misbehaving and disrupting the class. Peers often give encouragement in the form of smiles, comments, snickers, or subtle gestures. It is clearly to the teacher's advantage to turn this around and manage peer attention to encourage appropriate behavior. The most effective means of doing this is through the use of group contingencies that apply rewards and reductive consequences to the class as a whole.

peer influence + group contingencies/consequences

Is it fair to give or take privileges away from the classroom as a group? It is fair if there is evidence that peers are encouraging the misbehavior of Tough Kids. Teachers should look around their classrooms. Is a group of students fueling their Tough Kids' behavior problems? If teachers want to facilitate cooperation through peer attention for appropriate behavior, a group contingency can be a powerful approach. There are four basic types of group contingencies:

1. **Dependent Group Contingency.** This group contingency places all the responsibility for earning a group positive or reductive consequence on one student. This is the most severe form of group contingency and should rarely be used with Tough Kids because it puts so much pressure on one student. It can be used with a mixed contingency such as Chance Jars (see "How to Use Chance Jars" on p. 100), but only if the student is not identified.

2. **Independent Group Contingency.** We have already given an example of an independent group contingency earlier in this chapter when we discussed the What If? Chart. With this group contingency, there is a criterion. If the students independently meet this criterion, they are rewarded. Those who do not meet the criterion are not rewarded.

3. **Interdependent Group Contingency.** With this group contingency, students are interdependent on each other to meet a criterion to receive the reward. If the group as a whole meets the criterion, they are rewarded. If they do not meet the criterion, the entire group is not rewarded. The "Sure I Will" group contingency discussed at the end of this chapter is an example of an interdependent group contingency. Interdependent group contingencies work well with teams that compete against each other. With the use of teams, one team can lose and one win, both teams can win, or both teams can lose, depending on whether each team meets the group contingency's criterion.

When this type of group contingency is used, student "saboteurs" may be present. A saboteur is a student who deliberately misbehaves so the whole group will fail. Saboteur Tough Kids thrive on negative peer attention. If it is obvious that a student is trying to sabotage her group's chances of being rewarded, she should be removed from the group. Her misbehavior should not be held against the group. When this negative pattern occurs, the student should be made a group all by herself. The Tough Kid should lose the privilege of participating with the class until she demonstrates by appropriate behavior that she will not intentionally engage in sabotage.

4. **Mixed Group Contingency.** This group contingency may be one of the most powerful techniques for managing peer behavior. With a mixed group contingency, students do not know which group contingency (i.e., dependent, independent, or interdependent) is in effect until the end of the day. For example, with a rule-following program, an opaque jar that contains three slips of paper is placed on the teacher's desk. Each paper has written on it the name of one of the types of group contingencies. At the end of the day, the teacher (or a student) randomly selects one of the pieces of paper from the jar. The selected paper contains the name of the type of group contingency for the day (i.e., dependent, independent, or interdependent group contingency). The program presented in "How to Use Chance Jars" on pp. 99–100 is an example of a mixed group contingency.

The basic steps for implementing a group contingency are listed in "How To Implement a Group Contingency," with cautions.

Designing appropriate group contingencies and using them properly is critical.

First, never use a group contingency for a student who is learning a new behavior or skill but has not yet mastered it. Use group contingencies only for behaviors a student can already perform but chooses not to perform (e.g., following classroom rules, turning in homework, following teacher's directions).

Second, make sure the criterion is explained well to students and is attainable.

Third, publicly post feedback on how close students are to either gaining a reward or losing a privilege.

Fourth, we recommend that you not single out one student's performance on the behavior criterion. It is better to collect information on meeting the behavior criterion for the classroom as a whole (e.g., total number of talk-outs each day). Another option is to review whether one or more randomly selected students have met the criterion and evaluate their behavior or performance privately (e.g., select three students randomly, determine if they returned their homework, and grade it to determine if it is at least 80% complete and 80% correct).

When selecting random students, it may not be necessary for the class to know exactly who is being evaluated. You need only inform the class that three students were selected. Then reveal the students' average percentage of the performance (e.g., returned homework, on-task rates, number of talk-outs, tardies) and whether or not it meets the specified criterion.

Continued on p. 102

How to . . .

IMPLEMENT A GROUP CONTINGENCY

Step 1. Decide whether a group contingency is really necessary.

- Do peers contribute to the Tough Kid's misbehavior through encouragement or subtle behaviors?
- Is improved student cooperation necessary for this behavior?
- Have other positive approaches failed to change this behavior?

Step 2. Define the target behavior. Is it observable, measurable, and easily tracked?

Step 3. Is the student capable of the target behavior but unwilling to perform it?

- Make certain the student is not in the process of learning the behavior.
- Make certain the student can perform the behavior.

Step 4. Define the group contingency criterion.

- Will the criterion be based on the total number of behaviors (e.g., total number of talk-outs)?
- Will the criterion be based on the average of the classroom (e.g., 80% of homework returned by the class)?
- Will the criterion be based on the performance of one student (e.g., if any student goes to timeout)? Caution: Because of the severity of this criterion, it is generally not advised.
- Will the criterion be based on an average of a set number of randomly selected students? (For example, three students will be selected at random and not identified. If they have handed in their homework and the work is 80% complete and 80% correct, then the class will be rewarded.)

Step 5. Describe to the class the positive reinforcers that can be gained by the group. Ask for the group's input (e.g., class is permitted to select a reward from the reinforcer menu).

Step 6. Describe to the class a mild reductive consequence if the criterion is not met (e.g., class loses free-time period). Caution: Make sure the reductive consequence is not overly harsh or for too long a period (e.g., loss of privilege for a week is too long). The loss should be for a day or less.

Step 7. Post the rules for the group contingency. These rules might include:

- No threats or making fun of a student who has difficulty will be allowed.
- Students may encourage others to do their best.

Step 8. Publicly post the following group contingency information:

- The criterion for gaining a reward or losing a privilege—specific target behavior defined with the actual performance number (e.g., no more than five classroom talk-outs)
- How the students are doing (e.g., marks on the board for the number of talk-outs)
- What the students will win or lose

Step 9. Plan a backup procedure for a student who sabotages the group contingency—make the student a team by himself.

Step 10. Make certain the group contingency plan is written and that:

- All classroom staff understand the program.
- All students understand the program.
- The program is discussed with the school principal and has his or her support.
- Parents are informed.

Step 11. Emphasize the positive and cooperative aspect of the group contingency.

How to . . .

USE CHANCE JARS

The Chance Jars strategy was developed by Theodore, Bray, Kehle, and Jenson (2001) and reviewed in the book *School-Based Interventions for Students with Behavior Problems* by Bowen, Jenson, and Clark (2004). The Chance Jars strategy is a mixed group contingency that incorporates dependent, interdependent, and independent group contingencies to reduce disruptive behavior and improve classroom rule following. Variations of the program have been used in both elementary and secondary classrooms for students with emotional and behavioral disorders. The steps to setting up and implementing the program are as follows:

Step 1. Classroom rules must be in place. (See Chapter 1 for details.)

Step 2. Place three opaque jars on your desk. Label them *Group Jar*, *Student Jar*, and *Mystery Motivator Jar*.

- The Group Jar contains slips of paper. Each slip has one of the following types of group contingency written on it: *Whole Class, One Student, All Who Meet It*, and *Wild Card*.

- The Student Jar contains a slip of paper for each student in the class. Each student's name is written on a slip.

- The Mystery Motivator Jar holds slips of paper with various reinforcers written on them, such as free time, a treat, a homework pass, or a class game. You can ask students ahead of time to nominate rewards they would like to earn that do not take a lot of time or cost a lot of money.

Step 3. Create a Rule-Following Log with all the students' names listed on the left half of the log and spaces to the right of the names where you can record tallies for rule infractions and disruptive behaviors.

Step 4. Explain the classroom rules. Indicate that the class can earn rewards by complying with classroom rules and not engaging in disruptive behaviors such as touching other students, talking with other working students without permission, verbal put-downs, swearing or obscene language, playing with objects, or being out of seat without permission.

Step 5. Tell students that each time they break a rule or engage in a disruptive behavior, you will make a mark by their names on the Rule-Following Log.

Step 6. Each day, determine the criterion level for reinforcement—for example, three or fewer marks for rule breaking during the day.

Step 7. During the day, keep track (by putting a tally mark by the student's name on the Rule-Following Log) of every occurrence of disruptive or rule-breaking behavior.

Step 8. At the end of the day or class period, randomly draw a slip of paper from the Group Jar.

If the slip has the word *Class* written on it, the whole class must meet the criterion (e.g., three or less disruptive behaviors or rules broken) for reinforcement.

If the slip has the phrase *One Student* written on it, draw a slip with a student's name on it from the Student Jar. If that student has met the criterion, the whole class gets the reward. Note that this is a *dependent group contingency*—the whole class's reinforcement is dependent on one student. This student should remain anonymous when his name is drawn from the jar. The teacher draws a slip out of the jar, silently checks the name, and then tells the class if the anonymous student met the criterion. The student's name does not need to be revealed.

If the slip from the Group Jar has the phrase *All Who Meet* It on it, all the students who broke three or fewer (or the criterion for the day) rules or displayed three or fewer disruptive behaviors receive the reward. Those students who had more than three rule infractions or disruptive behaviors do not earn the reward.

If the *Wild Card* is drawn from the Group Jar, all students in the class receive the reward. The Wild Card option is used to help students remain motivated when they have had a bad day and exceeded the reward criterion by several rule infractions and disruptive behaviors. With the Wild Card, the student knows he still had something to lose if he continues to behave inappropriately.

Step 9. Randomly select a slip of paper with a reward written on it from the Mystery Motivator Jar. Depending on the type of group contingency selected from the Group Jar, students who meet the criterion receive this reward. Students who do not meet the criterion do not receive it.

Technique Option: In our example with rules, we set the criterion for rules broken or disruptive behaviors at three at the beginning of the day. A fourth jar could be added, a Rules Number Jar, which would contain slips of paper with a number (e.g., from 0 through 7) written on each. With this option, students would not know the criterion (number of rule infractions or disruptive behaviors allowed) until the end of the day. At that time, the teacher draws a slip of paper from the Rules Number Jar and announces the number of rule infractions allowed that day to still earn the reward.

Group contingencies can be used with a variety of consequences. They are particularly effective with more potent reductive consequences or with positive classroom systems such as the "Sure I Will" program to be detailed later in this chapter (pp. 115–119).

POTENT REDUCTIVE CONSEQUENCES

Up to this point, most of the reductive consequences suggested for a What If? Chart have been designed for general use in the classroom. In addition to these general consequences, more potent reductive consequences may be needed for Tough Kids. This section details three additional consequences: the Response Cost Lottery, timeout, and in-school suspension.

Response Cost Lottery

A response cost is simply a *fine* system, or losing something one has. Library fines, speeding tickets, and late penalties on loans are all examples of common everyday response costs. The problem with most response cost approaches used in classrooms is that teachers can take away most privileges only once. Then they are gone, and the teacher has nothing else to take away. For example, students can lose their recess or free time only a limited number of times in a day. Then what?

The Response Cost Lottery is a technique that research has shown to be especially effective with Tough Kids (Witt & Elliot, 1982; Proctor & Morgan, 1991). One advantage of this technique is that the number of times it can be used with

a Tough Kid is not nearly as limited as that of many other techniques.

For a Response Cost Lottery, tape an envelope to each student's desk. Each envelope holds five or more tickets. The student's name is written on each ticket. If a student breaks a rule or does not follow a request, remove a ticket from the student's envelope. At the end of the day, collect all tickets that remain in each student's envelope and put them in a bag or other container. The tickets are then mixed up, and three or four student names are drawn out, as in a lottery. The students whose names are drawn receive a reward (e.g., Mystery Motivator or choice of a reward from a reinforcer menu). Students quickly learn that the more tickets they have left in their envelopes, the more likely they are to win the lottery.

The effect of the Response Cost Lottery can be easily enhanced by combining it with an interdependent group contingency. For example, teams can be formed (e.g., all students in a row of desks, half the class on each team, or all students sitting at a table). Only one envelope is taped on one desk for each team (see Figure 3-5). When any team member misbehaves, a ticket is removed from the team envelope, thus reducing the whole team's

Figure 3-5 • Team Envelope With Tickets for the Response Cost Lottery

overall chances of winning the lottery. If you use group contingencies with the Response Cost Lottery, it is important to make sure the teams are balanced. Not all the Tough Kids should be on one team, or the procedure can backfire.

A Wild Card ticket can also be used with the group contingency Response Cost Lottery. A Wild Card is simply one ticket that is always in the container. If it is drawn, any team with a ticket in the container receives the reward. The Wild Card ticket works to keep teams that have low numbers of tickets left motivated and working. If they lose the last ticket in their envelope, they have no chance of winning the lottery. However, if they have even one ticket, there is a chance they can still win with the Wild Card.

THINK ABOUT IT

THINK

" Teachers cannot assign a timeout from a nonreinforcing environment. "

Timeout

Research shows that timeout is an effective technique with Tough Kids (Vegas, Jenson, & Kircher 2007). However, many teachers shy away from its use because they believe they need a timeout room and a set of complicated procedures. Timeout is not a *place*; rather, it is a *procedure* whereby a student is removed from a reinforcing environment to a less reinforcing environment when misbehavior occurs. If the student does not find the classroom reinforcing, by definition it is impossible to time him out from the classroom.

For example, if a teacher complains that a student would rather be in timeout in another location instead of the classroom, the reinforcement rate is undoubtedly too low in the classroom. Again, we cannot emphasize enough that teachers cannot assign a timeout from a nonreinforcing environment. It is impossible. The problem is that many classrooms are nonreinforcing environments. Timeout will not work in these cases.

NONSECLUSIONARY TIMEOUT
A student can often remain in the classroom when timeout is used. For instance, Bumpy Bunny Timeout is an in-class timeout procedure. If a student is reinforced by work materials but continues to misbehave, the materials can simply be removed and the student ignored (by the teacher and other students) for a short period of time. See "How to Implement a Bumpy Bunny Timeout" on the next page for more details.

SIT AND WATCH TIMEOUT
Similarly, a student may be removed to a timeout chair for *Sit and Watch Timeout*. With this type of timeout, the student is allowed to observe the classroom but not participate. If observing makes

How to . . .

P-4

IMPLEMENT A BUMPY BUNNY TIMEOUT

Bumpy Bunny Timeout is a timeout procedure that can be used with younger students—preschool through the fourth grade. It is called Bumpy Bunny Timeout because it is based on the desires of a little boy who wanted to take his toy bunny (Bumpy) to school to show his friends. However, a student's choice of any desired toy will do. Steps for implementing a Bumpy Bunny Timeout are as follows:

Step 1. Make a space in the classroom where toys can be displayed while students are working. For example, the top of a bookshelf is perfect.

Step 2. Tape off the last three feet of the bookshelf with red tape. Do not put toys in this area.

Step 3. Invite the students to bring a toy of their choice to the classroom to play with before class or during free time, breaks, or recess.

Step 4. The rules of toy selection and play are:

- Toys are brought to class on Monday. Students who do not bring a toy on Monday have to select a toy from the classroom box (supplied by the teacher) for the week.

- Only one toy can be brought to class each week. The same toy is used for the whole week. After a week's time, the old toy can return home and a new toy brought into the classroom.

- No toy weapons may be brought.

- Toys cannot be exchanged, sold, or borrowed. If a student violates this rule, she loses the toy privilege for one week.

- Fights over toys result in a loss of toy privileges for the next day.

- All toys are put away (but visible on the bookshelf) during classroom work times.

Step 5. If a student misbehaves or does not follow a teacher's request, her toy is placed in the timeout area (the red taped bookshelf area) for 3–5 minutes (see the illustration above) during the next toy-playing period such as recess or another break. During this time, the student must sit at her desk while other students are allowed to play. For multiple occurrences of noncompliance, the time can accumulate for toy timeout. For example, three occurrences of not doing what the teacher requested add up to nine minutes of toy timeout.

Step 6. After the timeout period, the student is allowed to join the other students with her toy and play.

the misbehavior worse, the chair can be turned to a wall or corner. In this case, the timeout becomes *Nonobservation Timeout*. Both of these timeout procedures are useful for students who are only mildly disruptive. If a student continues to misbehave or gets out of the chair, more potent forms of timeout may be necessary. Do not discount in-class timeout procedures without trying them first.

INTERCLASS TIMEOUT

More potent forms of timeout require a student to leave the classroom. *Interclass Timeout* is an excellent procedure for more difficult students (Jenson, Rhode, Evans, & Morgan, 2006). This technique has also been referred to as the *Think Time* technique (Nelson & Carr, 2000).

With this procedure, a student is removed to another classroom to work on an academic assignment for a limited period of time (generally 15 to 20 minutes). It is important, if possible, to pick a class one or two grade levels above the student's current grade level (e.g., a third grader goes to a fifth grade classroom). This ensures that the Tough Kid will not have same-age peers in the timeout classroom. It is also effective because students do not want to go into classrooms with older students. If this is not possible, pick a classroom one or two grade levels below the student. In this case, you must resist the temptation to say, "If you act immature, you have to go to a classroom for younger students." Such comments are not helpful.

It is also essential to preplan this procedure with the receiving teacher in the timeout classroom. One requirement is that an academic assignment for the student be ready and waiting in the other classroom. To return to his own classroom, the student must complete the assignment, behave

appropriately in the receiving classroom, and sign an agreement that he is ready to return to his own classroom and follow the rules.

3 things to complete

SECLUSIONARY TIMEOUT

Seclusionary Timeout is the most restrictive form of timeout to be used with a Tough Kid. It should be used only with great caution, written procedures (see "How to Implement a Seclusionary Timeout" on the next page), extensive training, and parent and administrator permissions. It should also be used only with the most extreme of behavior excesses.

Seclusionary Timeout is the form of timeout that most frequently results in misunderstanding by others, highly undesirable media coverage, and in some cases, legal action. In 2009, the Government Accounting Office (GAO) released a report outlining the abuses of both seclusion and restraint of children. While Seclusionary

How to . . .

IMPLEMENT A SECLUSIONARY TIMEOUT

1. Seclusionary Timeout should not be used unless all other procedures have been tried and failed. This should be a last-effort technique.

2. Seclusionary Timeout should *never* be used without a parent's written consent.

3. Seclusionary Timeout should be used only if the IEP Team has listed it as an approved and agreed-upon technique in a student's Individualized Education Plan (IEP). The student should be placed in timeout only for approved behaviors on the IEP, such as aggression, severe noncompliance, or destructive tantruming.

4. Seclusionary Timeout is defined as removing a student from a reinforcing classroom setting to a less reinforcing setting. This setting can be another classroom, a chair or desk outside the classroom, or a room specifically approved for timeout. If a room is used for timeout, it should be used only for timeout and for no other purpose (e.g., storage, counseling students, or a special academic work area).

5. The timeout setting should be well lit, well ventilated, nonthreatening, and clean. It must also have an observation window or device. Staff members should try the technique on themselves before using the room with a student, and the room should be shown to the student's parent prior to its use.

6. The entire timeout procedure should be explained to the student before it is implemented. This discussion should take place at a neutral time, not right after the occurrence of a misbehavior that will result in its use.

7. If misbehavior occurs, identify it. For example, tell the student in a calm, neutral manner: "That's fighting. You need to go to the timeout room." Tell the student to remove jewelry, belt, and shoes. Tell him to also empty his pockets to check for such items as pens, pencils, paper clips, knives, etc. The student's socks should be checked for these types of items also. If the student does not comply with these requests, call for help and then remove the items and check the pockets yourself. **No other conversation should ensue.**

8. When a student is placed in the timeout room, he must be constantly monitored by a staff member. The student must never be left alone.

9. When a student is placed in the timeout room, the following information should be entered in a Timeout Log:

   - Name of the student
   - Date
   - Staff member responsible for monitoring student
   - Time in and time out
   - Target behavior that warranted the procedure

10. The student should be placed in the timeout room for a specific period of time. A recommended formula is one minute per year of age (e.g., 10-year-old student X 1 minute = 10 minutes).

Timeout can be a powerful and effective tool for reducing extreme behaviors, it is also one of the most misused procedures.

With Seclusionary Timeout, a student is removed from the classroom and placed in a special timeout room. The room must be a room with no *other* purpose than use as a timeout room. It must be nonthreatening, clean, well lit, well ventilated, and of adequate size. (You may have read or heard media accounts of students being locked in "closets.") It must also have an observation

11. If a student is screaming, throwing a tantrum, or yelling, he should be quiet for 30 consecutive seconds before being released from the timeout room. This 30 seconds does not begin until the one minute per year of age time period has elapsed.

12. Communication between the supervising staff member and the student should *not* take place when the student is in the timeout room. In other words, do not talk with the student, threaten him, or try to counsel him at this time. Talking to the student while he is in timeout renders its use ineffective.

13. Do remain calm while taking a student to the timeout room. Do not argue with, threaten, or verbally reprimand the student.

14. If a student refuses to go to the timeout room, add on time to the specified timeout duration (e.g., one minute for each refusal up to five minutes).

15. If a student refuses to come out of the timeout room, do not beg or try to remove the student. Simply wait outside, and sooner or later the student will come out on his own.

16. If the student makes a mess in the timeout room, require him to clean it up before he leaves.

17. Once the timeout period has ended, return the student to the ongoing classroom activity, making sure he is required to complete the task he was engaged in prior to the timeout period. This will ensure that students do not purposely avoid unpleasant tasks by going to the timeout room.

18. All staff members should be trained in the appropriate use of Seclusionary Timeout, and the training should be documented before staff can use the procedure. Staff members should also pass both written and demonstration tests before using this form of timeout.

19. To ensure the effectiveness of timeout, the reinforcement rate for appropriate behaviors in the classroom should meet the recommended rate of *no fewer* than three or four positives to each negative (and never fewer than four positives per contact hour).

20. Data must be collected on target behaviors. If timeout is effective, these behaviors should decrease shortly after the technique is started. If they do not, check that the procedure is being used correctly and that the reinforcement rate for appropriate behavior in the classroom is high enough. Also consider another technique for possible use. Consider doing an ABC Functional Behavior Assessment on the behavior.

21. Timeout should not be used as a threat ("If you do that again, I will put you in the timeout room."). Rather, the technique should be combined with a Precision Request, such as "I need you to stop . . ." If the student persists, the timeout procedure should be used. When the student comes out of the timeout room, the Precision Request should be restated ("I need you to . . .").

22. The student should be reinforced for not needing timeout.

23. Use the timeout procedure on yourself. Put yourself in the timeout room for a specific period of time under actual conditions (with someone monitoring you, etc.). Using the procedure on yourself will be helpful when someone asks you, "Have you ever experienced this timeout procedure?"

window or device. A student must never be left unattended without a staff member outside the room monitoring his behavior inside. Thus, unless a staff member is available to supervise a student in the timeout room, this form of timeout is *not* an option. "How to Implement a Seclusionary Timeout" lists a series of procedures to follow.

One major danger of *not* using Seclusionary Timeout or not having it available for use with Tough Kids is that educators may use *physical restraint* as an alternative. When physical restraint is used, it is often abused (Fogt, George, Kern, White, & George, 2008). The authors view physical restraint as much more restrictive than

Seclusionary Timeout. We believe that using Seclusionary Timeout sparingly and with strong guidelines and training is far superior to physically restraining a student. When students are physically restrained, they are usually struggling and in physical contact with one or more adults. This situation has a much higher probability of injury and even death when compared with separating a struggling Tough Kid in a safe, dedicated room for a short period of time. Seclusionary Timeout must never be used with half measures (e.g., no dedicated timeout room, inadequate training and supervision). Remember, if ongoing timeout data shows that the problematic behavior is not decreasing, the technique is not working and must be reviewed or changed.

> THINK ABOUT IT
>
> **THINK** " *A good rule of thumb for elementary students is a timeout of no more than a minute per year of the student's age.* "

Timeout tips. The following tips can enhance the effectiveness of all timeout procedures:

1. **Make sure the reinforcement rate in the classroom is sufficiently high.** Remember, students cannot be given timeout from a nonreinforcing classroom—it is impossible.

2. **Combine the timeout with a Precision Request sequence.** This sequence will improve the overall effectiveness of timeout.

3. **When a student finishes timeout, restate the original request** ("Now I need you to . . ."). Do not allow a student to escape the request simply by experiencing timeout.

4. **Use a reasonable amount of time for each timeout episode.** A good rule of thumb for most elementary students is to limit the timeout length to no more than a minute per year of the student's age. For instance, if the student is seven years old, seven minutes is an appropriate timeout period. Frequently, smaller amounts of time can be used effectively.

5. **Reinforce Tough Kids for not needing timeout.** If a student is having difficulty with four timeouts per day, set a daily limit of two timeouts. If the student can manage to keep his timeouts to two or fewer per day, the student can earn a special privilege or small reward.

IN-SCHOOL SUSPENSION

In-School Suspension is a form of extended timeout to a preselected setting within the school. In-School Suspension is a reasonable alternative to more extreme consequences that can make things worse, such as suspension or expulsion from school. In-School Suspension is generally reserved for very difficult behavior, such as fighting, defiance, destruction of property, or repeated truancy.

"How to Implement In-School Suspension Procedures" lists the basic guidelines for setting up an effective In-School Suspension program.

The use of In-School Suspension requires a special physical location to detain students, monitoring by a trained staff member, and assigned academic work. Frequently, In-School Suspension can be used for relatively short periods of time,

How to . . .

IMPLEMENT IN-SCHOOL SUSPENSION PROCEDURES

In-School Suspension is an alternative to out-of-school suspension (being sent home). It should be reserved for very severe target behaviors (e.g., fighting, teacher defiance, arguing, property destruction, and repeated truancy or tardiness).

Step 1. Determine a physical place for In-School Suspension (e.g., another classroom, desk space in an office, or a carrel).

Step 2. In-School Suspension should always take place under the direct observation of a staff member. If students cannot be constantly supervised, In-School Suspension should not be used.

Step 3. Time lengths for In-School Suspension should typically be relatively short (45 minutes to 2 hours). In-School Suspension lengths of more than one day are not advisable. Try to assign time to coincide with something the student likes. For example, if a student is going to be in In-School Suspension close to the lunch period, schedule her suspension to run through lunch. In this case, have her eat her lunch while still in In-School Suspension.

Step 4. When students earn In-School Suspension, they should be placed in it immediately. No waiting lists should exist. Alternatively, In-School Suspension should be used for times of the day the student does not like to miss, such as lunch time, recess, or after school.

Step 5. In-School Suspension should have rules, including:

- No talking to other students
- No sleeping
- Stay in your seat
- Work on your school assignments

Step 6. Students should be given academic assignments to work on during In-School Suspension. This work can be actual classroom work or extra assigned work. The authors prefer actual classroom work so the student does not fall further behind.

Step 7. If a student refuses to go to In-School Suspension or shows up late, the time period can be expanded. For example, a student who refuses to go to In-School Suspension should have her time increased from two hours to half a day, then to three quarters of a day or a full day. If the student still refuses, the student's parent should be called.

Step 8. Before In-School Suspension starts, inform the student's parent and ask for consent, when possible.

Step 9. The next day after a student has been in In-School Suspension, she should be assigned to carry a Behavior Tracking Form to all her classes. (Elementary and secondary samples are depicted in Figure 3-7 on p. 111). The student should pick the form up in the morning from a supervising adult and check out with that adult at the end of the day. The Behavior Tracking Form should include the problem behavior being tracked, teacher ratings for the behavior, and a place for teacher signatures.

Step 10. Be aware that some chronic In-School Suspension students (three or more In-School Suspensions in a month) may be engineering their own In-School Suspensions to avoid certain classes (or situations) or to be with friends. Fill out an ABC FBA Tracking Sheet (Reproducible 1-1, p. 21) each time such a student is sent to In-School Suspension to assess these possibilities.

such as one hour or a single class period. More extended periods of one or more days are generally not needed. The goal is to assign only enough time for the student to regain composure and reduce the likelihood that the misbehavior will happen again.

On the day after an In-School Suspension, we recommend that the student carry an assigned tracking sheet to class to be signed by his teachers that day (see Figure 3-7). This works especially well with older students who have more than one teacher. The tracking sheet should include the problem behavior that resulted in the in-school suspension, a place to rate the student's performance for the subject or class period, and a teacher's signature line.

Tough Kids who chronically end up in In-School Suspension are often engineering the use of this technique for themselves. It has been estimated that up to 75% of chronic In-School Suspension students are using it to avoid classes or situations they do not like, to be with their friends who are also in In-School Suspension, or both. It is desirable practice to not allow students to avoid classes but rather to have them serve their In-School Suspension assignment at times they do not want to miss (i.e., lunch time, recess, or after school). Each time a student is sent to the In-School Suspension room, it is good practice to fill out an ABC Functional Behavior Analysis Tracking Sheet (see Reproducible 1-1 in **Chapter 1**, p. 21). When Tough Kids are chronic visitors to In-School Suspension (more than three times in a month), reviewing the tracking sheets can be especially helpful. This helps identify situations and classes the Tough Kid is trying to avoid. It may also provide useful information about why a Tough Kid would rather be in In-School Suspension than in the classroom.

Check-in/Check-out Program

Having Tough Kids check in and out with a supervising adult is a good technique to reduce problematic behaviors. With this strategy, a Tough Kid checks in with a supervising adult (e.g., teacher, counselor, school psychologist, attendance secretary) in the morning and picks up a tracking sheet. See Figure 3-7 for sample elementary and secondary Behavior Tracking Forms. *The Tough Kid Tool Box* contains blank versions of these and other tracking forms. For more information about this program, see Pointer Box 3-2.

POINTER BOX 3-2

CHECK OUT CHECK-IN

For a more extensive review of the Check-in/Check-out Program, the *Behavior Education Program* (Crone, Horner, & Hawkin, 2003) is an excellent resource. Also see *The Tough Kid Tool Box* (Jenson, Rhode, & Reavis, 2009) for additional details on monitoring student behavior and academic performance as well as ready-to-use tracking forms you can print out. Visit www.PacificNWPublish.com for more details.

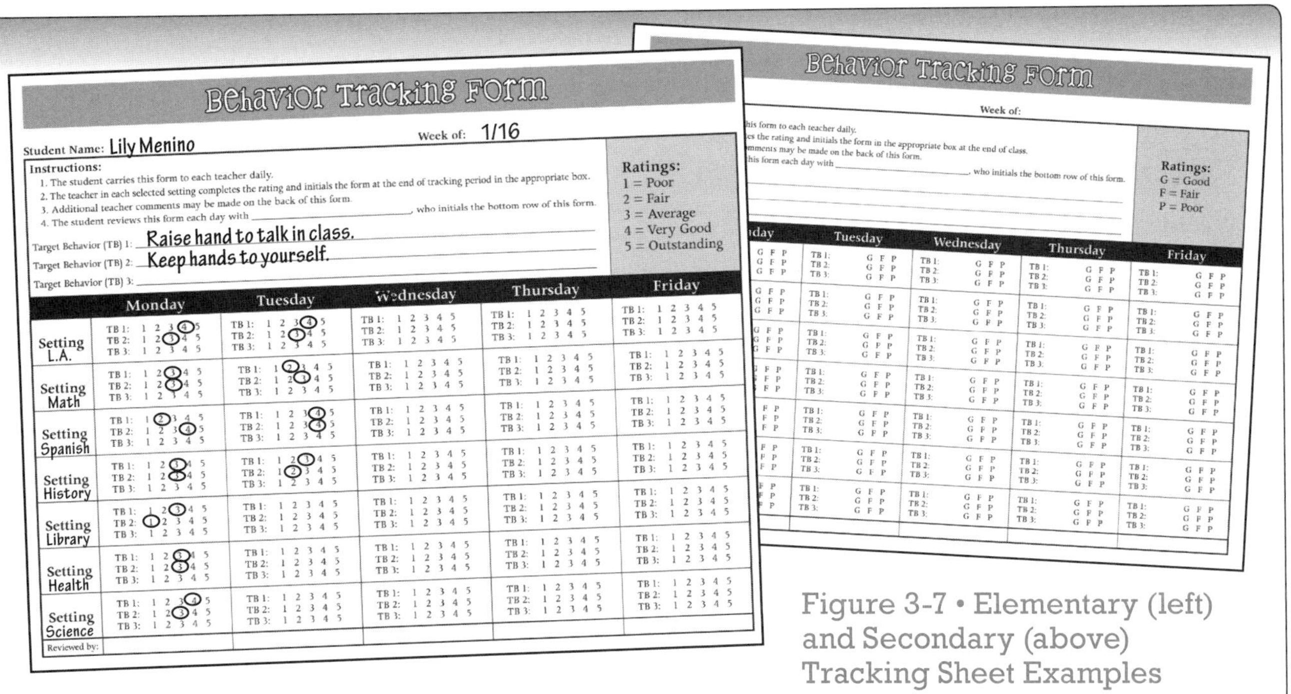

Figure 3-7 • Elementary (left) and Secondary (above) Tracking Sheet Examples

The tracking sheet has the behavior the Tough Kid is trying to improve, a rating for his performance, and a place for the teacher's signature. A younger student can check in with his teacher in the morning, get feedback on his tracking sheet at lunch, and get feedback again and check out at the end of the day. An older student can check in with a supervising adult to pick up the sheet in the morning, take the sheet with him to all classes, have each teacher sign it, and check out with a supervising adult at the end of the day.

TECHNIQUE TIP

As the student's behavior improves, gradually fade checking of the tracking form. An eventual goal is to replace Check-in/Check-out with some form of self-monitoring, which is discussed in detail in **Chapter 5**.

It is important to keep Check-in/Check-out positive with encouraging feedback. Even if the Tough Kid has problems during the day, his successes and the fact that he is working hard to behave appropriately should be emphasized. A Mystery Motivator Chart with invisible-ink pens or a Chart Moves strategy (see **Chapter 2**, pp. 64–69) can be awarded each time a student checks out with success.

POSITIVE REDUCTIVE TECHNIQUES

Positive reductive procedures for reducing inappropriate behavior may seem like a contradiction. However, several innovative techniques actually reward the nonoccurrence of misbehavior or actually interfere with misbehavior. The more potent reductive techniques may be needed initially with Tough Kids, but positive reductive techniques are especially useful in maintaining the positive balance in classrooms that serve Tough Kids.

Differential Attention

Many teachers naturally use *differential attention* and don't even know it. Or they may know this technique as *accentuate the positive—ignore the negative* or *proximity praise*. By whatever name, differential attention is an effective technique that helps reduce both common misbehaviors and the rate of teacher reprimands. The technique is called differential attention because the teacher differentially (separately) pays attention to appropriate behavior and ignores inappropriate behavior.

Differential attention combines two basic strategies. These are described below:

1. **When a misbehavior occurs, the teacher ignores it.** Ignoring is a difficult technique for teachers because it requires them to do nothing when an irritating behavior is occurring. Doing nothing is difficult, particularly when students are misbehaving in order to get their attention. Ignoring is also difficult because the misbehavior will usually get worse before it gets better. This predictable increase is called an *extinction burst* and is a sign the technique is working. To ignore, it helps if a teacher breaks eye contact, does not speak to the student, walks away, or engages in another behavior (e.g., reading, talking with another student, writing something, etc.). A mother in one of the author's parent training groups found the perfect ignoring activity to be vacuuming. She said it was a perfect ignoring activity because the machine made a lot of noise and drowned out the arguing, she broke eye contact with the child while she concentrated on the activity, and vacuuming made her move constantly.

2. **The teacher must find something the student is doing appropriately and praise that behavior.** Effectiveness is enhanced by using the IFEED-AV reward rules covered in **Chapter 2,** p. 61, especially "D," describing the appropriate behavior. This might mean having to wait for an appropriate behavior or even praising the smallest behavioral improvement.

Sometimes teachers complain that a student *never* does anything appropriate. There is always something to praise, however. Facetiously: "Good breathing! I love the way you get air into your lungs" or "Great taking up space! You fill volume better than anyone in this classroom." If a student is alive and breathes or takes up space, something the student does can be praised. Teachers must be creative and find even the smallest behaviors to praise. They are always there. Some examples include:

-   "I appreciate the way you are sitting."
-   "Nice paying attention."
-   "Now that's the way to get to work."

One way to use differential attention is to ignore the misbehavior of a student, wait, and then praise her appropriate behavior when she exhibits it. A second approach is to ignore the student who is misbehaving and praise a student seated nearby for his appropriate behavior (proximity praise). "How to Implement Differential Attention" gives the steps for both of these types of differential attention.

Some words of caution are required for differential attention. As we have already mentioned, it is important to remember that, when you ignore them, most misbehaviors will temporarily get

How to . . .

IMPLEMENT DIFFERENTIAL ATTENTION

Step 1. Is the behavior dependent on the teacher's attention (e.g., whining, complaining, clowning)? If so, differential attention will probably work. If the behavior does not require the teacher's attention (e.g., noncompliance, aggression), differential attention may not work.

Step 2. Ignore the inappropriate behavior by not paying attention to it, walking away, breaking eye contact, not saying anything to the student, or busying yourself with another activity.

Step 3. When the student stops the inappropriate behavior, wait a few moments and then catch the student behaving appropriately. Describe and praise the appropriate behavior—for example, "Bo, great working on your math assignment." Use the IFEED-AV rules for social reinforcement described in Chapter 2.

Step 4. When you ignore the bad behavior, you should be prepared for an extinction burst; it is temporary, but the behavior is likely to get worse before it gets better. Caution: If you break down during an extinction burst and pay attention to the student, you have just taught the student that if he misbehaves to an even greater extent, the misbehavior will be rewarded.

Step 5. Have a backup plan ready. For example, if the student's extinction burst is particularly bad, you can physically remove yourself from the student's presence by taking a break, walking away, or having someone take over the classroom for a few minutes. If the behavior becomes intolerable, a precision request ("Now I need you to stop . . .") should be issued, followed by a reductive consequence, if necessary.

Step 6. Be prepared for the student to misbehave immediately after being reinforced for an appropriate behavior. This is not uncommon and is usually only temporary. It may mean that the student is seeking negative attention simply because it is familiar. Ignore the new misbehavior and try again with positive attention when it stops. This takes patience. Many Tough Kids are so used to negative attention from teachers that they prefer it to praise.

Step 7. If differential attention with an individual student is difficult, you can include another student. Ignore the Tough Kid and praise a student that is nearby (proximity praise) for appropriate behavior. When the Tough Kid behaves appropriately, he can then be reinforced.

worse before they get better. Differential attention works best for behaviors that require your attention and thus make ignoring effective (e.g., complaining, whining, clowning, etc.). It is less effective for aggression or noncompliance when the student hopes the teacher will not notice him. Also be aware that if the ignored behavior gets out of hand, you may need to use a Precision Request followed by a more potent reductive consequence ("Now I need you to stop arguing," followed by a consequence). The beauty of differential attention is that it reduces the number of unnecessary teacher reprimands. Instead of a continuous stream of *Don't* reprimands, differential attention can be used. We suggest teachers routinely use a differential attention approach before giving a reprimand or a Precision Request for minor attention-getting behaviors.

Behavioral Momentum

Has a salesman ever tried to sell you a new roof, siding, or other home repairs? If he asked you directly to spend $1500 or more for such services, you would probably refuse. Instead he uses a momentum strategy such as:

- Do you value your home? (Yes.)
- Do you plan to stay in your home? (Yes.)
- Do you want to protect your investment in your home? (Yes.)
- Would you want your family to stay safe and protected in your home? (Yes.)
- Then he asks if you would like to buy the home repair services.

The salesman uses questions to increase your positive agreement momentum to get you to say *Yes*. Momentum is easily visualized if you imagine a large round rock at the top of a hill. Once inertia is overcome and you push the rock, it starts to roll down the hill, it picks up speed, and it continues to roll until it reaches the bottom. Behavioral momentum is the same. Once behaviors start to occur in a series, their momentum generally continues in the same direction.

Teachers can use behavioral momentum with Tough Kids, especially Tough Kids who walk into class with "chips on their shoulders" first thing in the morning. Behavioral momentum works by asking the Tough Kid to do two or three things you know he normally wants to do. (We refer to this as making a *high-probability request*.) Then follow this positive behavior flow with your desired *low-probability request*. For example, you might ask a Tough Kid to help pass out papers, answer a question to which you are sure he knows the answer, or sharpen pencils. Then follow the high-probability request with a lower probability request, such as working on an academic assignment or cleaning his desk. "How to Use Behavioral Momentum" lists the basic steps in setting up a behavioral momentum sequence for Tough Kids.

Many Tough Kids come from difficult home environments in which they are frequently punished. It is not unusual for these students to have problems at home in the morning before they come to school. They may be punished for being slow, not being ready, or arguing with their parent or siblings. In a sense, they have just experienced a stream of punishing, low-probability requests directed at them at home. This has the *opposite* effect of positive behavioral momentum. These are the students who arrive with chips on their shoulders, ready for a bad day that will only get worse. Using positive behavioral momentum first thing in the morning can help reverse this negative downward spiral.

We suggest teachers design their daily schedules to include several positive requests among the first activities of the day. Instead of reviewing the previous day's problems or having students report their progress (common practices in classrooms serving Tough Kids), several high-probability positive request activities should be substituted. For younger students, brief positive compliance games such as Simon Says, Seven-Up, or guessing games are recommended morning activities. These games get younger students following teachers' directions because they are fun. For older students, listening to music, reviewing a popular magazine, or reading part of an interesting book may be positive morning activities. Teachers can ask questions about the music, magazine, or book as a form of positive compliance requests. These positive activities can be as short as

How to . . .

USE BEHAVIORAL MOMENTUM

Step 1. Select a series of behaviors a student already likes to do (high-probability requests). These should be behaviors the student is at least 70% likely to do when asked.

Step 2. Ask the student to do several of the high-probability behaviors in a series before asking him to do the behavior he does not want to do (low-probability behavior). For example:

- "Tom, will you please help me hand out the papers?"
- "Thanks, Tom. Now please help me straighten the chairs."
- "Now, Tom, please sit down and do your math assignment."

Step 3. Requesting two or three high-probability behaviors before the low-probability behavior greatly enhances the momentum effect. However, asking for even one high-probability behavior before the unlikely behavior can help. For example, a teacher might say, "Tom, please help me erase the whiteboard" (high-probability behavior). She would then say, "Tom, please write your spelling words on the board" (low-probability behavior).

Behavioral momentum can be engineered into the classroom schedule. Instead of beginning the day with low-probability activities such as reviewing the previous day's work, completing a difficult academic assignment, or calendar review, we encourage you to begin with high-probability behavior games or activities, such as Simon Says, Seven-Up, team guess of a mystery animal you select, reading a high-interest story, or charades. Then follow this activity with low-probability behaviors such as completing academic work, problem review, or participating in group work.

5 or 10 minutes. After the positive activity, more low-probability activities such as individual seat-work or academic tasks can be assigned.

These activities can be programmed into activity schedules in the morning, after lunch, or after recess when compliance is frequently low and disruptive behavior is likely. The task for teachers is thinking of high-probability, positive behaviors, games, and activities. To find these positive behaviors, watch what students do naturally, pay attention to what students frequently request, or simply ask students what they like. Then incorporate these activities into your daily schedules for the whole class.

The "Sure I Will" Program

Teachers will punish a lot less if they can teach Tough Kids appropriate replacement behaviors that interfere with their inappropriate behavior. In simpler terms, they should find a behavior they like and reward it. If the behavior interferes with arguing, noncompliance, tantrum throwing, or aggression, these inappropriate behaviors will naturally decrease. The difficulty with noncompliance is finding an appropriate replacement behavior. The "Sure I Will" program, used in conjunction with Precision Requests, allows teachers to teach students an appropriate replacement behavior.

"Sure I Will" works like this. First, ask a student to do something such as "Please turn in your spelling assignment." Then the student is taught to respond with the words "Sure I Will" and begin the requested behavior. Once a student *begins* the requested behavior, she is likely to complete it. In this way, compliance increases. The student should be intermittently rewarded for saying "Sure I Will" to a request and beginning the behavior. When you make a Precision Request and the student responds with "Sure I Will" and begins the requested behavior before you repeat the Precision Request the second time ("Now I *need* you to . . ."), you will see marked improvement in compliance and a reduction in arguing and noncompliance. (See Figure 3-8 for a depiction of the "Sure I Will" request sequence.)

As you randomly reward students for saying "Sure I Will," do so not only intermittently, but also with specific social reinforcement paired with academic points or a chance to earn a small reward. Teachers should not reinforce every "Sure I Will" response, but do reinforce each third or fourth response on average.

teams

For whole classrooms, interdependent group contingency teams can be set up to compete with each other in saying "Sure I Will" or similar responses and complying with teacher requests. You might divide a classroom into two or more teams. Ask each team to pick a compliance phrase such as "Sure I Will," "Okey Dokey," "Glad You Asked," "Sure, Any Time," or "No Problem." Team names or numbers are then posted on a whiteboard or wall. Place a checkmark by a team's name when

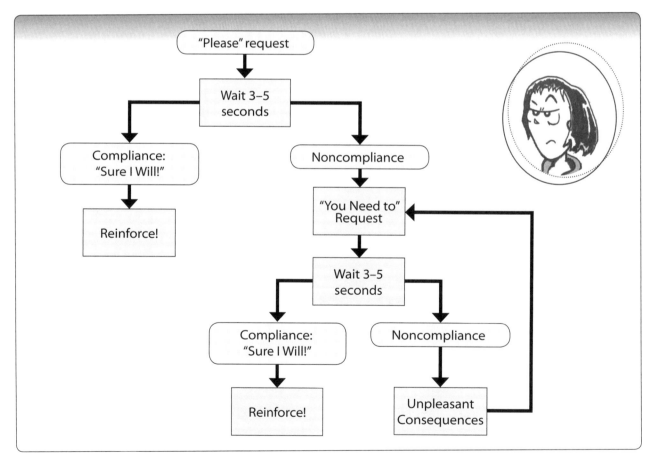

Figure 3-8 • "Sure I Will" Sequence

an individual team member makes a compliance response (see Figure 3-9).

For the program to be effective, begin the "Sure I Will" program by praising and awarding checks to teams liberally when the students respond with "Sure I Will" or their other assigned compliance responses. When student compliance has increased significantly (usually within two or three days), increase the criterion and gradually begin to fade the awarding of checkmarks. Over time, you will want to begin awarding checkmarks only for the most genuine responses or exceptional performance.

Teams can exchange their checkmarks for a chance at a Mystery Motivator or some other privilege. For example, you can write down a secret number. At the end of each day the number can be revealed to the class. If a team's number of checkmarks on the whiteboard or wall is the same as or greater than the secret number, the team receives the Mystery Motivator. Again, once compliance has increased significantly, the secret number can be revealed only every two or three days on average instead of every day. This will help maintain improved student performance over the long term.

The "Sure I Will" program can also be combined with a Response Cost procedure to make it even more effective. For example, you might erase one checkmark by a team's name if a student from that team engages in certain misbehaviors.

Figure 3-9 • Blackboard Example of "Sure I Will" Teams

How to . . .

IMPLEMENT THE "SURE I WILL" PROGRAM

The "Sure I Will" program is based on the idea that if a student verbally responds to a teacher's request with "Sure I Will," he is likely to begin the request and to comply. In a sense, the "Sure I Will" response interferes with noncompliance.

- The "Sure I Will" program is used with Precision Requests. The student must respond to a teacher's "Please" request with "Sure I Will" and start the behavior before the teacher issues the second request using the word *need* ("Now I need you to . . . "). If the student waits until *need* is used, he is not rewarded.

- Always socially reward a student's "Sure I Will" response.

- The student may also be rewarded randomly with a tangible reward such as academic points or a small toy.

"SURE I WILL" FOR TEAMS

The "Sure I Will" program can best be used with teams and a group contingency by following these steps:

Step 1. Each classroom team has a special response, such as "Sure I Will," "Okey Dokey," "Glad You Asked," "Sure, Any Time," or "No Problem."

Step 2. Select a secret number each day that is unknown to the students. One day it might be 20, then 15, then 19. Write it down on a piece of paper.

Step 3. Post the team names on the blackboard.

Step 4. Make a mark by each team's name when a team member responds with his team's preselected verbal response and begins the behavior. For example, you say, "Jeffery, please sit down in your seat." Jeffery says, "Sure I will, Mrs. Bolnick," and sits down.

Step 5. When the program first begins, be liberal in recording marks for teams. However, after several days of greatly improved compliance, accept only genuine efforts and sincere responses.

Step 6. At the end of each day, announce the secret number. If a team's number of marks is the same as or higher than the secret number, the team gets to participate in a class reward such as a Mystery Motivator or Grab Bag.

Step 7. If a team's number of marks is less than the secret number, they continue to do what is normally scheduled at that time of the day.

For instance, if a student goes to timeout, a checkmark can be erased from his team. Or if a student does not respond to a Precision Request after the *need* statement, a check can be erased. This Response Cost option should be used only rarely. The "Sure I Will" program should primarily be positive. It is not meant to be a program that threatens or frequently punishes students. If checks are often erased for the behavior of a particular student, you should determine whether or not the student can actually perform the behavior. Also determine whether or not the "reward" offered is actually positively reinforcing for that student.

One word of caution when using the "Sure I Will" program: Preliminary research has found the program to be exceptionally efficient at improving compliance (Martin-LeMaster, 1990). The problem is that repeated "Sure I Wills" can become tiring and repetitive. One teacher complained that she found high rates of repeated "Sure I Wills" to be tedious. We haven't ever had complaints about the compliance rates using this procedure, just the high rates and repetition of the same compliance response. To solve this problem, you should require students or teams to vary their compliance responses. Once they master one compliance response, students should choose another and then another. Once they are proficient with them all and any others you want to use, Tough Kids can be asked to use a different one each time they respond. This varied approach makes student responses sound far more natural. "How to Implement the 'Sure I Will' Program" summarizes the steps to take to use this program.

In a nutshell

A reductive technique is any research-validated procedure that temporarily stops or suppresses a behavior. The emphasis in this chapter has been on research-validated techniques. If there is no research evidence to support the use and effectiveness of a reductive technique, teachers are at risk professionally and ethically when using them.

Another emphasis in this chapter is that reductive techniques suppress a misbehavior only temporarily. They can give a teacher a window of opportunity to build in more functional social, academic, and self-management behaviors to replace the maladaptive behavior. If behaviors are merely suppressed with reductive techniques and students are not taught appropriate behaviors to replace them, the misbehavior will reappear.

Reductive techniques generally produce a rapid temporary behavior change that rewards their implementers and often results in their overuse. These procedures should be used sparingly with Tough Kids who make teaching difficult and disrupt the class. It is very easy to overuse punishment, which results in students disliking teachers and the educational setting in general.

(Continued)

In a nutshell *(Continued)*

This chapter presented several alternative positive programs that can be used to improve classroom compliance. Techniques such as "Sure I Will" and the Check-in/ Check-out program can be used to improve behavior. If possible, use these approaches first, with a major emphasis placed on positive replacement techniques.

If reductive techniques are required, teachers should be familiar with variables that allow them to use the procedures precisely and for the shortest possible period of time. Effectiveness variables reviewed in this chapter include establishing the teacher as likable and highly rewarding. Reductive techniques applied by someone who students like is far more effective than when they come from someone the students dislike. It is also important to reward appropriate behaviors that actually interfere with misbehaviors. For example, the "Sure I Will" program presented in this chapter actively interferes with noncompliance and is a highly valued behavior in and of itself.

Using reductive techniques early on in an aversive behavior chain also makes them far more effective. If a teacher waits until a student is out of control and at the peak of misbehavior, intervening becomes far less effective. Similarly, optimizing the antecedent variables of request making (e.g., no questions, up close, eye contact, requesting only twice, remaining unemotional, and making more start than stop requests) maximizes the use of several reductive procedures. Preplanning, consistency, and unique applications are the keys to using reductive procedures sparingly but effectively. Preplanning with a hierarchy of reductive consequences eliminates the likelihood that you will assign a consequence in the heat of a coercive interaction with a student. When teachers select a consequence during one of these coercive interactions, they tend to use overly harsh or unrealistic reductive consequences.

A publicly posted What If? Chart that lists a hierarchy of reductive consequences for increasingly severe misbehaviors is a good approach. The chart should also contain a serious behavior clause (i.e., procedures to temporarily remove a student from the classroom) for crisis or out-of-control behavior episodes. The What If? Chart must also contain a list of rewards for appropriate behaviors (e.g., no rule infractions for the day, everyone handing in their homework, perfect recess behavior).

Unique procedures reduce the need to use reductive techniques with Tough Kids. Simple but creative procedures such as differential attention, behavioral momentum,

In a nutshell *(Continued)*

and Bumpy Bunny Timeout are procedures students appear to enjoy. Enjoyment of the educational process is lacking in most Tough Kid's lives. These students have long histories of academic failure, have been overly punished for their misbehaviors, and have experienced rejection from peers. The essence of the goals of a good classroom is to help motivate Tough Kids to come to school, behave appropriately, learn new social skills, and achieve academically. Reductive procedures may be necessary, but they should be used sparingly and as an adjunct to an appropriate behavior-building, positive core program.

References

Bowen, J., Jenson, W. R., & Clark, E. (2004). *School-based interventions for students with behavior problems.* New York: Kluwer Academic/Plenum Publishers.

Crone, D. A., Horner, R. H., & Hawkin, L. (2003). *Responding to problem behavior in the schools: The behavior education program.* New York: Guilford Press.

Dishion, T. J., McCord, J., & Poulin, F. (1999). When interventions harm: Peer groups and problem behavior, *American Psychologist, 54,* 755–764.

Fogt, J. B., George, M. P., Kern, L., White, G. P., & George, N. L. (2009). Physical restraint of students with behavior disorders in day treatment and residential settings. *Behavior Disorders, 24,* 4–13.

Forehand, R. (1977). Child noncompliance to parental requests: Behavior analysis and treatment. In M. Hersen, R. M. Eisler, & P. M. Miller (Eds.), *Progress in behavior modification* (Vol. 5; pp. 111–148). New York: Academic Press.

Hamlet, C. C., Axelrod, S., & Kuerschner, S. (1984). Eye contact as an antecedent to compliant behavior. *Journal of Applied Behavior Analysis, 17,* 553–557.

Jenson, W. R., Olympia, D., Farley, M., & Clark, E. (2004). Positive psychology and externalizing students: Awash in a sea of negativity. *Psychology in the Schools, 41,* 67–80.

Jenson, W. R., Rhode, G., Evans, C., & Morgan, D. P. (2006). *The tough kid principal's briefcase: A practical guide to schoolwide behavior management and legal issues.* Longmont, CO: Sopris West Educational Services.

Jenson, W. R., Rhode, G., & Reavis, H. K. (2009). *The tough kid tool box.* Eugene, OR: Pacific Northwest Publishing.

Jesse, V. C. (1990). *Compliance training and generalization effects using a compliance matrix and spinner system.* Unpublished dissertation, University of Utah, Salt Lake City, UT.

Martin-LeMaster, J. (1990). *Increasing classroom compliance of noncompliant elementary-age students.* Unpublished dissertation, University of Utah, Salt Lake City, UT.

Nelson, J. R., & Carr, B. A. (2000). *Think time strategy for schools.* Longmont, CO: Sopris West Publishing.

Patterson, G. R. (1976). *The aggressive child: Victim and architect of a coercive system.* In E. J. Mash, L. A. Hamerlynck, & L. C. Handy (Eds.), Behavior modification and families (pp. 267–316). New York: Brunner Mazel.

Proctor, M. A., & Morgan, D. (1991). Effectiveness of a response cost raffle procedure on the disruptive classroom behavior of adolescents with behavior problems. *School Psychology Review, 20,* 97–109.

Theodore, L. A., Bray, M. A., Kehle, T. J., & Jenson, W. R. (2001). Randomized and group contingencies to reduce disruptive behavior of adolescent students in special education. *Journal of School Psychology, 39,* 267–277.

U. S. Government Accountability Office (2009). Seclusions and restraints: Selected cases of death and abuse at public and private schools and treatment centers (GAO-09-719T). Retrieved on February 2, 2010, from www.gao.gov/new.items/d09719t.pdf.

Van Houten, R., & Doleys, D. (1983). Are social reprimands effective? In S. Axelrod and J. Apsche (Eds.), *The effects of punishment on human behavior* (pp. 45–70). New York: Academic Press.

Vegas, K., Jenson, W. R., & Kircher, J. (2007). A single subject meta-analysis of the effectiveness of time out to reduce disruptive classroom behavior. *Behavior Disorders, 32,* 109–121.

Witt, J. C., & Elliot, S. N. (1982). The response cost lottery: A time efficient and effective classroom intervention. *Journal of School Psychology, 20,* 155–161.

 Evidence Base

The CD contains a file (Evidence_Base.pdf) that lists additional references to studies that demonstrate the effectiveness of the various strategies and techniques discussed in this book.

The Tough Kid® Book

CHAPTER 4

Advanced Systems for Tough Kids

Advanced systems are designed for use with the most difficult students teachers have in their classrooms. It is estimated that 1 to 2% of the school population will require the use of advanced systems. These procedures are extremely powerful in changing the behavior of students with severe behavior problems.

A core assumption in using any advanced system is that the target students are in a classroom setting with an appropriately implemented basic management system in place. It is also assumed that the teacher has already adjusted the basic classroom management system and found it to be ineffective in meeting the needs of these students. This is important for two reasons:

1. **Many students exhibit severe behavior problems as a result of ineffective, dysfunctional classroom management.** These are students whose behavior could be managed with a consistent basic management

THINK ABOUT IT

THINK

" *The target students should be in a classroom setting with a management system in place.* "

approach. When such an approach is absent, the inappropriate behaviors of these students escalate. In this case, the real problem is a *teacher problem* rather than a student problem.

2. **The goal with all Tough Kids is to sufficiently change their behavior so that ultimately they can be taught effectively using the basic classroom management plan.** Ideally, teachers will not want to use the more intrusive advanced systems indefinitely if students can be taught to work within the basic classroom management system. If a basic classroom management system is not in place, obviously there is nothing to maintain the positive behavior changes once advanced systems are faded from use. This chapter describes various advanced systems in detail.

In addition to classroom management issues, Tough Kids often experience difficulty in the area of academic instruction. Sometimes so much

How to . . .

DEVELOP A READING PROGRAM FOR TOUGH KIDS

Offer extra instruction. The more deficient the student's reading skills, the more extra instructional time she should be receiving.

Provide early remediation. Help should be made available as soon as deficits are identified.

Careful instruction. The more deficient the reading skills, the more explicit, direct, and focused the instruction must be.

Implement a well-designed program. Reading instruction must focus on essential skills and concepts.

Emphasize rapid progression. The greater the student's deficits, the more rapid her progress must be.

Monitor progress. Regular, frequent progress monitoring must be in place to determine whether the student is on target for meeting goals or whether adjustments must be made to instruction.

Motivate. Address the student's motivation with strategies described in Chapter 2. Progress and success are in direct proportion to student motivation.

Always include a compliance rule. You will get the behavior you post in the rules. If you want to improve compliance in the classroom, include a rule such as: Do what your teacher asks immediately.

Reading

effort and energy are devoted to managing their behavior that their academic instruction is not given careful consideration. In designing effective advanced systems for Tough Kids, their academic instruction must also be taken into account if long-term improvement is to be sustained.

ACADEMIC INSTRUCTION

An appropriate approach to teaching Tough Kids involves planning and implementing the behavior management they require within the context of teaching them the academic skills they need. Without improvement in academic skills, even the most "advanced" behavior management

system will not decrease behavior problems in the long term. It is a fact that many Tough Kids are significantly behind their peers when it comes to academic performance, particularly in the area of reading. Because reading is so critical to a great deal of learning, reading instruction should be assessed very carefully for Tough Kids who have a history of learning difficulties. Guidelines for providing reading instruction for these students are provided in "How To Develop a Reading Program for Tough Kids."

Academic Learning Time

Literature on effective schools tells educators to minimize the amount of class time spent on housekeeping tasks. The majority of time must

Tough kids generally more behind in reading.

How to . . .

INCREASE ACADEMIC LEARNING TIME

To increase academic learning time, assess and adjust the following variables:

Always begin on time. While this may seem obvious, many teachers lose valuable instructional time by beginning class (or tasks) late. You must reinforce the expectation of beginning on time and recognize and reward students who meet that expectation.

Minimize "housekeeping" tasks. Teachers must always be looking for ways to streamline everyday housekeeping tasks that take away from instructional time. Simplifying tasks and having students assist with them can help.

Minimize transition time. When transitioning between different academic learning activities, you can waste a great deal of time if the transitions are not managed efficiently and smoothly. Do the following to minimize transition time:

- Have materials organized and ready.
- Confidently end one activity and begin the next.
- Increase monitoring of students during transition times (praise and recognize those who transition quickly).
- Plan activities at which students can succeed. They will then be enthusiastic about beginning the next activity.

KEY

Most time spent on Atleast 70%

be spent on academic instruction. Assuming the Tough Kid is skill deficient, the amount of academic learning time in his program is absolutely critical because rapid progress is essential to the amount of improvement that is typically needed.

Academic learning time refers to the amount of time students are actually engaged in and experiencing success in learning. The time must be spent on learning the essential skills Tough Kids need to acquire. Obviously, if academic learning time is spent on meaningless or irrelevant tasks, it will not be highly related to their learning. Increased achievement will occur only when sufficient time is spent on appropriate and effective instruction. To achieve a level of academic learning time of no less than 70%, teachers must

address several variables, detailed in "How To Increase Academic Learning Time."

Direct/Explicit Instruction

Research indicates overwhelming support for the use of direct/explicit instruction to teach basic skills to all students and, in particular, hard-to-teach students. In fact, large-scale meta-analyses and extensive literature reviews confirm that the positive effects of direct instruction are much larger than those obtained by other programs (Adams & Engelmann, 1996; Borman, Hewes, Overman, & Brown, 2003; White, 1988). Steps incorporated in direct instruction are well suited for use with hard-to-teach students. Not only are the teaching strategies themselves

POINTER BOX 4-1

RECOMMENDED DIRECT/EXPLICIT INSTRUCTION PROGRAMS

MATH

Corrective Mathematics (ages 5–14)
Available from McGraw-Hill, www.sraonline.com

Seven modules provide teacher-directed instruction on the following skills and concepts: addition, subtraction, multiplication, division, basic fractions, decimals and percents, ratios, and equations. Structured practice develops student skills in learning and retaining facts, understanding place value, solving problems, and discriminating among various types of story problems. The focus of *Corrective Mathematics* is on core content and breaking the content into a series of small conceptual steps and embedded skills. This program teaches mathematics skills, rules, and strategies efficiently and effectively.

READING

Read Well (grades K–2)
Available from Sopris West Educational Services, www.sopriswest.com

This program's research-validated approach has demonstrated effectiveness across diverse student groups and implementations. Students must master skills, as demonstrated by ongoing assessments and progress monitoring, before moving on in the program. *Read Well* features multiple entry points and small group differentiated instruction to accommodate different skill levels. Continuous instruction features a unique scope and sequence to eliminate gaps in student learning. Complementary spelling and composition programs are also available.

REWARDS Program (grades 4–12)
Available from Sopris West Educational Services, www.sopriswest.com

REWARDS is an intense, short-term reading intervention program designed for students who have mastered basic reading skills only through first and second grade. It teaches flexible strategies for decoding multisyllabic words in order to build students' reading accuracy and fluency. The original program consists of 20 lessons that last 40 to 50 minutes each. Implemented by teachers or paraprofessionals in a whole-class setting, lessons are explicit with a high level of teacher/student interaction. *REWARDS* improves student skills in decoding, fluency, vocabulary, comprehension, test-taking skills, content-area reading and writing, word choice, and sentence writing and revision.

applicable for Tough Kids, but direct instruction maximizes academic learning time and provides a very structured learning environment in which Tough Kids simply have little opportunity to disrupt and engage in misbehavior. There is no single type of direct instruction—in fact, some are considerably more "direct" than others. What research indicates, however, is the more direct the instruction, the more effective it is. Also, more direct instructional time is associated with greater achievement. Pointer Box 4-1 lists available commercial instructional materials

Corrective Reading (ages 7–14)
Available from McGraw-Hill, www.sraonline.com

Corrective Reading features two major strands that can be used separately as a supplemental reading intervention or combined for use as a comprehensive reading intervention program. The Decoding strand is appropriate for students who do not read accurately or whose oral reading is choppy, as well as for less fluent readers who lack comprehension when they read. The Comprehension strand is suitable for students who need to develop vocabulary, background information, and reasoning skills that form the foundation of comprehension. *Corrective Reading* provides multiple entry points and fast-cycle options to accommodate skill levels from grade 4 to adult. Integrated assessments guide student movement through the program.

Reading Mastery (ages 6–14)
Available from McGraw-Hill, www.sraonline.com.

Reading Mastery features strategy-based instruction that helps students learn more efficiently. It covers all five essential components of reading: phonemic awareness, phonics and word analysis, fluency, vocabulary, and comprehension. Emphasis is placed on developing decoding, word recognition, and comprehension skills that transfer to other subject areas. Ongoing assessments and guidelines for remediation help teachers make effective instructional decisions.

SPELLING

Spelling Mastery (ages 5–14)
Available from McGraw-Hill, www.sraonline.com

This program takes several approaches to teaching spelling. Beginning spellers learn the phonemic approach to generalize the spellings of words and word parts that follow regular spelling patterns. More advanced spellers learn to use the morphemic approach to spell meaningful prefixes, bases, and suffixes, and combine words and word parts to form multisyllabic words. The whole word approach teaches students at all levels to memorize the spelling of potentially troublesome irregular words.

LANGUAGE

SRA Language Programs (ages 5–18)
Available from McGraw-Hill, www.sraonline.com

The *SRA Language Programs* are designed to develop language skills and give young children and ESL students a solid foundation for literacy. Students learn to group objects in different ways, to see the logic behind rules and strategies, and to know how and when to apply these rules.

recommended for a direct instruction approach to academic instruction.

Direct instruction is a teacher-centered instructional approach that is most effective for teaching basic or isolated skills (Kroesbergen & Van Luit, 2003). The most direct of the approaches involves a scripted, systematic program with step-by-step sequencing that requires mastery at each step before moving to the next one. With this approach, the teacher follows the sequence of steps. She begins by telling the students the objective of the lesson with a rationale for why they need the skill that they are about to be taught. According to Swanson (2001), the teacher reviews skills needed for new information, questions students, and provides group instruction and independent practice. She assesses performance and then provides additional practice. Swanson identifies twelve criteria associated with direct instruction and suggests that direct instruction is occurring when any four of them are present.

1. Breaking down a learning task into small steps
2. Administering probes
3. Providing repeated feedback
4. Providing a visual presentation
5. Including independent practice and individually paced instruction
6. Breaking down instruction into simpler parts
7. Instructing in a small group
8. Teacher modeling the skill
9. Providing structured materials at a fast pace
10. Giving individual instruction
11. Teacher asking questions
12. Teacher presenting new skills

According to the results of several meta-analyses (Ellis, 1993; Karp & Voltz, 2000; Swanson, 2001), using a combination of direct instruction and strategy instruction has a greater positive effect than either one alone. The purpose of strategy instruction is to teach students how to learn information and access it as needed. To gain the maximum benefit from both direct instruction and strategy instruction, teachers should use both in every lesson they teach. First they should teach basic skills to students using direct instruction. Then they should teach students strategies to store and retrieve the information.

Direct Instruction

"Direct instruction is teacher centered and focused on helping students learn basic skills and information. Strategy instruction is student centered and teaches students how to learn information and then retrieve that information when it is needed. Learning strategies are taught during strategy instruction as ways of organizing information so that it can be retrieved."

—The Access Center (2009)

Strategy Instruction

A strategy is a tool, plan, or method used to accomplish a task. Strategy instruction teaches students about strategies, how and when to use them, and how to identify what strategies are effective for them. Students are encouraged to make strategy use part of their continued learning. When students who have difficulty learning and retaining information are taught strategies and given sufficient encouragement, feedback, and opportunities to use them, they process information better, which in turn results in improved learning (Comford, 2002; Najar, 1999; Pressley, 1990; Vacca & Vacca, 2005).

According to the ERIC Clearinghouse on Disabilities and Gifted Education (2009), the most essential strategies to teach include:

Most essential strategies to teach:

1. **Computation and problem solving:** verbalization, visualization, chunking, making associations, use of cues

2. **Memory:** visualization, verbalization, mnemonics, making associations, chunking, writing (usually more effective when used in combinations)

3. **Productivity:** verbalization, visualization, self-monitoring, use of cues

4. **Reading accuracy and fluency:** finger pointing or tracking, sounding out unknown words, self-questioning for accuracy, chunking, using contextual clues

5. **Reading comprehension:** visualization, questioning, rereading, predicting

6. **Writing:** planning, revising, questioning, use of cues, verbalization, visualization, checking and monitoring

Strategy instruction should not be treated as a separate subject. It should be an <u>integral part</u> of ongoing instruction regardless of the content being taught. Strategies should be taught throughout the entire school year, with the teacher modeling and explaining them. Teachers must encourage students to use strategies when it is appropriate to do so and recognize and reward students when they do.

Steps for teaching strategy use include:

STEP 1 <u>Describe</u> the strategy. Tell students when the strategy can be used, how to use it, and why it is important to use it.

STEP 2 <u>Model</u> its use. Model the strategy and explain to students how to do it.

STEP 3 Provide ample time for guided <u>practice</u>. Monitor student practice, providing cues and feedback. Sufficient practice is essential for strategy use to become automatic.

STEP 4 Introduce student <u>self-monitoring and evaluation</u> of their strategy use. Teach students how to self-monitor and evaluate their use of strategies they learn. Match your evaluation of the strategy use with the student's and provide feedback on differences and similarities.

STEP 5 <u>Encourage continued use</u> and generalization of the strategy. Encourage and prompt students to use strategies in different content areas and in different settings. Brainstorm with them the varieties of ways and situations where the strategies can be helpful. Recognize and reward students when they continue to use strategies they've learned and when they use them in new ways.

Strategy Instruction should be integrated!

See Pointer Box 4-2 for additional resources for teaching study skills and strategies.

Monitoring and Evaluation of Academic Progress

Because most Tough Kids have no time to lose in making academic progress, it is essential that regular monitoring and evaluation take place. It is not sufficient for teachers to record unsatisfactory scores and grades week after week and then conclude at the end of the year that students were unsuccessful.

Achievement tests can provide feedback to teachers once or twice a year but are insufficient for ongoing progress monitoring. At least weekly or biweekly progress probes, mini tests, or mastery tests keyed to the instructional programs in use or to a standard are essential.

If a student hasn't mastered a skill that was just taught, the teacher who regularly monitors progress knows right away that additional and/or adapted instruction must be provided. If the Tough Kid is not sufficiently motivated to do his best in learning new skills, the teacher will also need to provide effective positive reinforcement for learning them.

Note: See **Chapter 1** for additional information related to progress monitoring.

POINTER BOX 4-2

RESOURCES FOR TEACHING STUDY SKILLS

Skills/Advanced Skills for School Success (grades 3–7+)
Available from Curriculum Associates, www.curriculumassociates.com

Students learn study and work strategies through this research-based program. Skills covered include time management, use of text and reference books, and interpretation of graphic organizers. Students also learn to organize their assignments and study for tests.

ADDITIONAL RESOURCES

www.amazon.com/Books-on-study-skills/lm/308PAL7ANANHD
www.soe.ku.edu/Donald-Deshler/
www.learningstore.org

Cooperative Learning Strategies

Cooperative learning strategies are successful teaching strategies in which small teams of students with differing ability levels are taught to use a variety of learning activities to improve their understanding of a subject. Each student on a team is responsible for personally learning what is taught as well as helping others on the team learn. Each student is assigned a specific job role for the group. All group members work through the assignment until everyone in the group has learned and completed the assignment. See "How to Use Cooperative Learning Procedures" for more details.

Cooperative learning structures are appealing for use with Tough Kids for a number of reasons:

- They have been shown to increase achievement, especially in low-achieving students.
- They have been shown to be helpful in successfully integrating Tough Kids into general education classrooms.
- They promote positive social relations and development.

How to . . .

USE COOPERATIVE LEARNING PROCEDURES

Step 1. Identify the academic objectives and cooperative learning objectives (e.g., social or cooperative skills) to be taught and recognized.

Step 2. Decide on the size of the groups (4–6 students is typical), composition of groups, how long the groups will function (e.g., for a specific project, a week, a month), and the physical arrangement of the classroom to facilitate small group work.

Step 3. Assign roles to group members (e.g., checker, accuracy coach, team manager, cheerleader). Emphasize to group members that their team is collaborative and that they must rely on one another for success or failure. Over time, the roles can be rotated among students.

Step 4. Explain the learning task and cooperative goal structure to the students. The cooperative goal structure usually includes:

- An academic group goal as well as a social or cooperative goal
- Criteria for success
- Understanding that all group members receive the same grade
- Awareness of the cooperative learning skills required for the task
- A reminder that everyone is to help others in the group

Step 5. Monitor, encourage, provide feedback, and intervene as needed as students work collaboratively. Provide assistance when requested.

Step 6. Evaluate individual student learning, group products, and individual and group cooperative learning and collaboration skills.

Sources: Johnson & Johnson, 2001; Kagan & Kagan, 2009

- They have been shown to increase students' social development and learning.

Cooperative learning consists of dividing the class into small teams of students who are made interdependent on each other, in a positive way, by the use of a reward and task structure.

"How To Structure Cooperative Learning" describes several types of popular cooperative learning structures. With cooperative learning, students are most often evaluated with individual quizzes so that the teacher can continue to monitor individual progress. Students generally earn points for their teams based on improvement over past performance. The teacher then uses newsletters, bulletin boards, and other social rewards and forms of recognition for teams' performances. Recognizing individual students who have performed extremely well or who have made sufficient improvement is also important.

Pointer Box 4-3 provides additional sources for information about how cooperative learning can help with homework completion.

Students still monitored individually

How to . . .

STRUCTURE COOPERATIVE LEARNING

Jigsaw. Form groups of up to five students. Each student is given a different but related assignment and then asked to teach her material to all the other students in her group. Students from different groups who have the same assignment may be given time to work through it together and to decide how to teach it to others in their own groups.

Three-Step Interview. Each team member pairs up with another student in the group. First, one partner asks the other partner questions related to the assignment for clarification. Then partners switch roles. Finally, each team member shares his partner's response with the group.

Three-Minute Review. Stop any time during instruction and ask established groups to take three minutes to review what you have been teaching and ask questions of one another.

Team-Pair-Solo. Students are first given problems to work through as a team, then with a partner, and ultimately on their own. This allows students to complete problems they could not do alone initially and fades help as the process progresses.

Think-Pair-Share. This strategy includes three steps. First, instruct students to think to themselves about a question or problem you have presented. Next, students are paired up to exchange ideas and thoughts. Finally, each pair shares their responses with other pairs and then with the entire group.

Numbered Heads Together. Assign students to groups of four. Each group member is given a number: 1, 2, 3, or 4. A question or problem is then presented to the group. Ask them to work together until all students in the group can answer the question or solve the problem. Then call on a number from each group (e.g., "3" or "1") to give the answer.

Source: Kagan & Kagan, 2009.

POINTER BOX 4-3

GETTING TOUGH KIDS TO DO THEIR HOMEWORK USING COOPERATIVE GROUPS

"Using student-managed interventions to increase homework completion and accuracy" by D. Olympia, S. Sheridan, and W. R. Jenson (1994). *Journal of Applied Behavior Analysis, 27,* 85–99.

ADDITIONAL HOMEWORK RESOURCES

Homework Success for Children With ADHD: A Family-School Intervention Program (2001)
by T. J. Power, D. F. Habboushe, and J. L. Karustis
Available from Guilford Press, www.guilford.com

Pacific Northwest Publishing is currently revising and updating a guide for parents who want to help children with homework, by Tough Kid author William R. Jenson and others. Visit www.PacificNWPublish.com for updates on this project.

SOCIAL SKILLS TRAINING

By definition, Tough Kids exhibit significant social skills deficits when they are compared with their successful peers. There are those who propose that students with severe behavior problems need only spend time with their normal peers to learn desired social behaviors. However, Tough Kids are poorly accepted by their "normal" peers, resulting in minimal interaction between them even when they do spend time together. When interaction does occur, it is often negative. It becomes clear that if exposing Tough Kids to their normal peers is all that is needed for them to acquire appropriate social skills, they would have already acquired acceptable social skills.

Lack of appropriate social skills affects Tough Kids not only while they are in school but also in their adult lives. Students who are noncompliant, manipulative, disruptive, and act out during their school years grow up to be noncompliant adults with similar problems. As a group, they have multiple marriages, lose jobs frequently, and break society's laws. Clearly, if these problems are not addressed during their school years, Tough Kids and society as a whole will suffer their effects indefinitely.

Many Tough Kids also lack the minimal behavioral skills necessary to promote their academic learning. Research indicates that most teachers have fairly rigid standards of behavior to which students are expected to conform. When students fail to do this, the whole learning process is disrupted and their classroom success is impeded. Thus, it is essential that Tough Kids receive specific social skills training in their school programs to break this cycle of failure. When Tough Kids have not acquired necessary social skills vicariously, they must be taught them directly, with a focus on specific problem areas.

Box 4-1 describes the elements found in most effective social skills training programs for Tough Kids. These programs generally use a direct or explicit instruction approach that uses many of the same components found in academic programs. A number of very effective social skills programs on the market can be incorporated into the Tough Kid's school program to directly teach needed social skills. Pointer Box 4-4 on pp. 136–137 provides information about recommended social skills programs. All those listed

BOX 4-1

Components of Effective _Social Skills_ Programs

○ **Instructions and Rationales.** Inform students about the specific skills they will be taught and how the skills will help them be more successful in daily interactions. Provide a definition of the skills along with examples.

○**Modeling.** Incorporate modeling by using films, videotapes, audiotapes, live demonstrations, puppets, books, and mental imagery.

○**Concept Teaching.** Concept teaching involves presenting the critical and irrelevant attributes of a social skill concept and determining whether the student can distinguish between examples and non-examples of the concept. Examples of a skill might include a videotape that depicts several scenes of the student "promptly doing what the teacher asks." Non-examples might include videotape depictions of students not promptly doing what the teacher asks.

○**Role Playing/Behavior Rehearsal and Practice.** The student rehearses how to behave in situations that have caused difficulty in the past or may cause difficulty in the future. The teacher first models the appropriate behavior and then provides prompts, coaching, and feedback to the student during the rehearsal. As is the case with any skill, the amount and quality of practice time is a critical variable in acquiring it.

○ **Coaching.** Coaching involves verbally instructing students by focusing on relevant cues, concepts, and rules.

○ **Contingent Reinforcement.** To effectively teach social skills, teachers must know how and when to praise, ignore, and give students corrective feedback. A positive reinforcement system needs to be in place to help Tough Kids acquire and maintain the social skills they need to learn.

have been well researched and their effectiveness documented when used as directed by the publisher.

There is no doubt that even Tough Kids can be taught social skills within the confines of four classroom walls. The real trick is to get them to use the social skills that they are taught in the classroom in other settings. It is a big mistake for teachers to assume that Tough Kids will exhibit social skills in other settings once they have been taught to use them in the classroom. Teachers must incorporate a number of procedures to encourage the generalized use of social skills by Tough Kids in other settings where they are needed and desired. "How To Enhance Social Skills Generalization" outlines these procedures.

How to . . .

ENHANCE SOCIAL SKILLS GENERALIZATION

- Teach behaviors that will maximize success and minimize failure. Teach behaviors that are needed and will be used in other settings. *Needed skills to be successful*

- Make classroom training realistic by using relevant examples and non-examples. Role-play and rehearsal activities should reflect what actually happens in students' lives. *Relavance*

- Make sure students learn the skills in the classroom training part of the program. The teacher must provide lots of supervised practice opportunities. *Learn → practice → application*

- Provide social skills "homework" assignments. This will allow the students opportunities to practice outside the classroom setting.

- Require self-reporting following a homework assignment. Provide positive reinforcement for accuracy of the self-report and actual achievement on the homework assignment. If the student has failed at either of these, the teacher should use problem-solving strategies to resolve them before the next training session.

- Program other settings to support the new skills, whenever possible. Other school staff, peers, and parents must help reinforce and prompt newly learned social skills.

- Gradually fade special positive reinforcement programs to eventually approximate the actual reinforcement available in real life. *Fade*

- Teach self-management skills to help the student maintain improved social skills. See the "Self-Monitoring" section of this chapter (pp. 160–163).

- For more difficult cases, you may need to go the extra mile and actually follow students into other settings to prompt, coach, correct, and reinforce new skills. You then fade out of the outside settings.

- Use periodic booster sessions if the student's behavior deteriorates or as a preventive measure. Re-teach or review appropriate lessons.

Source: Morgan & Jenson (1988).

POINTER BOX 4-4

RECOMMENDED SOCIAL SKILLS PROGRAMS

ELEMENTARY POPULATIONS (GRADES K–6)

The Tough Kid Social Skills Book (grades 3–8)
Available from Pacific Northwest Publishing, www.pacificnwpublish.com

The book presents an overview of Tough Kids' problematic social behaviors, describes how to assess social skills, and discusses small group, classroom, and schoolwide training options. Lesson plans cover eleven major social skills with materials provided in the book and on CD.

SMART Kids (grades K–1)
Available from Pacific Northwest Publishing, www.pacificnwpublish.com

This program provides instruction in social grace, old-fashioned manners, and how to talk respectfully. It includes direct instruction lessons and age-appropriate activities and games.

Cool Kids (grades K–3 [Level 1] and 3–8 [Level 2])
Available from Sopris West Educational Services, www.sopriswest.com

Teachers can use instructional strategies *before* problems occur to create a caring environment, identify social skills deficits, and uphold consistent standards for behavior. The program can be used with individual students, small groups, or an entire school.

Getting Along With Others: Teaching Social Effectiveness to Children
Available from Research Press, www.researchpress.com

The program guide introduces 32 training activities, five main teaching strategies, and nine additional techniques for teaching social skills. Each skill lesson contains teacher scripts, role-plays, group activities, relaxation training, and a home note and homework assignment.

Skillstreaming the Elementary School Child
Available from Research Press, www.researchpress.com

This program covers 60 specific prosocial skills and addresses the needs of students who display aggression, immaturity, withdrawal, and other problem behaviors.

Teaching Social Skills to Youth, Second Edition (ages 8 and up)
Available from Boys Town Press, www.boystownpress.org

Step-by-step component behaviors are provided for 182 skills ranging from basic (following instructions and introducing oneself) to complex (managing stress and resolving conflict). A CD contains social skills steps for display and more information for skill generalization.

The Walker Social Skills Curriculum: The ACCEPTS Program
Available from Pro-Ed Publishing, www.proedinc.com

ACCEPTS is a curriculum for teaching classroom and peer-to-peer social skills to children with or without disabilities. Its nine-step instructional procedure is based on principles of direct instruction and includes scripts for teaching and placement tests.

SECONDARY POPULATIONS (GRADE 7 AND UP)

Aggression Replacement Training
Available from Research Press, www.researchpress.com

This approved Safe and Drug-Free Schools Program teaches adolescents to understand and replace aggression with positive alternatives. It includes training in prosocial skills, anger control, and moral reasoning.

The Prepare Curriculum: Teaching Prosocial Competencies
Available from Research Press, www.researchpress.com

This program is designed for use with students who are chronically aggressive, withdrawn, or otherwise weak in prosocial competencies. The curriculum includes ten course-length interventions.

Skillstreaming the Adolescent: New Strategies & Perspectives for Teaching Prosocial Skills
Available from Research Press, www.researchpress.com

This curriculum provides training in 50 prosocial skills in six major skill groups. The program is appropriate for students who display aggression, immaturity, or withdrawal.

Teaching Social Skills to Youth (2nd ed.)

See description in elementary section

The Walker Social Skills Curriculum: The ACCESS Complete Program
Available from Pro-Ed Publishing, www.proedinc.com

This curriculum teaches social skills to students at middle and high school levels. Twenty-eight lessons cover 15 social skills. Contracting and self-reporting are used to transfer newly learned skills to other school settings.

Chapter 5 covers two social skills programs designed for use with Tough Kids in special placements. The Teacher Pleasers Program is intended for use with small groups, and Meeting Individual Teacher's Expectations focuses on individualizing instruction to address a Tough Kid's specific deficits. Though neither is a comprehensive program designed for general classroom use, you may wish to review them for tips on teaching social skills to Tough Kids. Materials needed to implement both are included on the CD provided with this book.

ADVANCED STRATEGIES

Advertising for Success

Advertising for Success is a public posting strategy that is effectively used with Tough Kids to decrease disruptive behaviors and improve academic motivation. It consists of posting measures of behavior or academic progress on a conspicuous bulletin board or wall in the classroom. Postings for behavior may include being on time to class, being prepared to work, appropriate transitions from class to class, and the like. Academic postings may include handwriting samples, story writing, number of books read, and contributions made in class.

Teachers must use caution so as not to violate the Family Educational Rights and Privacy Act (FERPA, 1974), which does not permit teachers to post graded work with student names or ask students to call out their scores. These practices must be avoided, and teachers should treat grade books and student work confidentially unless they have parents sign a form ahead of time to

No grades!

give permission to publicly post grades, scores, points earned, or other personally identifiable information.

For Advertising for Success to be effective, several components are essential:

- Some type of visual feedback system must be present and must be visible from students' desks. A conspicuous bulletin board, wall, poster, or display case are all appropriate for public posting.
- Accurate and meaningful information must be publicly posted. The more recent the information and the more immediately it is posted, the more effective the public posting will be.

> ### Advertising Success
>
> When Advertising for Success is used, students in the bottom half of the class academically benefit and improve the most.

An engineered reaction to the posting is very important. This refers to the responses of other school personnel, peers, the principal, and parents to the public posting system. Because public posting usually has no other reward associated with it other than its prominent display, the positively reinforcing reaction of others is critical. If this is not likely to happen naturally, the teacher needs to do everything possible to structure it.

To effectively implement a public posting system, we recommend that you follow the steps listed below:

STEP 1 Select a visual feedback system to display prominently in the classroom so students can see it from their desks. Lettering should be large and bold. We suggest that charts be erasable (e.g., laminated poster board) and contain a week's worth of data (Monday through Friday). Keep the system simple!

STEP 2 Decide on positive improvement to post. Students should be compared against their own performance rather than against each other. Thus, improvement is emphasized.

STEP 3 Decide on a specific, meaningful daily measure, such as daily points (with prior parent permission) earned for appropriate behavior.

STEP 4 Give feedback immediately. The more immediately the feedback is given, the more effective the posting system will be.

STEP 5 Develop a system to score or evaluate the students' work or behavior so that it can be posted immediately. Self or peer grading or rating can be used rather than waiting for the teacher to do the grading (and yes, the Supreme Court decision we mentioned above does permit this practice).

Method 1. Give students special colored pencils or pens for grading to prevent cheating. The teacher may randomly grade papers for accuracy after students have graded them.

Method 2. Set up grading stations with answer sheets and special colored pencils or pens

Like this method!

for grading. Allow students to bring only their answer sheets to the grading station. No other pencils or papers are allowed.

Method 3. Have students exchange papers and put their initials at the bottom as the grader. It may help to have students rotate papers two or three times so that students are not next to their graders. Again, the teacher can randomly grade a few papers after students have graded them to check for accuracy.

STEP 6 Give positive feedback for student improvements over their own best scores rather than for some absolute level or near-perfect goal. In this way, students compete against themselves.

STEP 7 Praise improvements on the posting chart, using descriptive praise statements such as "Billy, what a great job on your math assignment. You beat your best weekly score again!" It is also important to praise students who are having difficulty but are still improving.

STEP 8 Encourage peer comments and interaction about publicly posted information. When students compete against themselves rather than each other, spontaneous student comments will be positive.

Method 1. Acknowledge students' comments. For example, when a student makes a positive comment about a peer, you might say, "Sarah, you are sharp. You noticed what a super job Mary did on her math."

Method 2. Provide additional information regarding student comments. For example, if a student makes a positive comment about a peer, say,

How to . . .

ENHANCE ADVERTISING FOR SUCCESS

ADVANCED STRATEGY 1

— **Add a tangible reward for students who have improved.** In addition to the teacher's and peers' praise, the effect of public posting can be strengthened by adding Mystery Motivators, Spinners, or Grab Bags. For example, you can have all students who posted improvements for a particular day write their names on pieces of paper and put them in a container. Then draw a name and give the daily reward to the student whose name was drawn.

ADVANCED STRATEGY 2

— **To keep motivation high even when you cannot immediately grade or evaluate the performance of all students, randomly select several students at the end of the day and evaluate their performance.** Post the work of those students who have made improvements on a specially designed posted chart and make them eligible for the reward described in Advanced Strategy 1.

ADVANCED STRATEGY 3

— **Divide the classroom into teams and post team averages.** The team approach does not require that individual student names be posted, only a team name. However, both team and individual performance can be posted together, if desired.

ADVANCED STRATEGY 4

— **Combine Advertising for Success with a team-based group contingency.** Divide the class into teams as described in Advanced Strategy 3. In addition, add a reward for team performance. For example, each team may be given ten points each day. If a student breaks a rule or engages in misbehavior, deduct one point from his team's total. Publicly post the points each team has earned at the end of the day. Provide a reward or treat for teams that are able to maintain a certain number of points over a week's time.

"You're right, Bob. Tim not only finished more math problems today, but he beat his best score as well!"

Method 3. Recognize and praise students for making positive comments about other students.

Method 4. Enlist several popular students in the class to make positive comments about how others are doing. Stress to them that the comments must be sincere. With popular students making positive comments, others will soon follow suit.

In addition to these basic steps for implementing a public posting system, several advanced strategies can improve the effects of a good public posting system even more. These strategies are described in "How To Enhance Advertising for Success."

Some teachers have expressed concern that students may feel uncomfortable if their work is displayed. Most students prefer an Advertising for Success system when it is used correctly and when positive rather than negative information is displayed. The more negative the system, the less effective it will be. Advertising for Success, of course, should never be used to humiliate students. If teachers are concerned about posting student names, secret codes can be assigned instead.

Back-to-School Night is a good time for teachers to inform parents about their total classroom management plan, including the Advertising for Success system. The principal's support and permission should be obtained prior to presenting it to parents or students.

The Teacher's 100 Club

The Teacher's 100 Club is one of the powerful positive behavior support systems for a classroom. This positive behavior support system is just one component of a more extensive classroom behavior management system. Used successfully in dozens of elementary, middle, and junior high schools, the Teacher's 100 Club effectively increases positive behavior and rule following in the classroom. The purpose of the club is to "catch" students following the Classroom Rules and behaving appropriately. It is easy to use and involves the teacher, students, and parents.

The Teacher's 100 Club also provides an element of positive variability to keep Tough Kids motivated. It includes a dynamic feedback system that continually informs students and the teacher about who is following the school rules. The term *dynamic feedback* means the contents of the information system are constantly changing, and students are never quite sure when they might be caught and recognized for good behavior. The backbone of the Teacher's 100 Club is a system of Classroom Rules or expectations, along with additional positive behavior management systems.

SETTING UP THE TEACHER'S 100 CLUB

The materials needed to set up the Teacher's 100 Club are listed below and are described in more detail later in this section:

- The Teacher's 100 Club Chart (Reproducible 4-1 on the CD)
- Classroom Rules poster (see **Chapter 1**)
- 100 disks numbered 1–100 (inexpensively purchased in craft stores; you'll need to number them yourself)
- *Teacher's 100 Club Celebrity Book* (several lined sheets of paper in a three-ring binder with the title on the cover)
- Water-based marker
- A master sheet of Teacher's 100 Club tickets (Reproducible 4-2 on the CD)
- Mystery Motivator (see **Chapter 2**)

GETTING STARTED

 **STEP 1** Post the Classroom Rules in a conspicuous place in the classroom. For an example of a Classroom Rules poster, see Reproducible 1-4 on p. 29.

STEP 2 Post the Teacher's 100 Club Chart (Reproducible 4-1 on the next page) right next to the Classroom Rules. This is simply a chart with a 10 x 10 matrix of numbered squares. Reproducible 4-1, found on the CD, can be printed on 11″ x 17″ paper, or you can create your own chart from easel paper or posterboard. We suggest you laminate the chart and use water-based ink so you can erase and reuse the chart. Wait a day or two before giving any explanation. This allows students to see the chart and wonder what it is.

 **STEP 3** Copy a supply of Teacher's 100 Club tickets on colored paper, usually about five sheets to start with. Cut the sheets into individual tickets. You will notice that each ticket has a space for the name of the student who receives it, the behavior for which the ticket was awarded, and the date. Reproducible 4-2 on the CD is a master sheet of Teacher's 100 Club tickets.

STEP 4 Write a group reward on a slip of paper and seal it in a Mystery Motivator envelope. Place a Mystery Motivator envelope near the posted Teacher's 100 Club Chart. Refer to **Chapter 2** for information on using and posting the Mystery Motivator and for ideas for positive reinforcement.

 **STEP 5** Place the *Teacher's 100 Club Celebrity Book* in the classroom. In some classrooms, it has been placed on a dictionary stand right by the door coming into the room, where parents can easily find it when they visit the classroom.

STEP 6 After several days, refer to the Teacher's 100 Club in the morning after you take roll or make morning announcements. You might say something like, "You may have noticed the big chart with all of the squares on the wall by the books." Make a game of it by inviting several students to guess what the chart is for and how it works. Keep the mystery going by telling students you will tell them what it is before class is out for the day and you will begin using it the next morning.

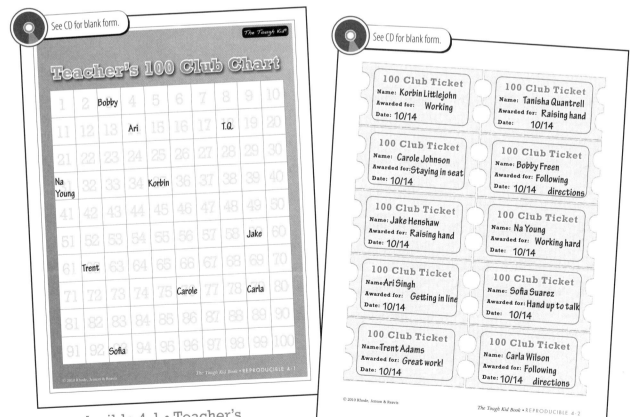

Reproducible 4-1 • Teacher's 100 Club Chart

Reproducible 4-2 • Teacher's 100 Club Tickets

STEP 7 When you are ready to explain the Teacher's 100 Club, begin by asking for additional guesses from students about what the chart is and how it works. Make sure you call only on students who raise their hands. After several guesses from students, explain the system to the class. Tell students that throughout each day you will be watching for students who are following the Classroom Rules. Periodically, but students will never know when, you will award a Teacher's 100 Club ticket to a student who is following the rules. When a student is given a ticket, you will congratulate her and tell her why she is receiving the ticket. You will ask her to write her name on it along with the behavior that earned her the ticket.

STEP 8 Let students know that you will keep their earned tickets in a container on your desk until just before lunch (or the end of the day). At that time, students who have earned tickets will sign the *Teacher's 100 Club Celebrity Book*. Each of the students will then select a disk from an opaque container. (These are the plastic disks you purchased from a craft store and numbered from 1–100.) Have each student look away, reach into the container, and select a disk. Each student then writes her name with a water-based marker on the numbered square on the Teacher's 100 Club Chart that corresponds to the number on the disk she selected. This is Advertising for Success at its best! *Do not put the selected disks back in the container!* The selected numbers must be kept in a manila envelope or another receptacle separate from the container from which students select their disks. That way, no other student will select the same number while the program is in progress.

TECHNIQUE TIP

Keep the *Teacher's 100 Club Celebrity Book* in a prominent location in your classroom, and be sure to invite all classroom visitors (parents, other teachers, the principal, etc.) to take a look at it.

STEP 9 After a student signs the *Teacher's 100 Club Celebrity Book* and when the teacher has a moment or two, the teacher calls the student's parent at home or work with the student beside her. When the parent answers the phone, the teacher says, "Congratulations! This is Mrs. Gabardi. I only have a minute, but I just wanted to let you know what a good job Kiera did following the rules at school today."

Describe specifically what the student was doing right and then invite the parent to stop by the classroom to take a look at her child's name in the *Teacher's 100 Club Celebrity Book* the next time she is in the neighborhood or at the school. Then, the teacher hands the phone to the student so she can speak to the parent for a moment. "How to Contact Parents" on the next page provides some tips to make this step successful.

STEP 10 As you keep awarding Teacher's 100 Club tickets each day, the numbered squares of the Teacher's 100 Club Chart will be randomly filled in by students. The first ten students whose names appear in a row, column, or diagonal are winners. When the tenth box in any of these configurations

How to . . .

CONTACT PARENTS

- Most parents of Tough Kids expect to hear negative information about their child when the school calls. This is why it is important to immediately say, "Congratulations!" when a parent answers the phone. This procedure turns a contact that the parent expects to be negative into a positive one.

- Some teachers say they do not have time to make the parent call. They need to remember how important it is to make time. It takes only a few minutes and provides huge returns! Our experience with this aspect of the Teacher's 100 Club is that it has a dramatic impact on parent-school relations over time. Parents think teachers who positively recognize their children are more capable teachers.

- More than 50% of the time, parents will not be available (e.g., they are running errands or away from their desks at work) when you call. If they have voicemail, leave a message. If no one answers or there is no voicemail option, use a prestamped postcard to notify them. To save time, consider having "What I Was Doing Right Today" printed on the cards. Have the student fill one out with the behavior for which she was recognized, her name, and the date. Add your signature and mail the postcard. Many PTAs are willing to fund postcards for such a positive program.

is filled in with a student's name, the ten names on the winning row, column, or diagonal are announced as winners. All ten students receive the Mystery Motivator contained in the Mystery Motivator envelope. We suggest you announce that there is a winning row at the moment it happens, but if it is not a convenient time to have the winning students open the Mystery Motivator envelope, let them know they will receive the Mystery Motivator just before they go home or at some other specified time. This is your choice. Once winners have been announced, erase all the names on the Teacher's 100 Club Chart, return the numbered disks selected by students to the container, and start the entire process again.

OTHER HELPFUL INFORMATION

The Teacher's 100 Club sounds simple, and it is. Our experience shows that if ten tickets are awarded each day, it takes about one week to get a winning row, column, or diagonal of ten winning names. As your 100 Club progresses, you will see students congregating around and looking at the 100 Club Chart, especially the more it fills up. Just as you find with any other game, the closer you get to having a win, the higher the interest there will be in the game.

TECHNIQUE TIP

The Teacher's 100 Club can easily be adapted into a schoolwide motivation system—The Principal's 200 Club. For more details, see *The Tough Kid Principal's Briefcase* (Pacific Northwest Publishing, www.pacificnwpublish.com, in press).

What the chart does at this point is advertise or show off the names of students who are following the Classroom Rules to the entire class and class visitors. Students whose names are on the chart but not on the winning row, column, or diagonal are still rewarded by having their parents notified and their name written in the *100 Club Celebrity Book* and publicly displayed on the 100 Club Chart.

....

Contracts

When adults see the word *contract*, they generally think of corporate mergers or sports stars signing agreements for millions of dollars. Contracts also have everyday meaning for most adults in terms of buying or renting cars, getting married, and business and employment agreements. Contracts are used in conjunction with many adult behaviors because they are explicit and set expectations. For similar reasons, contracts can also be used effectively when working with Tough Kids.

Following are a number of characteristics of contracts that must be present in order for them to be effective:

1. **Agreeing.** This means both the teacher and the student have negotiated the positive and negative consequences for specific behaviors. The negotiation aspect of a contract is one of its major advantages, particularly in working with adolescents who want to be adult-like and independent. Negotiations should not be one-sided in the sense that the teacher dictates terms to the student.

2. **Formal Exchange.** The contracting equation is Desired Behavior = Reward. It is always a mistake for teachers to relax the behavior requirement midway through a contract, to not give the agreed-upon reward after the behavior has been produced, or to give the reward before the behavior is produced.

3. **Reward or Penalty.** The positive consequence is the motivating component of a contract. However, it may also increase effectiveness to include a penalty clause if the agreed-upon behavior is not produced within a certain time frame or to offer a bonus reward if behavior is exceptional or produced before the specified deadline.

4. **Behavior.** The expected behavior must be objectively defined (that is, easily measured or observed). It must include the standard that is expected (e.g., "B" grade or better) and the time deadline (e.g., by 3:00 p.m. next Friday). specific

Following are two approaches that further enhance the effectiveness of contracting with Tough Kids.

- **Goal Setting.** Contracting can be combined with goal setting by having a student help set his own goals. If this procedure is used, we recommend a bonus reward for reaching the goal before the deadline and a penalty clause for not reaching the goal on time.

- **Public Posting.** This procedure includes contracting for improvement and displaying the contract on a public bulletin board.

whole class
Group Contingencies. A contract can be designed for a total classroom or for class teams instead of for an individual student. If this method is used, the teacher must be certain that each student in the group is capable of

Map racing

performing the expected behavior. An example of a group contingency is the teacher formulating class teams that race each other across a United States map from Los Angeles to New York. Each completed assignment contributes so many miles to the team (e.g., 100% = 100 miles; 75% = 75 miles). Teams can receive speeding tickets when members are tardy or don't turn in homework. Speeding tickets result in deducted miles. Bonuses can be awarded on randomly selected days for the most miles earned that day by a team.

The steps for implementing effective behavioral contracting are listed below:

STEP 1   Define the specific behavior for which the contract is being implemented.

POOR EXAMPLES:

- "Improving classroom responsibility"
- "Showing respect for authority"

BETTER EXAMPLES:

- "Hand in work by the end of the period without being asked."
- "Talk in a calm voice to classmates with no arguing."

It may be necessary in the initial contract to break a behavior into smaller steps so the goal seems attainable to the student. It is important for the student to be successful at first in earning the contract reward so that she will be motivated to continue. Reproducible 4-3 shows an example of a completed contract. A blank version of Reproducible 4-3 is provided on the CD that accompanies this book. Additional contract forms are available in *The Tough Kid Tool Box* (see Pointer Box 4-5).

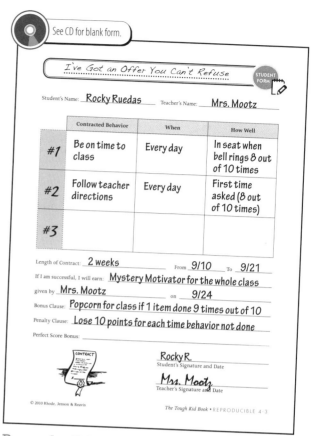

See CD for blank form.

Reproducible 4-3 • I've Got an Offer You Can't Refuse

STEP 2   Select contract reinforcers. The student should assist in this selection. Reinforcers should not take a lot of time to deliver, nor should they be expensive.

STEP 3   Define the contract criteria. Generally, contract criteria include the (quantity of behavior, (quantity of reinforcer,) and (time limits.) There are two basic types of contract criteria: consecutive criteria and cumulative criteria.

- *Consecutive criteria* are the less desirable type. For example, the student may be told that he will receive the contract reward if he earns 7 out of 10 recess points for ten straight days. In this case, the student may earn 7 points or more on nine days but earn 6 on the tenth, thus not receiving the reward.

- *Cumulative criteria* are preferred. With cumulative criteria, the quantity of behavior adds up with each student success but does not decrease for student failures. Cumulative criteria allow the student some days of not meeting the criteria.

Many contracts are defined so they pay off at the end of the week. However, contracts can also be designed to pay off each day. Contracts that extend payoff over two weeks are generally ineffective because a Tough Kid can seldom wait that long for payoff, at least initially. A rule of thumb for an initial contract is to pay off at least by the end of the week for a student with specified cumulative criteria.

STEP 4 For a particularly unmotivated Tough Kid, consider adding a bonus reward and a penalty clause. A bonus reward is a helpful incentive for the student to reach his cumulative criteria quickly. Though contracts should primarily be designed to be positive, a penalty clause may be added if the initial contract does not work even though the rewards are valued and the payoff time is short. An example of a penalty clause might be requiring the student to complete four homework assignments of "B" grade quality or better to receive the contract reward for the week (based on daily homework assignments for a five-day period). However, if the number of homework assignments completed is less than three for the week, the student loses television privileges at home for the next week. A penalty clause may be needed to give added incentive when all else fails.

STEP 5 Negotiate contract terms with the student. The basic sub-steps of negotiation are:

1. Discuss a specific set of contract behaviors and rewards with the student.

2. Indicate to the student why a contract is necessary and say you would like to help.

3. Indicate that several of the contract components are negotiable (e.g., rewards, behaviors, criteria). Emphasize, however, that a contract is needed and its implementation is not negotiable.

POINTER BOX 4-5

THE TOUGH KID TOOL BOX

Many of the examples shown in this book appear in *The Tough Kid Tool Box*, a companion volume that features ready-to-use reproducible materials for implementing behavior management strategies with Tough Kids. The book and accompanying CD contain tools in both English and Spanish, along with detailed directions for using them. *The Tough Kid Tool Box* provides an assortment of Contracts, Home Notes, Home Note Icons, and more. The book is available from Pacific Northwest Publishing, www.PacificNWPublish.com.

4. Tell the student what you would like to specify in the contract and ask for the student's input.

5. Do not allow the student to set unrealistically high standards for himself. Encourage the student to begin slowly and then expand.

6. Indicate that you want and expect the contract to work, but if things do not improve, a penalty clause will be added. Within limits, the penalty clause may be negotiated with the student.

7. Tell the student the contract is open to renegotiation at any time. The teacher should give the sense that she values the student's input.

STEP 6 Put the terms of the contract in writing. Writing and signing a contract prevents misunderstandings and indicates agreement with the terms at the time all parties sign the contract. Also, a good written contract will have a section that summarizes data on the student's progress (regardless of whether or not the contract criteria have been met). By including these data, the contract will serve as a self-recording instrument. A written contract may also be publicly posted, further enhancing effectiveness.

TROUBLESHOOTING CONTRACTS

No technique will work in all situations with Tough Kids. Although contracts can be powerful behavior change strategies when they are properly implemented, there can be problems with their use.

Problem: The student starts out working hard and then loses motivation.

Solution: The reward payoff may be too delayed. Cut the time period before the reward can be earned in half. Delaying the reward too long is one of the most frequent problems with contracts.

Problem: The student appears confused and never really gets started.

Solution: The required behavior may not be defined or explained clearly enough, or too much of the required behavior may be expected initially. Discuss the expectations thoroughly with the student. If necessary, model and role-play the behaviors. If the student understands, the requirement may be too great. Try reducing the behavior requirement for one week (half the problems, half the points, etc.). After at least one week when the student has received the contract reward, gradually begin to increase the contract requirement again.

Problem: The student still appears unmotivated and uninterested, even after the teacher has checked the delay in earning the reward, checked for the student's understanding of the expectations, and the student has earned the contract reward at least once.

Solution: A penalty clause may be needed to get the student to actively participate.

Problem: The student began the contract excited about it, but appears frustrated and anxious before finishing.

Solution: Check the criteria. Student frustration can result from expectations that are too difficult. Use cumulative criteria rather than consecutive.

Problem: The student is openly defiant and will not participate in the contract.

Solution: Indicate to the student that you want to negotiate the terms of the contract and that you value the student's input. If possible, invite an adult who is important to the student to participate in the negotiations, especially if a penalty clause is set. This person may be a parent, a coach, a favored teacher, a counselor, etc. Make certain the invited person supports the idea of a contract.

Problem: The parent offers extremely large rewards with too long a time period before they are delivered (e.g., bicycle, four wheelers, trips, remote-control vehicle, money).

Solution: Talk to the parent and express your concern about the promised big reward. Help the parent compile a list of smaller rewards to be given within a much shorter time period, and suggest the large reward as an additional bonus.

CAUTIONS WITH CONTRACTING

Teachers must remember that most contracts operate with a delayed reward payoff system. With Tough Kids, delays frequently destroy initial steps that are needed to get them started. Contracts are most useful when:

> THINK ABOUT IT
>
> **THINK**
>
> " With Tough Kids, delays frequently destroy initial steps that are needed to get them started. "

- They are used as a way of fading out more frequent rewards or after a student has started to perform appropriately, or
- They are used with older or more motivated students. Contracts with long delays are ineffective with younger or highly unmotivated students. In these cases, it is better to start with an hourly, twice daily, or daily reward system.

Parents and other professionals may object to a contract, believing the student should just be responsible on her own. The problem is the Tough Kid is *not* responsible. Thus, strategies are needed to jump-start the student to begin to be responsible. Objectors may also see a contract as an artificial crutch. However, contracts should be designed to enhance initial motivation and eventually be slowly faded from use.

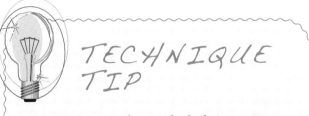

TECHNIQUE TIP

Contracts can be included in a Home Note program (see the "Home Note" section in this chapter). For example, when a student accumulates four weeks' worth of acceptable Home Notes, she receives an agreed-upon reward or earns a Mystery Motivator.

Some teachers may view contracts as too complex and time consuming. A well-designed contract is like a good investment. Most sound financial investments require initial start-up capital in order to return greater dividends later. Similarly, a well-designed contract will take more time to implement than doing nothing. However, the potential dividends from implementing a contract are great.

Home Notes

A Home Note program can be one of the most effective techniques for improving elementary and secondary students' motivation and classroom behavior. It is also one of the most underutilized and mismanaged techniques. A Home Note program consists of a note that is:

- Periodically completed by the teacher
- An assessment of academic and/or behavioral progress
- Sent home for a parent to review, apply consequences to, and sign
- Returned to school

"How To Implement a Home Note Program" outlines the steps in setting up an effective Home Note program.

Problems can occur with even the best-implemented Home Note program. The Home Note program is particularly prone to problems because it relies on a student to carry the note. However, most problems are readily resolvable if the program is well designed and the teacher is working with a cooperative parent.

TROUBLESHOOTING HOME NOTES

Problem: The student keeps losing the note.

Solution: Ask the parent to take away a privilege at home or initiate a penalty when notes are not brought home. For example, the parent may have the student go to bed one hour early or miss television or outside play time each day the note is not brought home. It is important the teacher and parent both emphasize to the student that no excuses are accepted and that it is her responsibility to ask the teacher for the note at the end of the school day and to bring it home.

Problem: The student changes the ratings or forges the teacher's initials.

Solution: Changing a rating or forging initials should be handled like a lost note. No excuses should be accepted, and the student should receive a penalty at home.

Problem: The student refuses to take the note home.

Solution: If the student flatly refuses to take the note, have the parent consistently implement the procedures for a lost note. Be sure to be a support for the parent in the event this occurs. Most students will come around within a week

How to . . .

IMPLEMENT A HOME NOTE PROGRAM

Step 1. Design or select a simple Home Note. Examples of Home Notes (Figures 4-2 to 4-4) appear on page 154. Reproducible 5-5 in Chapter 5 is a Home Note designed for use with a level system. Model your note after one of these examples. *The Tough Kid Tool Box* (see Pointer Box 4-5 on p. 147) includes four ready-to-use Home Note templates.

Step 2. Decide which behavior(s) will be targeted for change. Limit the selection to no more than five academic and/or social behaviors.

Step 3. Make contact with the student's parent either in person or by phone to gain her cooperation and explain the system. With parental input, determine what positive or mild negative consequences the parent is willing to deliver at home in response to the student's Home Note performance.

Ask the parent to read the note each day, make certain it is initialed by the teacher, and sign it. Convince the parent to accept no excuses if the student does not bring the note home.

Step 4. Decide when the Home Note program will start and how frequently a Home Note will be given. It is generally more effective to begin by giving a Home Note daily and slowly fade to giving the note only on Fridays. Eventually fade to no note.

Step 5. Explain the program to the student and answer questions the student has about the program.

Step 6. Implement the program. After marking the note, give the student specific feedback about what he did right and what needs to improve. Encourage the student!

Step 7. Once the program has been implemented, call the parent at least twice the first week and once a week for the next two weeks. The calls can help troubleshoot problems and provide support to the parent for her part in the program.

Step 8. After the program has been in place for four to six weeks, arrange for another parent conference or talk with the parent by phone to review the student's progress. Be optimistic and emphasize the gains the student has made. Discuss any concerns you or the parent has with the program, make any needed adjustments, and plan to continue the program as needed.

after having consequences applied consistently. The program may also be enhanced by providing reinforcement within the classroom for the student using the note properly in addition to the reinforcement provided by the parents.

Problem: The parents are willing to look at the note, but they are incapable of applying consequences at home for the program.

Solution: Put together a reinforcer kit and deliver it to the home. Include items such as candy, stickers, and little toys that the parent can give the student for a good note.

An alternative is to tell the parent that you would like to begin applying the consequences for the note in the classroom. The parent is still expected to review and sign the note at home. When it is returned the next day, class reinforcers such as a

Mystery Motivator, Spinner, or Grab Bag may be given to the student. If a penalty is warranted, a mild negative consequence such as missing recess, staying after school, or eating lunch in the classroom may be delivered.

Problem: The teacher suspects that the parent may be abusive to the student if she receives a poor note.

Solution: Set up a meeting with the parent and ask for her cooperation in applying agreed-upon consequences (both positive and negative). Tell her if she punishes too severely, the program will fail and the student will learn to dislike school. If abuse continues, the program may have to be discontinued or authorities called. Although this is a serious problem when it occurs, it rarely comes up.

Problem: The parent refuses to participate in the program and will not even sign the note.

Solution: Set up a meeting with the parent. Address any concerns she has with the program. Explain the program is not designed to punish the student, but to give the student feedback about her performance and to keep the parent informed. Ask if she would be willing to try the program for two weeks. If she still refuses, tell her you would like to give the student the note anyway and hope the parent will look at it. (In this case, try to make the notes as positive as possible for the first week.)

MAKING HOME NOTES EVEN BETTER

1. **Combine the Home Notes with the 30-item Importance of Classroom Behaviors form (Reproducible 5-7) shown in Pointer Box 4-6.** This combination improves the performance of the Home Notes program, especially in combination with the picture icons shown in Figure 4-1. Rate the 30-item behavioral checklist for the student. Pick three to five of the behaviors rated as most important to you and the family. Use these items as the target behaviors to rate for the Home Note.

   Each item in the checklist has a corresponding picture icon (e.g. picture icon #7 corresponds to behavioral checklist item #7). Each picture icon actually depicts the appropriate behavior for the checklist item. To use the picture icons, write the behavioral definition from the checklist on the Home Note, cut out its corresponding picture icon, and paste it on the note (see Figure 4-3 on the next page). You can do this the old-fashioned way with a copier and scissors, or you can electronically cut and paste using the electronic versions of these icons provided on the CD. See the "Using the CD" file on the CD for more detailed directions. You may have to reduce the size of some of the picture icons to make them fit on the Home Note. After a note is made with pasted icons, make several copies of the note and keep the original.

2. **When selecting behaviors for the Home Note, include some academic subjects.** For example, add some items specific to reading or math to be rated along with target

THINK ABOUT IT

> " *The program is not designed to punish the student, but to give feedback about performance.* "

POINTER BOX 4-6

IMPORTANCE OF CLASSROOM BEHAVIORS

A checklist of behaviors that you rate according to their importance can help you identify behaviors to focus on with a Home Note program. You can then paste photos or drawings, such as those shown below, onto the Home Notes to illustrate the desired behaviors.

For example, you might fill out the Importance of Classroom Behaviors form (Reproducible 5-7) in Chapter 5 to identify those behaviors that are most important to student success in your classroom. Then use the corresponding icons on any Home Notes you use (see the example in Figure 4-3 on the next page). You can also use the icons with self-monitoring forms.

See Chapter 5 for more information about using the Importance of Classroom Behaviors form and the behavior icons. The form and icons are provided on the CD; the icons also appear in Appendix A as part of the Individual Skill Cards used in implementing Meeting Individual Teacher's Expectations.

From *The Tough Kid Tool Box.* See Pointer Box 4-5, p. 147.

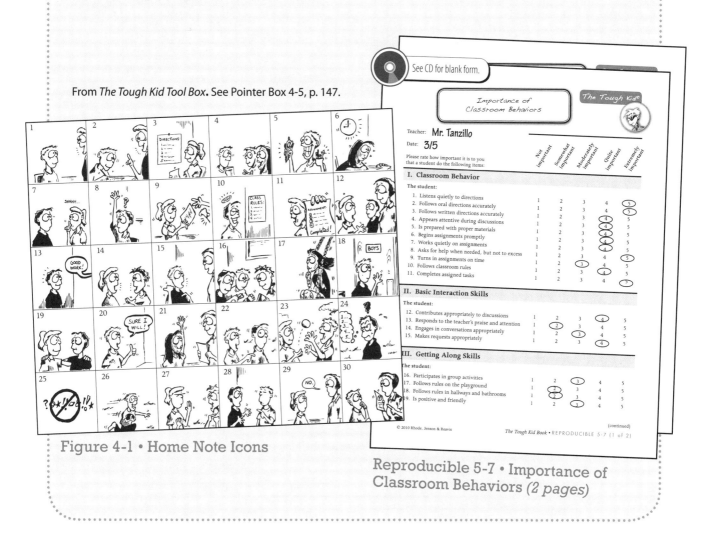

Figure 4-1 • Home Note Icons

Reproducible 5-7 • Importance of Classroom Behaviors (*2 pages*)

behaviors. An *all-behavior* or *all-academic* note is less effective.

3. **For secondary students, use a note similar to the Information Note (Figure 4-4).** This note has seven areas for seven periods in a junior high or high school. The subjects and teachers' names should be written in each space in the order the student attends classes. The Information Note can be either a daily or weekly note. For a weekly note, write Weekly in the blank space in the upper left hand corner. For a daily note, staple five notes together and write MON in the space for the first note, TUE for the next note, and so on for the whole week.

The Information Note can also be used with elementary students. It is particularly useful because it includes spaces for assigned homework, upcoming tests, and missing work.

4. **Combine the Home Note with the Mystery Motivator program.** For each day the student returns the note signed by a parent, she is permitted to color in a Mystery Motivator square with a magic decoder pen. See **Chapter 3** for more details.

5. **Have the student save good Home Notes for a behavioral contract reward.** For example, when the student has three good weeks of signed Home Notes, he is allowed a special treat (e.g., lunch with the teacher, a popcorn party, free time).

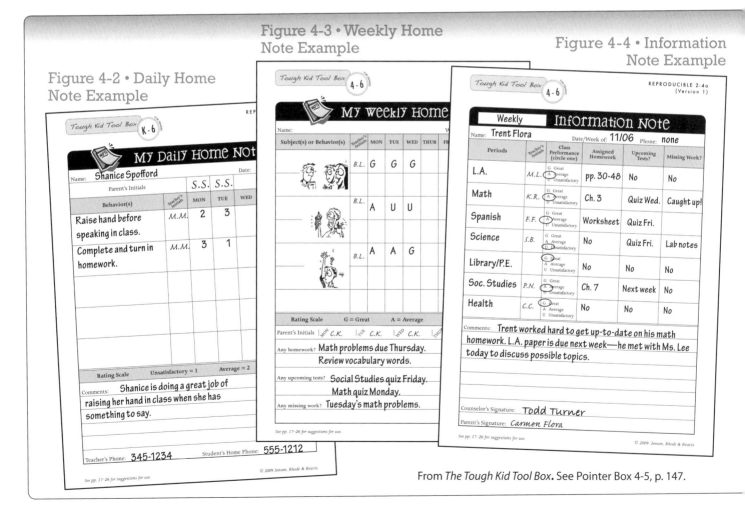

Figure 4-2 • Daily Home Note Example

Figure 4-3 • Weekly Home Note Example

Figure 4-4 • Information Note Example

From *The Tough Kid Tool Box.* See Pointer Box 4-5, p. 147.

POINTER BOX 4-7

WHERE TO FIND GET 'EM ON TASK

The Get 'Em On Task computer program is available from Sopris West (www.sopriswest.com). It comes on a CD with a 44-page instruction manual. Minimum requirements are a Pentium II running Windows 98/2000/ME/NT/ XP or a Macintosh Power PC running Mac OS 8.6–X. You also need 320MB of disk space.

Get 'Em On Task

Tough Kids exhibit many behaviors that interfere with their learning and interpersonal relationships in the classroom. Given independent assignments to complete in their seats, Tough Kids often talk to their classmates, leave their seats, disrupt the class, or worse. During group instruction they may not watch or listen while the teacher presents a critical new skill, avoid responding when called on to do so, and disturb students around them so they cannot profit from the instruction either. Get 'Em On Task is an auditory computer signaling program that provides a way to improve the classroom behavior of Tough Kids by teaching them attending and self-management skills (Althouse, Jenson, Likins, & Morgan, 1999). The program can be used effectively with an individual student or groups of students in grades K-12. It can be used to support any positive reinforcement or self-management program.

Get 'Em On Task systematically provides positive reinforcement for increasing amounts of appropriate behavior. Once appropriate behavior has been established and stabilized at acceptable levels, the program is then used to fade reinforcement to lower levels. Fading reinforcement is necessary to avoid students'

dependence on the program and to enable them to function successfully with less supervision and in other school settings.

HOW TO USE THE GET 'EM ON TASK PROGRAM

1. Install the program on your computer. See Pointer Box 4-7 above for information on where to purchase the program.

    Go to the main screen and tell the program:

    - How long to run
    - How many audible signals to give
    - How to space the audible signals (see Step 3 below for further information)
    - The total number of points you want students to earn during the period
    - The hours and minutes for the time period you want the program to run

2. You may choose between evenly spaced or randomly spaced signals. Evenly spaced signals are more predictable and may result in students pausing in their work or participation right after a signal occurs. Randomly placed signals are less predictable, usually resulting in more student engagement between intervals. The Get 'Em On Task system is designed so some of the Tough

Kid's appropriate behavior, but not all of it, will result in positive reinforcement. This is referred to as random or intermittent reinforcement. Behaviors that are positively reinforced on a random or intermittent basis are more likely to be maintained in the long run. When intermittent reinforcement is used correctly, the Tough Kid learns to delay gratification and maintain appropriate behavior over longer and longer periods of time.

3. Individual students, small groups of students, or an entire class can earn a point or token (such as poker chips, marbles, or class "money") each time a signal sounds, and they are doing what they are supposed to be doing. Select reinforcers that you will make available to students in exchange for the points or tokens they earn by being on task and following classroom rules when an audible signal goes off. (See **Chapter 2** for reinforcement ideas.)

STEPS FOR IMPLEMENTING GET 'EM ON TASK

STEP 1   Explain to target students (or the class) the specific behaviors they are expected to demonstrate in order to earn a point or token when the signal sounds. Then explain how the program works.

STEP 2   Establish a schedule on the computer with the number of audible signals you have selected. In designing a schedule, begin with an average length of time between signals that approximates or is slightly greater than the amount of time students follow classroom rules before engaging in inappropriate behavior.

TECHNIQUE TIP

For unique auditory signaling sounds, replace the beeps on the Get 'Em On Task program with other sounds you can download from the Internet. To do so, search the Internet to locate and download WAV files by theme (e.g., movie or television sounds, a bar of music from a song, dog barking).

Example: *Reuben currently breaks classroom rules an average of six times during each 30-minute reading session. This amounts to one rule infraction every five minutes. Mr. Angilau selects a schedule with five beeps per 30 minutes (an average of one beep every six minutes) because this schedule approximates the time frame of misbehavior that Reuben currently exhibits.*

STEP 3   Select a method for recording points or tokens that students (or the class) earn. This may be an individual point card taped to each student's desk or carried by each student. When a signal sounds, you can mark the cards or have students mark their own when you ask them to do so.

An alternative is to carry a group point sheet on a clipboard and mark points for individual students as they are earned. Each time a signal sounds, you must tell students whether they have earned a point for being on task. If you are recording points for all students on a clipboard, you will need to transfer points earned onto students' individual cards at the end of the work session.

VARIATIONS
- Trade points earned for Chart Moves.
- Have the class earn points collectively toward a class reward.

 Decide what reinforcers points or tokens may be traded for. (**Chapter 2** has many suggestions from which to choose.) Initially, rewards should be earned daily if students are earning 85% of their points or better.

STEP 5 When a signal sounds, give immediate and specific verbal praise to target students (or the class) who are doing what they are supposed to be doing and inform them that they have earned a point or token.

Note: The old adage to "let sleeping dogs lie" is never appropriate when using the signal program. The beep sound is the teacher's cue to immediately praise deserving students.

Examples: *"Jaxon, Owen, and Xenith, you've just earned a point for working on your math assignment. Great job!"*

"Ashley, I appreciate that you are watching me and listening. That's a point for you."

"Wow, the whole class was practicing the reading paragraph just now! Everyone earns a point."

STEP 6 As appropriate behavior increases, set Get 'Em On Task schedules with longer intervals and fewer signals. When should you move to a new, less rich (in terms of reinforcement) schedule? Whether you are using the program for only one or two students or for the entire class, you should move

---

BOX 4-2

Cautions When Using Get 'Em On Task

- For some students, you will need to adjust the number of points required for payoffs as longer intervals of appropriate behavior are demonstrated. In other words, if a student demonstrates appropriate behavior for longer intervals but still needs daily payoffs to meet criteria, you will need to continue to provide daily payoffs for the time being.

- You should never discontinue using specific praise statements for appropriate behavior, even when audible signals have been reduced or eliminated.

---

to a slightly less rich schedule when payoff criteria of 85% of possible points has been earned for three consecutive days.

Any time a teacher begins using a new, less rich schedule and students are not meeting criteria within the first three days, our rule of thumb is to drop back to the previous signaling schedule at which students were successful. If dropping back is necessary, you should again require three days of students meeting criteria before using a less rich schedule again.

Get 'Em On Task payoffs automatically become less frequent as longer intervals are introduced and there are fewer audible signals. In this way, positive reinforcement will gradually be reduced. Box 4-2 offers two cautions for teachers using the audible signal program.

How to . . .

TROUBLESHOOT AN AUDIBLE SIGNAL PROGRAM

If students are not meeting audible signal criteria after three days with a particular schedule, consider the following suggestions:

- Examine classroom expectations. Do students know exactly what you want them to do?

- Change or adjust positive reinforcement students can earn for meeting criteria.

- Lower the number of points needed for payoff.

- Drop back to a signal schedule with smaller intervals between signals.

- Eliminate students from the group payoffs if they are deliberately sabotaging group efforts. Keep the rest of the class on the same payoff schedule, but place the single student on an individual payoff schedule.

It is assumed that if teacher praise alone were positively reinforcing enough for Tough Kids to begin with, a teacher could simply praise them for their appropriate behavior in order to increase it. If this were the case, an audible signal program would not be needed. For many Tough Kids, however, teacher praise simply is not powerful enough to be effective initially. Rather, they must actually be taught to find it reinforcing. Thus, with Get 'Em On Task, praise must be paired with the awarding of points or tokens. Points or tokens must then be exchangeable for items or activities the Tough Kids already find to be positively reinforcing.

Gradually, as audible signals (and thus points) are reduced and eventually withdrawn, teacher praise will retain the positive reinforcement qualities students have learned to associate with it. Teacher praise, then, must never be completely eliminated—it is the praise that will continue to maintain students' newly improved behavior.

Teachers must let Tough Kids know what they are doing right and that they appreciate it. "How To Troubleshoot an Audible Signal Program" offers some suggestions for dealing with problems you may encounter.

WEANING TOUGH KIDS FROM AN AUDIBLE SIGNAL PROGRAM

When Tough Kids can successfully work and follow classroom rules for at least 15 consecutive minutes, a teacher may begin moving toward a less cumbersome means of increasing appropriate classroom behavior:

- Without the use of an audible signal program, the teacher awards points earned at the end of productive 15-minute work periods (e.g., if a maximum of five points can be earned, the teacher might award four points if the student talked out or broke another rule during that time). The teacher

Exchangeable points

gradually increases work periods to 20 minutes, 30 minutes, 1 hour, etc.

- When students are working successfully for 15 minutes with an audible signal program, the teacher may have the students begin to monitor and evaluate their own work and behavior. In this way, responsibility will gradually be shifted from teacher to students. (See the "Self-Monitoring" section on pp. 160–163 for further details.)

Peer Tutoring

There are a number of benefits for both Tough Kids and their peers from a good peer tutoring program in the classroom. Academic gains, improvement in classroom behavior, and cooperative peer relations have been common positive outcomes of peer tutoring programs. Teachers should note, however, that peer tutoring techniques are most effective when they are used to supplement teacher instruction rather than take its place. To maximize the effectiveness of peer tutoring, Tough Kids must be carefully taught the specific procedures to be used, and the teacher must monitor the program very carefully.

Classwide peer tutoring programs are relatively easy to implement. "How To Implement a Peer Tutoring Program" provides step-by-step instructions.

An initial time investment by the teacher to thoroughly train students in their roles will pay big

How to . . .

IMPLEMENT A PEER TUTORING PROGRAM

- Decide on a subject for tutoring and select a 30-minute period of the day for the program. (Within the 30 minutes allotted, the peer will tutor the Tough Kid for 10 minutes, the Tough Kid will tutor the peer for 10 minutes, and 10 minutes will be spent by both counting points and posting results.)

- Tough Kid and peer pairs will be selected and reassigned once each week. They will sit next to or across from each other during tutoring sessions. Tell each pair who will tutor first. The tutor will monitor performance (e.g., oral reading), correct errors, and award points for correct performance. Signal at the end of 10 minutes for students to reverse roles.

- Circulate among pairs of students during peer tutoring sessions and award points for tutoring correctly. You may also divide the class into two teams (e.g., rows one and two compete with rows three and four).

- When both 10-minute tutoring sessions are over, the Tough Kid and his peer should each count their own and each other's points. Call on each pair and ask them to report points earned. Publicly post scores at the front of the room on a bulletin board or poster. Tally points and announce the winning pair or team. Change the composition of the pairs or teams each week. Provide small rewards both on a daily basis (as needed) and a weekly basis.

- Conduct your own evaluation of each student's progress on skills practiced with peer tutoring teams at least once each week.

Sources: Greenwood, Terry, Arreaga-Mayer, & Finney, 1992; Maheady & Harper, 1987

dividends in the long run. Each step must be carefully explained to students, and they must have the opportunity to ask questions and gain clarification. Supervised role-playing with corrective feedback from the teacher as well as discussion may be helpful. Specific error correction procedures and the use of tokens or points must be carefully reviewed and demonstrated.

Self-Monitoring

Self-monitoring is a process in which the student observes and collects data on his own behavior. Monitoring one's own behavior is an important part of self-management. Self-monitoring techniques have been used successfully with Tough Kids to increase appropriate behaviors such as improving academic skills and on-task behavior. They have also been very effective in decreasing Tough Kids' inappropriate behaviors (Briesch & Chafouleas, 2009).

THINK ABOUT IT

THINK

" *Self-management skills are 'portable' in that they rely mainly on students themselves for implementation.* "

The ultimate goal of self-monitoring procedures is for Tough Kids to manage or control their own behavior—a goal most educators wholeheartedly support! While Tough Kids may monitor and manage their own behavior in the long run after using these techniques, initially the teacher needs to be the primary manager. However, the teacher's objective during the course of the intervention is to gradually transfer as much management of Tough Kids' behavior as possible from the teacher to the students themselves.

One advantage of teaching Tough Kids to monitor and evaluate their own behavior, of course, is they then depend less on the teacher for guidance, reinforcement, and control. Emphasis on this self-management approach is relevant to teacher concerns about time demands placed on them by interventions that rely solely on their own efforts. Tough Kids who learn to self-monitor and manage are not only active participants in their own improved performance, but they perceive themselves as more competent as well. In addition, self-management skills are "portable" in that they rely mainly on students themselves for implementation. For teachers, this is much of the appeal of teaching self-management skills to Tough Kids. Below we list the necessary steps to teach Tough Kids to self-monitor their own behavior.

STEP 1 Specifically define the behavior the student will monitor and evaluate. Self-monitoring may be effectively used to reduce behaviors such as talk-outs, not following class rules, tardiness, and being off task. Behaviors to increase with self-monitoring may include studying independently, following class rules, completing assignments on time, remaining seated, and raising a hand to speak.

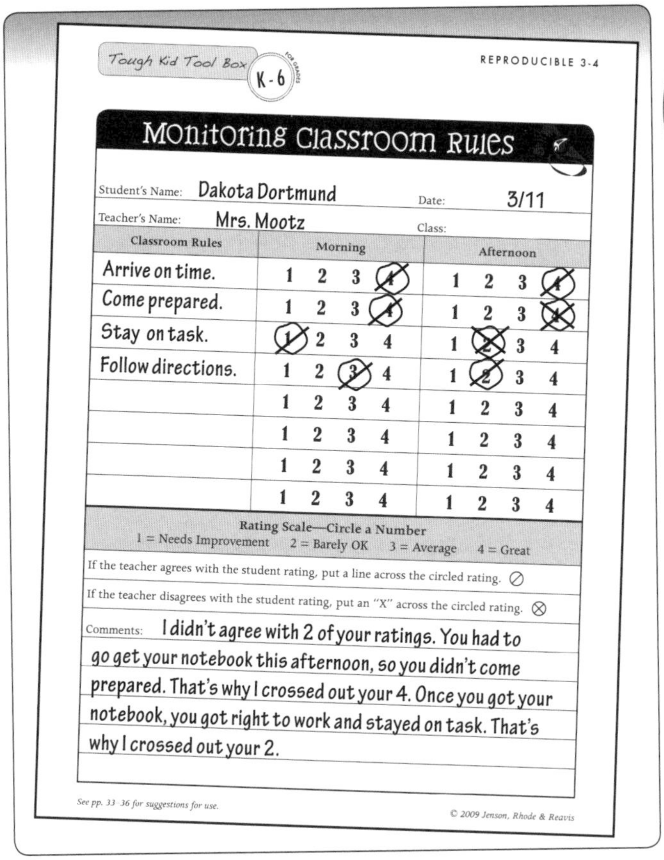
Tough Kid Tool Box K-6 REPRODUCIBLE 3-4

Monitoring Classroom Rules

Student's Name: Dakota Dortmund Date: 3/11
Teacher's Name: Mrs. Mootz Class:

Classroom Rules	Morning	Afternoon
Arrive on time.	1 2 3 4	1 2 3 4
Come prepared.	1 2 3 4	1 2 3 4
Stay on task.	1 2 3 4	1 2 3 4
Follow directions.	1 2 3 4	1 2 3 4
	1 2 3 4	1 2 3 4
	1 2 3 4	1 2 3 4
	1 2 3 4	1 2 3 4
	1 2 3 4	1 2 3 4

Rating Scale—Circle a Number
1 = Needs Improvement 2 = Barely OK 3 = Average 4 = Great

If the teacher agrees with the student rating, put a line across the circled rating.
If the teacher disagrees with the student rating, put an "X" across the circled rating.

Comments: I didn't agree with 2 of your ratings. You had to go get your notebook this afternoon, so you didn't come prepared. That's why I crossed out your 4. Once you got your notebook, you got right to work and stayed on task. That's why I crossed out your 2.

See pp. 33–36 for suggestions for use. © 2009 Jenson, Rhode & Reavis

Figure 4-5 • Monitoring Classroom Rules Form Example

STEP 2 Select or design an appropriate recording form for the student to use. Figure 4-5 shows an example from *The Tough Kid Tool Box* (see Pointer Box 4-5 on p. 147). That book also includes forms for monitoring on-task behavior and talk-outs.

STEP 3 Define the target behavior for the student and give examples and non-examples of it. Typically, it is more effective to have the student record only one behavior at a time. The exception may be having the student record how well she is following classroom rules. Model and role-play the target behavior.

STEP 4 Define the time period in which you want the student to self-monitor the behavior. Predetermine periods of 15, 30, or 60 minutes during which the student will count and record his target behavior. It is better to give the student a specific time such as during math instruction, at recess, or the first half of the day until lunch. Most students will find indefinite monitoring of their behavior too overwhelming. Begin with a small period of time and gradually increase it as the student becomes more proficient. Match your counting and recording of the student's behavior with his on a frequent basis. Discuss any differences between the two ratings.

STEP 5 Give the student the recording form for a trial run during the time period in which you want him to self-monitor. You may need to prompt the student to record the behavior during this period. If the student talks out and does not mark it down, tell him to mark it down. Prompt students to record appropriate as well as inappropriate behaviors. (For example, "Samuel, you are studying. Please mark it down on your sheet.")

TECHNIQUE TIP

Select recording intervals that are not too short (e.g., 10 seconds). Short intervals are too complex and frequent for the student to learn. It is much easier to have the student record the behavior:

- Each time the behavior occurs (e.g., talk-outs)
- When he thinks of it (e.g., "In history class, record a mark when you realize you are on task and studying.")

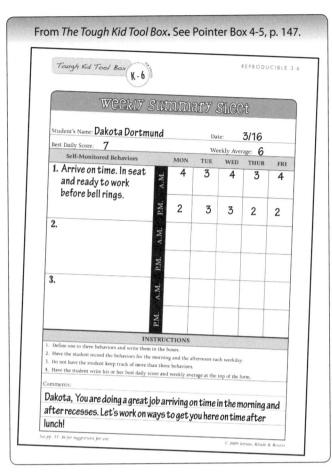

From *The Tough Kid Tool Box*. See Pointer Box 4-5, p. 147.

Figure 4-6 • Weekly Summary Sheet Example

STEP 6   If the student is monitoring the number of times a target behavior occurs, have the student write down the actual number on a summary sheet at the end of the recording period. Figure 4-6 shows an example of a Weekly Summary Sheet that can be used for this purpose.

STEP 7   Self-monitoring changes a behavior only temporarily. To make the change permanent, tie the self-monitoring program to some type of contingency. For example, if the student keeps his talk-outs below two during a specified time period, he may earn a small reward or privilege. The contingencies may be gradually withdrawn over time. However, the teacher should continue to praise appropriate behavior.

Some self-management techniques are very simple to use. For example, Tough Kids may be given a piece of paper with 20 or so squares marked on it. They can be taught to make a plus sign (+) in one of the squares each time they "think about" and "recognize" they are working or behaving appropriately. They can also be taught to mark a minus (–) sign when they think they are not working or behaving appropriately.

Pluses can be converted to points that can later be exchanged for rewards. With very young children, a smiley face may be used to denote appropriate behavior or working, while a frowny face indicates poor working or behavior. A neutral face indicates OK or fair behavior or working.

One way teachers can enhance the use of self-management procedures is through the use of a "matching" procedure. Once a teacher has transferred at least some responsibility for rating and recording the student's behavior to the student himself, the teacher may continue to rate and mark the behavior some of the time. If this is done on a random basis, the student will not know ahead of time when teacher ratings will take place. When the teacher "matches" ratings with a student, a bonus point is given for exact matches, the student keeps his own ratings when the difference between teacher and student ratings is only one or two points, and the student loses all points for the rating period when there is a difference of more than one or two points between teacher and student ratings.

Another way the teacher can maximize self-management is by combining contracting with a matching self-monitoring procedure. Figure 4-7 depicts a form for doing this.

From *The Tough Kid Tool Box*. See Pointer Box 4-5, p. 147.

REPRODUCIBLE 3-1

Tough Kid Tool Box K-6

Contract for Self-Monitoring

Student's Name: Dakota Dortmund   Date: 3/11

Teacher's Name: Mrs. Mootz   Class:

Definition of Behavior to Be Monitored: Stay focused and on task when
I work with my group and by myself. Follow directions the first
time the teacher gives them.

Criterion for Monitored Behavior: Two or fewer "Needs Improvement"
ratings in a week. I will mark "Needs Improvement" if Mrs.
Mootz has to speak to me more than twice about the rules.

Over What Time? Each week

What do you get if the criterion is met? Spin the Spinner for a reward.

What do you lose if the criterion is not met? I will eat lunch in the
classroom the next Monday.

Optional Bonus Clause: I will get 15 minutes of computer game
time for every week I don't have any "Need Improvements."

Signature of Student: Dakota Dortmund

Signature of Teacher: Mrs. Mootz

Comments:

See pp. 33–36 for suggestions for use.   © 2009 Jenson, Rhode & Reavis

Figure 4-7 • Contract for Self Monitoring Example

Self-management skills are not a panacea. However, there is good evidence that they can be very helpful in working with Tough Kids when:

- Tough Kids receive very specific instruction on how to use the program.

- Control of how the students behave and work is gradually transferred from the teacher to the students.

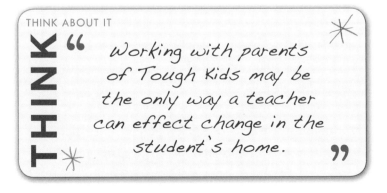

THINK ABOUT IT

THINK " *Working with parents of Tough Kids may be the only way a teacher can effect change in the student's home.* "

- The teacher continues to carefully monitor students' correct and accurate use of the program.

Parent Training

Working with parents of Tough Kids may be the only way a teacher can effect change in the student's home. However, many teachers simply give up working with parents because they believe it is too difficult. Most parenting programs actually lose about 50% of parents once they begin. But why? It may not be because parents are too difficult to work with. It may be that educators train them ineffectively and/or with the wrong materials. There are several other common mistakes made by teachers that result in parents not coming to training sessions:

1. **The biggest mistake is to make the parents of Tough Kids feel they are the cause of the problem.** Most parents of Tough Kids have had years of negative contact with school personnel who insinuate that their family lives are at the root of the students' problems. Parents must be made to feel comfortable and part of a team effort at the first meeting.

2. **The second basic problem with parent training is that many parenting programs focus on mild issues and problems.** But parents of Tough Kids are plagued by the same problems at home as their children's teachers are at school. Good programs for parents of Tough Kids focus on changing arguing, aggression, noncompliance, tantrums, poor school performance, and problems with social skills.

3. **Third, many parenting programs are far too technical and complex.** Professional jargon, theoretical concepts, and difficult data collection requirements result in parents dropping out. Parents should be made to feel comfortable, competent, and helped to see the immediate connection with what is included in training and meaningful behavior change.

There are several "tricks of the trade" that make parent training effective.

- The teacher should disclose a little about herself. If she has children, the teacher should talk about them in human terms. We recommend she also talk about personal difficulties and how she applies the techniques she is suggesting to other parents. If the teacher does not have children, she should talk about using the suggested solutions in the classroom. The teacher must present herself as not perfect, but working to manage problems.
- The teacher should be humorous. Getting parents to laugh breaks down barriers and makes the training session enjoyable.
- If possible, parents should be trained in a group (although individual training can be effective). Working with parents in a group maximizes the teacher's efforts and helps parents see that other parents have similar problems with their children. During the first training meeting, parents should describe their child (age and sex), what they like about him, and what they would like to change.
- The teacher should use a structured curriculum or set of materials that focuses on meaningful behaviors such as arguing, noncompliance, aggression, and academic problems.

- The teacher should use as many prompts and techniques as possible to keep parents interested. For example, DVDs, video clips (audiotapes are not recommended), PowerPoint slides, cartoons to illustrate points, and role-playing all help.
- The teacher should give parents homework assignments after each meeting so they build a system of behavior change. They must bring back their assignment to the next session so the teacher can help them problem solve what didn't work, congratulate them for their efforts on what did work, and encourage them to keep going.

If the teacher finds she is losing parents, particularly low-income parents, it may help to:

- Call before each parent group.
- Supply baby-sitting (volunteers).
- Supply some type of transportation or a gasoline coupon (donation from a gasoline company) or bus pass.

A sample weekly training sequence is listed in "How To Conduct Tough Kid Parent Training." This sample sequence closely parallels the procedures presented in this book and is also the specific content presented in *The Tough Kid Parent Book* (Jenson, Rhode, and Neville, 2009). This sequence focuses on recruiting parents as part of the school-home team. The first night of training is spent on parents describing their children and learning what causes childhood problems. The goal is to make parents feel comfortable and not accuse them of causing students' difficulties.

During the second meeting, improving the overall positive interactions with the children and teaching differential attention as an

How to . . .

CONDUCT TOUGH KID PARENT TRAINING

WEEK 1: INTRODUCTION—MAKING PARENTS PART OF THE TEAM

- Setting the tone (humor, self-disclosure, and practical target behaviors)
- Parents describe their child (what they like, what they want to change)
- Temperament and its effects on behavior
- *Parent homework:* Select three behaviors to increase and select reinforcers to use

WEEK 2: INCREASING POSITIVE AND DIFFERENTIAL ATTENTION

- Homework review
- IFEED-AV reinforcement rules
- Differential attention
- *Parent homework:* Using differential attention

WEEK 3: DECREASING NONCOMPLIANCE

- Homework review
- The coercive process explained
- Using antecedents (effective request making) to reduce noncompliance—Precision Requests
- Using reductive consequences to stop noncompliance—timeout
- *Parent homework:* Giving precision requests followed by reductive consequences for noncompliance

WEEK 4: THE "SURE I WILL" PROGRAM AND NONCOMPLIANCE IN PUBLIC SETTINGS

- Homework review
- Reducing noncompliance in public settings
- The "Sure I Will" program
- Unique motivators (Mystery Motivators, Spinners, Grab Bags)
- *Parent homework:* Setting up a "Sure I Will" program

WEEK 5: THE HOME-TO-SCHOOL CONNECTION

- Homework review
- The Home Note program
- Learning to design a behavioral contract
- *Parent homework:* Setting up a Home Note program

WEEK 6: SOCIAL SKILLS, HOMEWORK, AND PARENT TUTORING

- Homework review
- Learning about social skills curricula
- Learning to set up an effective homework program
- Learning to set up an effective parent tutoring program
- Finishing the group

The sixth meeting covers advanced techniques, including an overview of social skills curricula that can be used at home and how to set up an effective homework or parent tutoring program.

In providing parent training to parents of Tough Kids, an important overall goal is to recruit parents as part of a coordinated team that works between the students' homes and the classroom. The closer the parent training interventions parallel what the teacher does in the classroom, the better the overall result for students will be. Parents are valuable resources that teachers should involve whenever possible.

Administrative Intervention

Administrative Intervention is a strategy used by school administrators or other trained support staff (school psychologist, counselor, social worker) when a student is out of instructional control. We have chosen to include it here for teachers who ultimately require additional support when an out-of-control student is taking so much teacher time that instruction for other students in the class has virtually come to a standstill. Over the years, the authors have found the tool described in *Administrative Intervention: A School Administrator's Guide to Working With Aggressive and Disruptive Students* to be very effective for regaining student instructional control and returning the student to the classroom (Black & Downs, 1997). Even though the book is no longer in print, we have obtained permission from the original authors to include enough information here for its implementation.

alternative to reprimanding is stressed. During the third meeting, coercion and how to reduce children's "pain control" through effective antecedents (Precision Requests) and practical reductive consequences are explained. The timeout technique for use at home is also introduced.

During the fourth meeting, use of Precision Requests in public places is explained, and the "Sure I Will" program, a method for positively reinforcing compliance, is introduced. The use of Mystery Motivators, reinforcement Spinners, and Grab Bags as rewards is explained.

During the fifth meeting, the home-to-school connection is introduced with the Home Notes program (see pp. 150–154). Parents are taught to design and begin the Home Notes program as a method of communicating with the teacher and helping manage their Tough Kids' behavior in the classroom.

Administrative Intervention is a strategy that takes a step-by-step approach to dealing with behavior problems from the time the student must leave his classroom to the time of reentry back into the classroom. Using the prescribed process, the administrator models appropriate behavior, shows the student how to be successful, engages in a consensus-building process regarding appropriate and inappropriate behavior, and provides constant feedback during the intervention.

The session is viewed as an opportunity to teach the student the skills he did not display in the classroom that resulted in his removal from class. Administrative Intervention essentially assists the administrator in filling a vital leadership role.

Before the student leaves the administrator's office at the conclusion of the intervention, he will know:

- How to accept criticism
- How to follow instructions
- The appropriate posture and voice tone when in a conference with an authority figure
- How to formulate and deliver an apology
- How to accept a penalty (and other social skills)

The Administrative Intervention process consists of procedures to:

- De-escalate disruptive behavior
- Obtain and maintain instructional control
- Teach alternative behaviors
- Prepare students for classroom reentry

We will describe each stage below.

DE-ESCALATE DISRUPTIVE BEHAVIOR (Crisis State)

STEP 1 When a student is sent to the office:

- Call him by name.
- Thank him for coming.
- Ask him to come into your office.

STEP 2 Get between the student and the door.

STEP 3 Ask him to take a chair. Do not engage him in discussion as to why he is there. You will obtain that information from his teacher.

STEP 4 Track him physically: Stay an arm's length from the student. Keep your hands by your sides or in back of you. Don't point or gesture with your hands. If the student doesn't sit down, move parallel to him, and always stay between him and the door. If the student moves to a corner, move more than an arm's length away so as not to make him feel trapped or in need of lashing out.

If the student pushes you aside, let him go. Track him out of the building if need be. Always encourage the student to return to your office. If he does not return, notify parents, police, or whoever needs to be notified. Very few students will leave the office, particularly if the administrator remains between the student and the door, keeps his arms at his sides, tells the student he appreciates his coming in so he can be helped, thanks him for eye contact, and continues to talk in a calm, low voice.

STEP 5 Track the student verbally using a calm, rational voice tone. No matter how the student behaves, always remain calm. Ask him to have a chair so you can help him. Tell him which chair you want him to take. (For example, "Ty, please sit down in this chair so we can talk.") Keep a calm, low voice tone even if the student yells, calls you names, or swears at you. Remember, you are modeling the behavior you want from him. Track the student verbally by saying what he is doing. ("Ty, you are swearing.") Give him specific instructions. ("Ty, stop swearing.") Identify the inappropriate behaviors one at a time. Give him specific instructions to engage in alternative appropriate behavior and specifically to stop talking.

When the student finally sits in the chair, stops talking, and gives you a verbal commitment to remain in his chair while you leave the office, you then prepare to leave the student to discuss his behavior with the teacher who sent him. When the student reaches this state, we would say his behavior is under gross control.

STEP 6 When the student first enters the office, the administrator should offer him the chair furthest from the door. When the student is seated in the chair and has stopped talking, the administrator should place a chair between the student and the door and sit in it. Remove potentially dangerous objects from sight.

STEP 7 Leaving the office to check with the teacher gives the student time to further de-escalate. Before visiting with the teacher, check your database regarding previous referrals. When you ask the teacher why she sent the student from the classroom, she must be specific enough in her description for you to identify the social skills the student needs to learn to be successful in such a situation. Terms like "bad attitude," "he knows how to push my buttons," or "he just won't be responsible" do little to help. What you want is a description such as "When I asked him to take out his book, he rolled his eyes at me, threw his book to the floor, and swore at me." When talking to the teacher, let her know the possible consequence the student might earn as a result of his poor behavior. This is for her information and not for her input. Let her know you will be back to discuss the student's reentry to class before the student comes back to class. Your goal is to have the student back in the classroom working appropriately. The teacher's goal should be the same. After this visit, you now have the information needed to continue working with the student.

OBTAIN AND MAINTAIN INSTRUCTIONAL CONTROL (Intensive Teaching)

The next step is the Intensive Teaching sequence. This step is designed to help the student learn the skills necessary when talking to a "boss." It also helps you gain complete instructional control so you can teach him the social skills he needs to learn. Let the student know that he is expected to follow these directions:

- Refrain from talking without being asked or instructed to do so.
- Sit up straight.
- Have good eye contact.
- Maintain appropriate facial expressions.
- Keep his hands on his knees.
- Keep his feet flat on the floor.
- Do not engage in any limit-testing behavior.

Once the student follows these directions, tell him that he may relax by moving his feet backward or forward slightly and place his hands in his lap. Ask him to now describe his inappropriate behavior that got him sent to the office. If problems are encountered and progress is not made, take another break for about ten minutes to allow the student to de-escalate further. **Under no circumstances should you permit the student to avoid following your directions and manipulate you into allowing him to return to his classroom before he has successfully gone through the entire process.** You are now ready to begin the Teaching Interaction.

THINK ABOUT IT

THINK

" You teach the student the appropriate social skills he did not demonstrate in the classroom. "

TEACH ALTERNATIVE BEHAVIORS (Teaching Interaction)

The Teaching Interaction process is likely to go rapidly since you have already taught the student the behaviors he needs to have for receiving feedback from his "boss." He knows to sit up straight, listen, maintain eye contact, and other skills.

This process is the means by which you teach the student the appropriate social skills he did not demonstrate in the classroom. This process includes the following steps:

- Express good will toward the student by using the student's first name in a pleasant voice.
- Give the student praise in the form of describing a positive behavior the student recently demonstrated.
- Describe the student's specific inappropriate classroom behavior that resulted in the referral to the office.
- Describe in specific terms the alternative appropriate behavior the student should have demonstrated.
- Give a rationale or reason why the student needs to engage in the specific desired behavior in the classroom.
- Ask the student for understanding and gain acknowledgment by a "Yes" or "OK."
- Practice rehearsing the appropriate behavior in a role-play reenactment of the classroom situation.
- Give the student specific feedback about what he did right and what needs improvement in the social skill he has just practiced.
- Describe to the student the consequence he has earned as a result of his behavior.
- Again, praise the student, recognizing his appropriate behavior during the Teaching Interaction. Let him know you are finished teaching him the social skill.

"How To Teach Selected Major Social Skills" on the next page provides the steps to teach common social skills. The two social skills programs discussed in **Chapter 5** provide steps for other skills that may be appropriate to teach.

The undesired consequence the student has earned is delivered next.

How to . . .

TEACH SELECTED MAJOR SOCIAL SKILLS

HOW TO FOLLOW INSTRUCTIONS

- Look at the person.
- Say "OK" or "Yes."
- Do the task immediately.
- Check back. (This step is not necessary under most conditions.)

HOW TO ACCEPT CRITICISM OR A CONSEQUENCE

- Look at the person.
- Say "OK."
- Don't argue.

HOW TO ACCEPT "NO" FOR AN ANSWER

- Look at the person.
- Say "OK."
- Don't argue, whine, or pout.
- If you don't understand why, ask calmly for a reason.
- If you disagree or have a complaint, bring it up later.

HOW TO MAKE A REQUEST

- Look at the person.
- Use a pleasant tone of voice.
- Say "Please."
- State the request specifically.
- Say "Thank you" after the request is granted.

HOW TO GET THE TEACHER'S ATTENTION

- Look at the person.
- Raise your hand.
- Wait for acknowledgment.
- After acknowledgment, ask your question in a quiet tone of voice.

HOW TO GREET A GUEST

- Stand up.
- Look at the person.
- Smile.
- Use a pleasant tone of voice.
- Give a verbal greeting and introduce yourself.
- Shake hands—this may not be used in every situation.

HOW TO GREET A PERSON YOU KNOW

- Look at the person.
- Smile.
- Use a pleasant tone of voice.
- Give a verbal greeting and state the person's name (e.g., "Good morning, Mrs. Roderick.").

Adapted from *School Social Skills Manual* by L. J. Brown, D. D. Black, and J. C. Downs, 1984. For additional social skills, see *Teaching Social Skills to Youth* (Dowd & Tierney, 1992) listed in Pointer Box 4-4 earlier in this chapter.

PREPARE STUDENTS FOR CLASSROOM REENTRY

Finally, conduct the process of preparing the student for classroom reentry. Begin by teaching the student how to deliver an appropriate apology to the teacher. The student must do this before he is allowed to return to class. The apology is delivered in the student's own words and must contain four parts:

- Call the teacher by name.
- Make a statement of remorse, including specifically what the student is sorry about.

- Make a statement letting the teacher know the behavior won't happen again.
- Make a request to come back to class.

First, practice the apology with the student sitting in his chair. Then practice the apology with both of you standing. Prepare the teacher to accept the apology. Let her know ahead of time that you will signal her as to whether she should accept or reject the student's apology. When she accepts the apology, she must make the student feel welcome back in the class and treat the student positively. Practice the apology standing one last time with the student. Walk the student back to class to deliver the apology to the teacher just outside the classroom door. Return the student to class.

In a nutshell

Critical information necessary to design and implement effective programs for teachers' toughest students has now been covered. Once effective interventions have been selected from this book and implemented, what can and should be done to keep things working? One of the most common errors teachers of Tough Kids make is to set up interventions and assume their effectiveness will continue almost indefinitely. The key to managing Tough Kids effectively is to view planning for their program as an ongoing process that requires regular attention. *constant monitoring*

After initial implementation, there are bound to be problem areas that do not continue to work as well as they should. The teacher will want to review relevant parts of this book to identify problem areas early on, analyze them, make adjustments to the Tough Kid's program, continue implementation, continue to analyze, and so on. Only by engaging in ongoing evaluation and adjustments based on that evaluation will the program continue to meet the Tough Kid's needs.

References

Adams, G., & Engelmann, S. (1996). *Research on direct instruction: 25 Years beyond DISTAR*. Seattle, WA: Educational Achievement Systems.

Althouse, R. B., Jenson, W. R., Likins, M., & Morgan, D. P. (1999). *Get 'em on task: A computer signaling program to teach attending and self-management skills*. Longmont, CO: Sopris West Educational Services.

Black, D. D., & Downs, J. C. (1997). *Administrative intervention: A school administrator's guide to working with aggressive and disruptive students*. Longmont, CO: Sopris West.

Borman, G. D., Hewes, G. M., Overman, L. T., & Brown, S. (2003). Comprehensive school reform and achievement: A meta-analysis. *Review of Educational Research, 73*(2), 125–230.

Briesch, A. M., & Chafouleas, S. M. (2009). Review and analysis of literature on self-management interventions to promote appropriate classroom behaviors (1988–2008). *School Psychology Quarterly, 24*(2), 106–118.

Ellis, E.S. (1993). Integrative strategy instruction: A potential model for teaching content area subjects to adolescents with learning disabilities. *Journal of Learning Disabilities, 26,* 358–383.

Family Educational Rights and Privacy Act. 20 U.S.C. Section 1232 (g) (1974).

Greenwood, C. R., Terry, B., Arreaga-Mayer, C., & Finney, R. (1992). The classwide peer tutoring program: Implementation factors moderating students' achievement. *Journal of Applied Behavior Analysis, 25*(1), 101–116.

Jenson, W. R., Rhode, G., & Neville, M. H. (2009). *The tough kid parent book: Practical solutions to tough childhood problems.* Eugene, OR: Pacific Northwest Publishing.

Johnson, D., & Johnson, R. (1994). An overview of cooperative learning. In J. Thousand, A. Villa, & A. Nevin (Eds), *Creativity and collaborative learning.* Baltimore: Brookes Press. Retrieved from: http://www.co-operation.org/pages/overviewpaper.html on November 9, 2009.

Kagan, S., & Kagan, M. (2009). *Kagan cooperative learning.* San Clemente, CA: Kagan Publishing.

Karp, K. S., & Voltz, D. L. (2000). Weaving mathematical instructional strategies into inclusive settings. *Intervention in School and Clinic, 35,* 206–215.

Kroesbergen, E. H., & Van Luit, J. E. H. (2003). Mathematical interventions for children with special educational needs. *Remedial and Special Education, 24,* 97–114.

Maheady, L., & Harper, G. F. (1987). A class-wide peer tutoring program to improve the spelling test performance of low-income, third- and fourth-grade students. *Education and Treatment of Children, 10*(2), 120–133.

Morgan, D. P., & Jenson, W. R. (1988). *Teaching behaviorally disordered students: Preferred practices.* Columbus, OH: Merrill Publishing.

Najar, R. L. (July 1999). *Pathways to success: Learning strategy instruction in content curriculum.* Paper presented at HERDSA Annual International Conference, Melbourne.

Pressley, M. (1990). *Cognitive strategy instruction that really improves children's academic performance.* Cambridge, MA: Brookline Books.

Swanson, H. L. (2001). Searching for the best model for instructing students with learning disabilities. *Focus on Exceptional Children, 34,* 1–15.

Vacca, R. T., & Vacca, J. L. (2005). *Content area reading: Literacy and learning across the curriculum.* Boston, MA: Allyn & Bacon.

White, W. A. T. (1988). A meta-analysis of the effects of direct instruction in special education. *Education and Treatment of Children, 11*(4), 364–374.

CHAPTER 5

Getting Tough Kids Back to General Education Settings

Successfully placing a Tough Kid back into a general education setting either part time or full time is often very difficult for the Tough Kid. It is also difficult for the classroom or school that receives him.

There are several reasons why general education placement can be difficult and often fails:

1. **Many Tough Kids return from restrictive special placements.** These placements include self-contained classrooms, resource rooms, special schools, alternative schools, hospital settings, and juvenile detention centers. Tough Kids were often placed in these special settings for disruptive externalizing problems such as noncompliance, aggression, oppositional behaviors, arguing, and temper tantrums. These disruptive behaviors may concern some teachers who assume or even expect the Tough Kid will regress to his previous behavior patterns when he returns. Some teachers also think that once a Tough Kid has been referred to a specialized placement, he is no longer general education's responsibility (translation: the student is not their problem anymore). The student is now the property of the receiving placement, whether it is special education, juvenile justice, or mental health. This, of course,

makes adjustment back to general education even more difficult. In essence, the Tough Kid is returning with a Bad Reputation.

2. **Most likely, the Tough Kid still has some significant behavior deficits in social skills and the ability to self-manage his behavior.** (See **Chapter 1** for more details.) For example, a Tough Kid may have a deficit in the social skills needed to successfully make and keep friends, cooperate with others, and follow school and classroom rules. When Tough Kids are simply placed with their normal peers without appropriate preparation and support, the peers often reject them in a very short time. A socially rejected Tough Kid regularly seeks out other Tough Kids when placed in new settings. If a Tough Kid's main peer group is other Tough Kids, it will be only a matter of time before he is in trouble again.

3. **Tough Kids often return to general education classrooms with academic deficits that have plagued them for years.** This is

especially true for reading skills. If a Tough Kid is placed in a general education setting that demands academic performance beyond her capabilities, it will not be long before she reverts back to her previous disruptive behaviors. Disruptive behaviors often serve a Tough Kid well in escaping an unsuccessful and punishing environment. Who can blame her? If the Tough Kid is frustrated, punished for poor performance, and humiliated or embarrassed, she will often use opposition, noncompliance, and other disruptive behaviors to get out of the situation. Academic adjustments, accommodations, and supports are critical for the Tough Kid if she is to survive and achieve real success in a general education setting.

4. **Other serious adjustment problems can occur when the Tough Kid has been isolated from mainstream general education for a long time.** Even if her special placement was housed in a regular school, she may be unfamiliar with the common school stimuli (the everyday trappings) and expectations of a general classroom or school. For example, general classroom schedules, seating arrangements, classroom rules, class sizes, textbooks, and academic materials may all be unfamiliar to the Tough Kid. The Tough Kid may have no idea about the behavioral expectations of her new general education teacher. It is natural for her to experience anxiety and fear in a new, unfamiliar environment where she is not sure what to expect. Why would any student look forward to going to such a setting? Thus, a Tough Kid may act out in an attempt to sabotage her return to a regular school environment. For a Tough Kid to be successful, she must be systematically reintroduced to the

variables that make up the general education everyday environment, including the behavioral expectations to which she is returning. She must also be specifically taught the behaviors she will need in the new setting.

5. **Another area of difficulty is the "fix-it" mentality of many general educators.** They may believe, or at least hope, that when a Tough Kid is successfully placed in an alternative educational setting where she receives special services, she will be permanently fixed, with no future behavior problems. Frequently, if the Tough Kid's placement in a general education placement environment fails, it may be assumed that the previous special placement simply did not work. Obviously, the Tough Kid must not have been ready to come back to the regular school or general education classroom.

As we stated in **Chapter 1**, working with a Tough Kid is a management issue, most often an ongoing one, and not an issue of a permanent cure or fix. The most common treatment model for a Tough Kid in a special setting is still to train and hope. The Tough Kid receives training and services in a special setting with additional support, and when placed back into a general education settings, educators hope she will be successful. There is nothing magic about mainstreaming or using an inclusion model.

THINK ABOUT IT

THINK

"Working with a Tough Kid is a management issue, most often an ongoing one."

To be successful at re-entering a general education setting, Tough Kids need intensive special preparation and training, such as lessons about behavioral expectations, training on the social skills required by the new setting (for example, making new friends), academic preparation, and accommodations. She must also be taught the self-management skills needed to cope with new problems when they arise. If her academic skills are below grade level, she needs to have appropriate supports, adjustments, and accommodations in place. Academic accommodations might include reducing assignment length (see Dots for Motivation in **Chapter 2**), allowing more time to complete assignments or take tests, providing a study guide or outline, or alerting the Tough Kid to important points—for example, "This is important, so listen carefully." These will be explained in detail later in the chapter. As the Tough Kid is increasingly successful in her general education setting, many supports may gradually be faded over time. The idea is to not fade these more quickly than the student's increasing skills permit.

MAINSTREAMING AND INCLUSION AS A GENERALIZATION PROCESS

It is not the mainstreaming or inclusion processes by themselves that lead to successful re-entry of Tough Kids. Rather, it is systematic training and preparation with continued support that ensures a Tough Kid's successful return. We refer to this systematic process as generalization. *Generalization* is defined as the extension of newly trained or learned behaviors to new environments in which the behaviors have not been trained or learned (Wahler, Berland, & Coe, 1979). In essence, generalization for Tough Kids means they demonstrate in their new general education settings the adaptive behaviors (e.g., social skills, coping skills, self-management skills) they learned in their specialized placements. The newly learned and trained behaviors transfer from the special setting to the general education setting with new teachers, new students, and new expectations. Achieving this generalized transfer requires specialized preparatory procedures in the special setting with consistent follow-up and support in the new general education setting.

A number of evidence-based generalization strategies have been published in the research literature over the last three decades. Some of these adapted strategies are listed and described in Box 5-1 on the next page (Morgan & Jenson, 1988). These strategies have been identified as useful for generalizing Tough Kids from specialized settings such as self-contained classrooms and special schools back to general education environments. They have been incorporated into the generalization model outlined in this chapter.

BOX 5-1

Generalization *Strategies*

Sequential Modification. Teach and reinforce the behavior in many different settings.

Natural Contingencies of Reinforcement. A newly taught behavior is valued and naturally reinforced by people in new settings.

Sufficient Number of Teaching Examples. Instead of teaching only one form of the behavior, teach many forms that will be reinforced.

Train Loosely. After new behavior is learned under tight learning conditions, vary the learning conditions to be looser.

Use Indiscriminable Contingencies. Make the conditions under which the newly learned behavior will be reinforced indiscriminable, or unpredictable. The Tough Kid is never sure when or where he will be reinforced for the behavior. The Get 'Em on Task program described in Chapter 4 is a good example of an indiscriminable contingency.

Programming Common Stimuli. Make the training setting more like the natural setting that the Tough Kid will be returned to.

Teach Required Behaviors in the Natural Setting. Teach the behaviors that will be required and valued by people in the natural setting that the Tough Kid will return to.

Self-management Skills. Teach the Tough Kid to self-monitor, self-instruct, self-evaluate, and self-reinforce when he is back in the natural setting.

Lucky Charms. Let the Tough Kid take something from the training setting into the natural setting.

Think of systematic generalization as a treatment or educational insurance plan. Why spend so many resources and so much money on Tough Kids' special placements only to lose those gains when Tough Kids return to general education settings? The "train and hope" model of sending Tough Kids back to general environments is wasteful of resources and harmful to Tough Kids. A little planning and preparation can spare the Tough Kids and the educational system one more failure.

Another very important point must be made about returning Tough Kids to general education settings. A Tough Kid cannot be successfully returned from a poor or ineffective special placement. Spending time in a poor special placement does nothing but give the adults in the original placement a brief reprieve. If the Tough Kid has not made any real progress, there are no skills or gains to be generalized back to a general education setting. The Tough Kid must have made genuine progress in decreasing his behavioral excesses (e.g., noncompliance, arguing, tantrums, disruptive behaviors). He must also have made genuine progress in improving behavior deficits (e.g., social skills, academic skills, and self-management). Otherwise, the special placement was useless.

As we have stated earlier, there is nothing magic or rehabilitating in mainstreaming or including an unprepared Tough Kid in the general education environment. He must have made positive behavioral changes and academic gains before he can be successfully generalized back to general education.

There is no 100% accurate test to judge a Tough Kid's readiness to reenter a general education setting. However, the following guidelines can help you judge readiness.

GUIDELINE 1

First, The Tough Kid must be compliant and follow appropriate adult requests 80–85% of the time. Severe noncompliance is the hallmark behavior of a Tough Kid. It is not unusual for a Tough Kid to comply with adult requests less than 50% of the time. If he is coercive and noncompliant with adult requests, the Tough Kid will fail in a general education setting and most other settings as well.

GUIDELINE 2

Another readiness indicator is the percentage of time the Tough Kid is on task and working in the classroom. If the Tough Kid is off task and not listening or working, she will not be successful.

TECHNIQUE TIP

An easy way to get an objective measure of compliance is to administer the Teacher Compliance Probe described in Chapter 1, p. 23.)

The average Tough Kid is on task less than 50% of the time in the classroom. This needs to be increased to 80% or more time on task for both individual and group work in the classroom. If the Tough Kid is on task and working, it is difficult for her to engage in disruptive or troublesome behaviors at the same time. An objective measure of on-task behavior may be obtained by conducting a response discrepancy classroom observation using the Behavior Observation Form (Reproducible 1-3) provided in **Chapter 1**. This observation system is especially useful because it provides:

- The on-task rate for the identified Tough Kid
- A sample of on-task rates for other students in the classroom
- A breakdown of the Tough Kid's problematic off-task behaviors

It is more difficult to judge the Tough Kid's progress in social skills, academic ability, and self-management skills. However, the generalization model given in this chapter can help assess a Tough Kid's readiness to return.

GUIDELINE 3

Our Tough Kid Generalization Model (discussed in detail beginning on p. 180) documents the progress the student has made in each of the six components of the model. For example, advancement through the program's level system is a good gauge of behavioral progress. Similarly, demonstrating substantial progress in the Teacher Pleaser Social Skills Program (see Appendix B) and learning appropriate responses to the teacher's expectations (see pp. 191–195) must be evident. The Tough Kid's progress with both the Teacher Pleaser Program and response to the teacher's expectations are good indicators of his or her readiness to be placed in settings with new teachers. (*Note:* Both programs are included on CD accompanying this book.)

When all indicators are positive for a Tough Kid to go back to general education, the administrator in the receiving school must address a number of important issues. Here is our Top Ten List of Considerations.

Ten Things Administrators Should Consider When Tough Kids Return to Their Schools

School administrators and related service personnel need to consider a number of issues before a Tough Kid returns to their school. These issues are important not only for the Tough Kid's successful placement but also for the well-being of the school.

1. **He's coming back.** It's important for administrators to acknowledge that the Tough Kid has a right to return to his neighborhood school when he does not require a more restrictive placement. These rights are federally guaranteed, particularly if the Tough Kid is a special education student with an Individual Education Plan and is not a danger to himself or others.

2. **There's always another one.** Even if the Tough Kid leaves your school permanently, there will always be a new Tough Kid to replace him. With a prevalence rate of 3–7%, Tough Kids will always be in your school or coming to it.

3. **A proactive approach for managing a Tough Kid is always better than a reactive approach.** We suggest that the school administrator proactively plan for the Tough Kid's return by selecting a positive, structured teacher; having a contingency plan in place if there is a crisis; and creating a plan to separate him from other Tough Kids.

4. **He's immune to punishment.** As we stated earlier in this book, Tough Kids are immune to punishment. They can take three or four times the punishment a general education student can. For a Tough Kid, a management strategy based on positive reinforcement is the best strategy.

5. **Supervision works.** One of the best pro-active management strategies is simply supervision. Supervision eliminates opportunities for trouble. If a Tough Kid is well supervised, he is far less likely to get into trouble. Positive Check-in/Check-out strategies like the Behavior Education Program (Crone, Horner, & Hawken, 2003) are excellent supervision programs.

6. **Suspension is the worst strategy.** Suspending Tough Kids out of school is usually a disaster. Tough Kids should not be suspended unless they are a danger to others. When a Tough Kid is suspended, the problem is shifted from the school to the community, where he will most likely not be supervised. Similarly, in-school suspension may not work with some Tough Kids because many of them engineer their own placements to get into in-school suspension to avoid classes and/or be with their friends.

7. **Tough Kids have academic deficits.** It is important to recognize that most Tough Kids have academic deficits, especially in reading and study skills. If a Tough Kid regularly fails in the classroom because he cannot do the required work, he will act out to escape that environment. Academic accommodations must be made to ensure the Tough Kid's academic success.

8. **Tough Kids have social skills deficits.** Because Tough Kids are socially deficit, they are often rejected by their normal peers when they first come to a new school. If they are rejected, they will seek accepting Tough Kids with whom they can hang out. During the initial adjustment to a new school, it is a good idea to assign a peer buddy to the Tough Kid for unstructured times such as lunch, recess, and showing him around school. It is also recommended that the administrator indicate to the Tough Kid that there is an open-door policy for the Tough Kid to meet with an accepting adult (e.g., school counselor, school psychologist, or principal) to discuss issues such as peer rejection, bullying, or not having friends.

9. **Pick the right teacher.** The teacher should be positive and structured, and have effective classroom rules that she follows through with consistently. She should also have a well-defined classroom schedule and excellent academic teaching skills. Above all, if she is not positive, nothing is going to work!

10. **Yes, you can work with the parents.** It is a "goodness of fit" approach where the teacher's approach and qualities fit the needs of a Tough Kid. Schools often blame parents for a Tough Kid's behavior problems. Interestingly, parents often blame the schools for their child's problems. Parents of Tough Kids often do not want to work with schools because they have been made to feel guilty about their child's problems. They often are blamed for the problems. They hear from the school only when there are problems, and they are often called upon to control the Tough Kid's behavior in school when they cannot control it at home.

Remember—what the Tough Kid is doing in school he is probably also doing at home. The research is clear. Parents can be effective partners with schools in managing Tough Kids' behavior (Maughan, Olympia, Jenson, Clark, & Christiansen, 2005). Thus, it is essential to treat them like partners by enlisting their help, making no blaming statements, calling them at home or work when things are going well (not just when there are problems), and teaching them effective behavior management skills. *The Tough Kid Parent Book*, a part of The Tough Kid series, is designed to train parents and incorporate them as partners in managing their child's behavior. It does so by teaching parents strategies that complement those discussed in this book.

COMPONENTS OF THE TOUGH KID GENERALIZATION MODEL

The Tough Kid Generalization Model is composed of research-validated generalization strategies. The model was developed, researched, and field tested in Utah with Tough Kids returning to general education settings from a specialized school for children with significant behavioral problems (Jenson, Christopolus, Nicholas, Reavis, & Rhode , 1991). The focus of the model is to teach Tough Kids the essential skills they need to survive in general education settings. The model also helps them acquire the self-management behavior they must have to demonstrate these skills when and where they are needed. This essential generalization model includes the following six components.

COMPONENT 1: SPECIAL PLACEMENT LEVEL SYSTEM

The level system provides systematic shaping of the Tough Kid's behavior. Through this system, behavioral excesses are decreased, and social and academic skills are taught. A good level system for Tough Kids must also teach the self-management skills of self-monitoring and self-evaluation so the Tough Kid learns to accurately judge his own performance.

COMPONENT 2: COMMON CLASSROOM STIMULI ASSESSMENT

This part of the generalization model assesses the common stimuli in the setting the Tough Kid is returning to as compared with those in his special placement. These stimuli include such things as academic materials, scheduling, classroom rules, routines, and the physical layout of the general education classroom. The student is then taught and exposed to these common stimuli while he is still in the special placement, before he returns to the general education setting.

COMPONENT 3: MEETING INDIVIDUAL TEACHER'S EXPECTATIONS (Individualizing)

The model also assesses the most important and frequent expectations of general education teachers. The Tough Kid is then taught the appropriate behaviors to meet these expectations. This process is designed to teach Tough Kids the necessary skills to meet their general education teacher's individual expectations.

COMPONENT 4: TEACHER PLEASER SOCIAL SKILLS PROGRAM

A Tough Kid often returns to general education environments with a bad reputation. Some teachers almost expect him to be a problem from the get-go. This bias can become a self-fulfilling prophecy. Our model teaches the student a set of social skills we view as the top five Teacher Pleasers. These five social skills are universally valued by teachers and are particularly helpful for the Tough Kid during the initial days of his return to the general education environment. Teacher Pleaser skills are designed to defuse his reentry and derail any biases and negative preconceived ideas a general education teacher might have. The Teacher Pleaser Social Skills Program is located in Appendix B.

COMPONENT 5: LUCKY CHARMS

No, Lucky Charms is not a breakfast cereal. Rather it is a generalization technique that makes use of an object or symbol that the Tough Kid has become familiar with in her special placement. The student then takes this object or symbol back to her new general education placement. It is like taking a token of the successful special placement and importing it into the new environment.

COMPONENT 6: SELF-MANAGEMENT SKILLS

This part of the model teaches the Tough Kid self-management skills, including self-monitoring and self-evaluation, to promote success. The student is systematically taught to evaluate and record her appropriate behaviors and match them for accuracy at a later time with a teacher or another adult. Gradually, the matching piece is faded as the student becomes more accurate in her self-evaluation. In this way, she becomes more and more responsible for her own behavior. The Tough Kid takes a reduced and less cumbersome form of this strategy with her back to the general school setting.

The Tough Kid Generalization Model uses all of these components and several more that will be explained in detail later in this chapter. The focus of the model is preplanning and pre-teaching skills to help ensure the Tough Kid's successful integration back into general education settings. Details of the model are provided below.

Component 1: Special Placement Level Systems

Behavior level systems are commonly used in special education classrooms, special schools, group homes, psychiatric hospitals, and other special placements. This type of system can be very powerful in changing the behavior of students with very severe behavior problems. When used appropriately, a level system is a comprehensive, data-based classroom management system that consists of a hierarchy of skills and behaviors a student is expected to master. It is a tiered program in which students earn higher degrees of privileges and freedom as they advance through the levels (steps) of the system. On the beginning levels, students are taught simple, fundamental skills that progress in complexity (and may be prerequisite to skills taught and required on higher levels) as the student moves through the level system. In addition, greater amounts of specific appropriate behaviors are required as a student progresses through the system. Thus, the level system shapes appropriate behavior by systematically teaching it. In this way, students earn access to new privileges and freedoms as they learn and demonstrate an increased ability to handle them successfully.

It does a Tough Kid no favors to expose him to situations and settings he is not yet prepared to handle. For example, if a Tough Kid is not yet able to demonstrate appropriate behavior in a small group, sending him to an activity like a schoolwide assembly is likely to be disastrous. However, this is the theoretical view. All too often, level systems used with Tough Kids are primarily punitive.

ADVANTAGES OF A CLASSROOM LEVEL SYSTEM

The basic advantages for using a classroom level system are:

- Classroom rules are explicit.
- Data for monitoring and evaluating student progress are built into the system.
- Students receive continual feedback about their performance.
- Classroom privileges and reinforcement are contingent on explicit and well-defined performance expectations.
- The system is used as a shaping and generalization tool to prepare students to be successful in other settings.
- Behavior change is systematic, with prerequisite skills taught first.
- The system can be very powerful in changing the behavior of students, even those with the most severe behavioral problems.

When level systems are used inappropriately, they may function as response cost systems for punishment. They may be viewed as a way to punish or fine Tough Kids through the withdrawal of privileges. Negative threats may be associated with level systems—"If you do that one more time, I'm going to drop you a level." When level systems are used in this punitive way, they destroy Tough Kid motivation and become ineffective. If a Tough Kid has made progress and gained privileges, losing those privileges because of impulsive, inappropriate behavior can be devastating. Tough Kids

THINK ABOUT IT

THINK " *Well-designed level systems should not include instant level drops because of a single misbehavior.* "

generally move slowly up the level system to gain their privileges. Well-designed level systems should typically not include instant level drops because of a single misbehavior. Level drops should also not be made in an arbitrary and capricious manner. The authors prefer level systems with behavioral recourse built into them. With such a system, a student who misbehaves does not immediately lose everything he has worked for. Tough Kids are impulsive by their nature and can misbehave without considering the consequences. Built-in behavioral recourse is a way for Tough Kids to stop their misbehavior, reevaluate what they are doing, and maintain hard-earned privileges.

A behavioral level system should be viewed mainly as a teaching, shaping, fading, and generalization system instead of as a response cost punishment system. The teaching component includes teaching the behavioral expectations of each level and the steps to learning these behaviors. A level system shapes behaviors through progressive steps where the Tough Kid learns more and more complex behaviors as he progresses through the levels.

It is a fading/generalization system because good level systems shift the behavioral control of the Tough Kid's behavior from the level system to the student himself through teaching self-management and self-evaluation skills. It should be noted that level systems work only when the rules and expectations for moving up the levels are objective, easily understood by the student, and measurable.

Behavioral level systems also have several other functions that serve the student and the teacher. Well-designed level systems give students feedback about how well they are doing in a program. A large copy of the level system should be posted on a wall so all students and the staff can see the behavioral requirements and the steps in the system (see Figure 5-1 on the next page). Some teachers place students' names above the various levels on the wall where the level system is posted. In this way, students can see their names, their current level, and how well they are progressing.

Teachers who do not want to post students' names might give each student a level card with his name on the card, his current level, and the required behaviors to be mastered for that level. The advantage in posting a large replica of the level system in a prominent place is that it clearly

TECHNIQUE TIP

USE CAUTION BEFORE POSTING
Before publicly posting students' names, points earned, behaviors, or placement on the level system, be sure to obtain written parental permission. Posting such information without permission may be viewed as a violation of the Family Educational Rights and Privacy Act (FERPA).

outlines and reminds students of the program requirements. The advantage to having students' names associated with their current steps on the level system (either posted on a wall or with a level card) is that it gives students constant visual feedback about their progress and motivates them to work their way up to the next level.

Figure 5-1 on the next page depicts a five-tiered level system for Tough Kids. Each level is color coded. It starts at the Red level with the most basic behavioral excesses of aggression, out of seat, and inappropriate hands. Subsequent levels focus on behavioral deficits and encourage students to exhibit positive behaviors such as paying attention (Yellow level), cooperating with friends (Blue level), and task completion (Green level). Note that focus behaviors carry over from one level to the next, so the Blue level, for example, includes the focus behaviors from the Red and Yellow levels as well.

A level system does not have to be color coded, as in this example. Other options include:

- Each level is numbered
- Each level is associated with an animal
- Each level represents a particular car (e.g., Morris Minor, VW Bug, Mustang, Porsche, Ferrari, etc.)

In our color-coded levels example, when a student has made appropriate progress at the Red level, he advances to the Yellow level, which includes appropriate behaviors such as following directions, paying attention, and raising his hand to make contributions.

The next level, Blue, emphasizes basic social skills such as using polite language, cooperating with friends, and reinforcing peers for

Figure 5-1 • Example of a Behavioral Level System

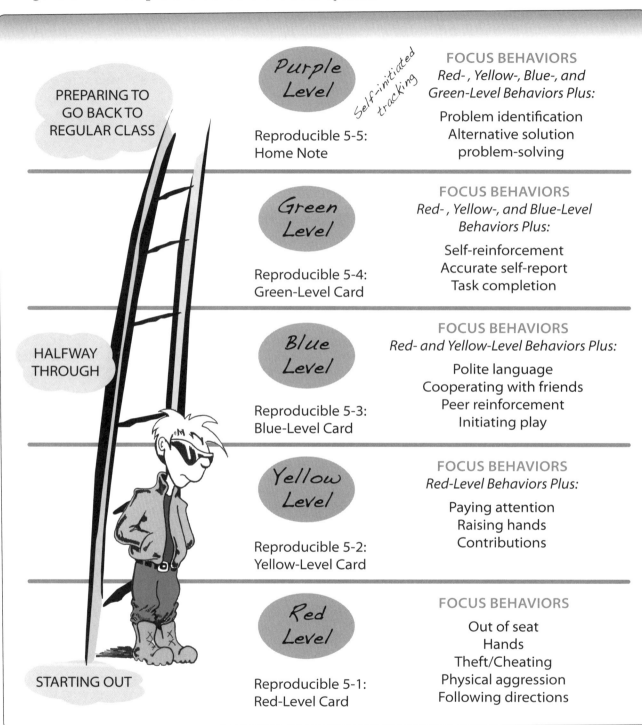

appropriate behavior (e.g., Put-Ups). At this level, a shift begins whereby the Tough Kid starts to self-monitor his own behavior and give an accurate report about how well he has done in the classroom. At the fourth level, Green, he also completes assignments and rates himself on how much reinforcement he thinks he has earned and how well he has done. His report is compared with the teacher's rating of his progress. If there is a match, the student earns classroom reinforcement. If his rating and the teacher's do not match, no reinforcement is earned.

On the fifth and top level, Purple, the Tough Kid continues to self-monitor, identifies problems that he may be having in the classroom, and generates alternative solutions to these problems. At this point he is much more independent. He has access to all the classroom privileges and is ready to spend more and more time in the general classroom.

BEHAVIOR MONITORING CARDS

The exact criterion a Tough Kid needs to meet to advance to the next level depends on the particular setting in which he is placed. However, the teacher needs to have some type of data collection system that allows accurate monitoring of various level system behaviors and documents the progress the student is making. The level system in Figure 5-1 was used in conjunction with a color-coded card and classroom points system to reinforce the student and also to document student progress. The cards are issued to students daily and are color coded according to the level the student is on.

Examples of the cards used at different levels are shown on the following pages (Reproducibles 5-1 through 5-5). Blank copies are provided on the CD for you to print. (If using color-coded level cards, you may wish to print on colored paper to match the level color). Also included is a card template that you can customize with your own level names and target behaviors.

The cards are designed to record a number of different items.

Missed points are marked on the card for behaviors that correspond to certain focus behaviors on the level system. For example, if a Tough Kid engages in one of these Red-level focus behaviors, it is marked on his card:

- OS = Out of seat
- PA = Physical aggression
- H = Inappropriate touching or use of hands
- T = Theft
- C = Cheating

Note that the focus behaviors for the Red level are all behaviors of excess that you are trying to decrease. In later levels the focus behaviors shift to deficit behaviors that you want to increase—for example, paying attention and raising hand at the Yellow level. For the purposes of tracking missed points, however, you will record instances where the focus behavior is absent. At the Yellow level, for instance, you will mark when the Tough Kid talks out without raising his hand and when he is not paying attention. Note that once they are introduced, focus behaviors appear on the cards across all subsequent levels except the Purple (top) level.

Following directions. Each card has a special section for FD (followed directions) and NFD (did not follow directions). If the Tough Kid follows a teacher's requests the first time it is given, he earns points. If he does not comply with directions, a mark under Did Not Follow Directions indicates that he missed points. This section also appears on all cards across all levels. Improving compliance is one of the major behavioral objectives of the Tough Kid program.

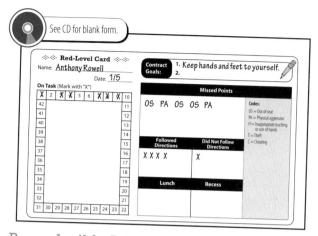

Reproducible 5-1 • Red-Level Card

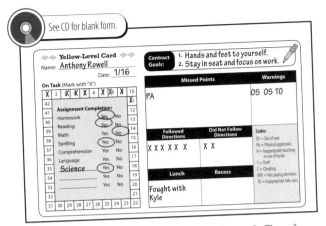

Reproducible 5-2 • Yellow-Level Card

On task. The squares on the left side of the card are intervals for being on task. Improving the Tough Kid's on-task behavior is the second major behavioral objective of the program. If a Tough Kid is on task (and compliant), there is far less chance he will have problems in the classroom. The perimeter squares on the cards are often used in conjunction with the Get 'Em On Task random signaling program discussed in **Chapter 4**. When the computer produces a random signal, such as a beep, all the students in the classroom who are on task and following the classroom rules are prompted by the teacher to mark the next square on their card with an earned point.

Contract goals. The card also has a section for special contracts for individual students. These are behavior goals on which a particular student is working. They may be different for each student in the classroom. The Contracts section allows individual programming for students.

Recess and lunch behavior. Use the Recess and Lunch areas to record the Tough Kid's behaviors during these special periods of the day.

Collecting data from the cards. At the end of each week, the cards are gathered and points earned, points missed for inappropriate behaviors, and on-task points are calculated. Note that the color-coded cards are used for the Tough Kid to earn points. But they are also valuable sources of data for the students across the week. The points earned and points missed, on-task behavior (as measured by points in the perimeter squares), following directions points (points marked in the FD square), special contract points, and particular problematic behaviors (indicated by points missed on the card) can easily be entered into an Excel spreadsheet to monitor student progress. Use the spreadsheet or other record-keeping system to determine when a Tough Kid meets your criteria for moving on to the next level.

Yellow-level card. The card for each level should reflect the new focus behaviors for that level as well as expectations from previous levels. The next color-coded card is for the Yellow level (Reproducible 5-2). This level adds these behaviors to the Missed Points section:

- NPA = Not paying attention
- TO = Inappropriate talk-outs

These correspond to the Yellow-level focus behaviors of Paying attention and Raising hands.

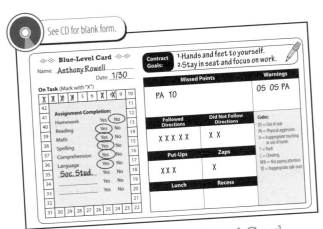

Reproducible 5-3 • Blue-Level Card

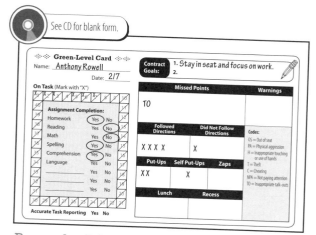

Reproducible 5-4 • Green-Level Card

One of the privileges of the Yellow level is warning the student once when he is engaged in certain inappropriate behaviors (see Warning box on card). After the first warning, the inappropriate behavior is marked as missed points.

Another addition at the Yellow level is the awarding of points for successful completion of academic assignments. These are listed in the center of the On-Task squares, with room at the bottom to add additional assignments. Points that are awarded for academic assignments can be tracked on a form such as Chart Moves (see **Chapter 2**).

Blue-level card. This card (Reproducible 5-3) adds areas for the new focus behavior of peer reinforcement. There is a box to record Put-Ups, which are expressions of praise to other students for their appropriate behavior. Put-Ups are the opposite of put-downs, or Zaps, which are critical statements to other students or staff in the classroom. Students will also record Zaps on the Blue-level card.

Green-level card. For the new focus behavior self-reinforcement, the Green-level card (Reproducible 5-4) adds a space to record Self Put-Ups, which are verbal self-rewarding remark for appropriate behaviors.

The boxes on the perimeter of the Green-level card are split. This is because the student starts to self-monitor his own on-task behavior without a prompt from the teacher. When a signal goes off from the Get 'Em On Task program, the student self-monitors whether he was on task or off task by marking an X in the left section of the box. The teacher also keeps track of the student's on-task behavior. The teacher may choose to give immediate feedback by marking the right side of the box at the same time. Or the teacher may keep track on a separate card and compare her ratings with the student's at the end of the day.

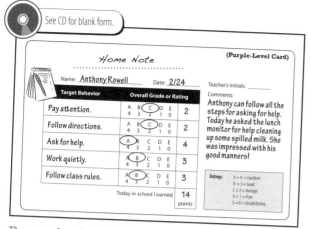

Reproducible 5-5 • Home Note (Purple-Level Card)

If the difference between the teacher's rating (number of checks for on-task behavior) and the student's on-task total is two or less, the student gets to keep the points he has earned. If not, the student does not earn any points.

Purple level. On the Purple level, the student is no longer subject to the constraints of the level system and is spending more and more time in a general class setting. A Home Note (as described in **Chapter 4**) is often implemented to inform the parents of the student's progress. Or the general education teacher can complete a class note on the Tough Kid's behavior when he is in the general classroom. Self-monitoring and matching the teacher's rating are important skills that can be used when the student returns to the general classroom.

The privileges associated with advancing to each level of a level system are one of its major motivating factors. Privileges are cumulative—the Tough Kid has access to all the privileges for his current level as well as for the lower levels that he has mastered. Box 5-2 gives some examples of privileges that can be used in conjunction with a level system.

If a student has a major behavior problem, a level system recourse system should be implemented. This recourse system gives the student a chance to correct the problem behavior without being dropped a level.

For example, if a Tough Kid impulsively becomes disruptive and defiant, she should be given time (e.g., 3 to 5 minutes) to cool down, correct her behavior, and commit to behave appropriately without a drop in level. Sometimes a signed behavioral contract can be used to gain student commitment to behave appropriately and comply with the classroom rules. The Administrative Intervention described in **Chapter 4** is a good model to follow as a recourse procedure. However, if the student continues to be disruptive or breaks the contract, the staff should convene and consider a level drop or other consequences.

TECHNIQUE TIP

Some classroom privileges are not really privileges (rewards based on appropriate behavior), but rather legal rights. Common sense is the rule here. Access to the restrooms, food, water, appropriate clothing, and other necessities should never be used as a privilege on a level system. The student has access to these irrespective of her behavior. However, special foods, activities, and the right to wear special clothing have been appropriately used as level system privileges.

BOX 5-2

Privileges for Level Systems

- Free time at desk after work is complete
- Gets to buy additional free time when others are working
- Special Friday activities (e.g., watching DVD, computer time, field trip, special art project)
- Gets to help select the Special Friday Activity
- Does not have to line up after recess
- Does not have to line up after lunch
- Gets to be in the group that leaves early (30 seconds) for out-of-class activities
- Is eligible for a surprise reward or Mystery Motivator
- Unrestrained recess (gets to play during morning or afternoon recess without having to stay near an adult)
- Choice of where to sit at lunch time

- Choice of where to sit in the classroom
- Gets to use the food machines (with own money) in the lunchroom
- Gets to do classroom jobs and help the teacher
- Gets to do office errands outside the classroom
- Gets to buy DVD or MP3 player (his own) listening time
- Gets to buy time on the class computer for games
- Gets to wear an article of clothing (e.g., a hat) that others are not allowed to wear
- Gets to work in the library
- Gets to read when work is complete
- Gets to leave seat to sharpen pencil (or get needed materials) at any time

Student progress as demonstrated by monitoring data should be used to advance or drop students in the level system. Staff can use weekly student data reviews to make these decisions. These level system gains or drops should be determined by data collected on progress across the week, not based on minor incidents or one staff member's impression of the student's progress. For example, advancements up a level might be based on one of the following:

- Student earns a certain number of points (e.g., 100 points equals an advance)

- Student has five consecutive good days.
- Student fulfills terms of a special contract.

Criteria for level drops might include:

- Student has three "rough days" in a week (e.g., fails to improve a problem behavior after given recourse opportunities for noncompliance, disruptive behavior, or repeated arguing).
- Student has three nonproductive days in a week (a nonproductive day is one in which a student fails to earn a minimum number of points—say, 20).

- Student displays extremely severe behavior, such as aggression, bullying, or property destruction (make sure there is staff consensus about the behavior—this should not be one person's opinion).

Level progress or level drops should be data-based decisions that are reviewed with the Tough Kid at the end of the week.

If the Tough Kid is not making progress, something is wrong with the system, not with the Tough Kid. Review the system and possibly make an ABC Functional Behavior Assessment of the behavior problem (see **Chapter 1**). Privileges, behavioral requirements, and academic requirements should be reviewed. Determine and document that the level system privileges are rewarding for the student and that the student is capable of performing the required behavioral and academic tasks. It is a level system failure when a Tough Kid is stranded on one level for a long period of time.

Component 2: Common Classroom Stimuli Assessment

Why assess common stimuli found in the receiving general education classroom? The reason is simple. For many Tough Kids, these stimuli are not common. Frequently, Tough Kids have been out of the mainstream educational environment for so long that they have very little idea what "general" education is going to be like. Many Tough Kids have been in self-contained classrooms, day treatment programs, alternative schools, or psychiatric hospitals for long periods of time. Even if they are in self-contained classrooms in a general education school, they may have little interaction with the common stimuli found in the rest of the school. They may have no idea what to expect when they enter a general education classroom.

In fact, it is not uncommon for a Tough Kid who is successful in a special education environment to sabotage his return to general education because he is unsure of and worried about what to expect. We all want to know what the future holds. What will the setting be like? Who will we meet? What are the rules? What does the classroom look like? What will be expected from us? The Common Classroom Stimuli Assessment helps Tough Kids answer these questions and prepares them for their receiving general education classroom.

General education classrooms vary. The classroom that the Tough Kid was referred from in the first place may be vastly different from the classroom to which she will be returning. On the CD included with this book is Reproducible 5-6, the Common Classroom Stimuli Assessment, adapted from Epps, Thomas, and Lane's (1985) generalization project from the Iowa Department of Public Instruction. This four-page form is completed through observing and interviewing the receiving teacher and carefully inspecting the new classroom. Details recorded on the form include the classroom's physical environment, teacher behavior, classroom behavior management system, classroom rules, and instructional

> THINK ABOUT IT
>
> " Tough Kids may have no idea what to expect when they enter a general education classroom. "

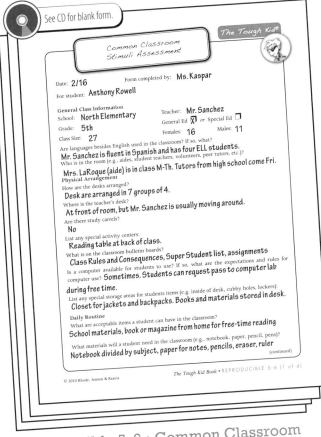

Reproducible 5-6 • Common Classroom
Stimuli Assessment (*4 pages*)

methods used in the classroom. In addition, photos, textbooks, sample assignments, and other materials may be collected.

Once the Common Classroom Stimuli Assessment information is gathered, the Tough Kid's current environment is made as similar to the receiving classroom's environment as possible. For example, curriculum materials and books from the receiving classroom can be used with the Tough Kid so he is familiar and successful with the academic materials. Similarly, the rules from the general education classroom can be implemented for him and the student treated with the same management and discipline strategies that are used by the receiving teacher. Even digital photographs of the receiving classroom can be taken and shared with the Tough Kid. In some

circumstances, it may not be possible to observe the classroom or interview the teachers because the teacher is new or has not been selected yet. In these situations, we suggest interviewing and observing in a similar general education teacher's classroom—from the same school and from the same grade level, if possible.

The main idea behind the Common Classroom Stimuli Assessment is to match the Tough Kid's environment as closely as possible to the general education environment to which he will be returning. This allows the Tough Kid to become familiar and more comfortable with the receiving classroom prior to the actual change.

Component 3: Meeting Individual Teacher's Expectations (Individualizing)

Everyone has his or her own expectations about other people's behavior and how they should behave socially. The difficulty with Tough Kids returning to general education is that they frequently have not been prepared to meet the expectations they will encounter there. Teachers have common as well as individual expectations for students' social behavior in their classrooms (Lane, Givner, & Pierson, 2004; Walker & Rankin, 1983). Common expectations include following directions, no talking out in class, attending to the teacher, staying in seat, and not engaging in disruptive behaviors (Nicholas, 1998). However, teachers also have expectations that are specific to them and to their classrooms. Some teachers may value students who work quietly, while others value students who actively participate in the classroom.

BOX 5-3

List of 30 Common Teacher *Expectations*

I. CLASSROOM BEHAVIOR

The student:

1. Listens quietly to directions
2. Follows oral directions accurately
3. Follows written directions accurately
4. Appears attentive during discussions
5. Is prepared with proper materials
6. Begins assignments promptly
7. Works quietly on assignments
8. Asks for help when needed, but not to excess
9. Turns in assignments on time
10. Follows classroom rules
11. Completes assigned tasks

II. BASIC INTERACTION SKILLS

The student:

12. Contributes appropriately to discussions
13. Responds to the teacher's praise and attention
14. Engages in conversations appropriately
15. Makes requests appropriately

III. GETTING-ALONG SKILLS

The student:

16. Participates in group activities
17. Follows rules on the playground
18. Follows rules in hallways and bathrooms
19. Is positive and friendly
20. Is cooperative
21. Gets the teacher's attention appropriately
22. Gets his or her peers' attention appropriately
23. Gets along with others on the playground

IV. COPING SKILLS

The student:

24. Expresses anger appropriately
25. Uses appropriate language (no swearing)
26. Enjoys competition in the classroom/on the playground
27. Resists peer pressure
28. Disagrees appropriately
29. Accepts "No" for an answer
30. Accepts criticism or consequences appropriately

Box 5-3 lists 30 of the most common behavior expectations that teachers have for students in their classrooms. When first placed in a new classroom, the Tough Kid must master and demonstrate the basic behaviors (e.g., following directions, listening to the teacher) that meet the new teacher's expectations. It is also important for the Tough Kid to demonstrate the individual behaviors that his particular teachers value. This needs to happen quickly when a Tough Kid is first placed because he is frequently on informal probation with his new teacher. The first three weeks of a Tough Kid's placement are usually critical.

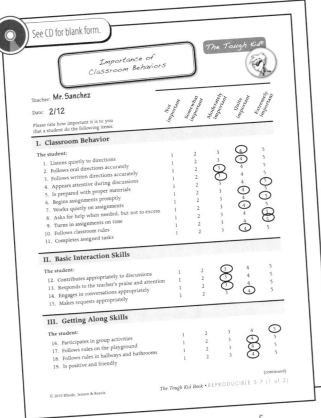

Reproducible 5-7 • Importance of
Classroom Behavior (*2 pages*)

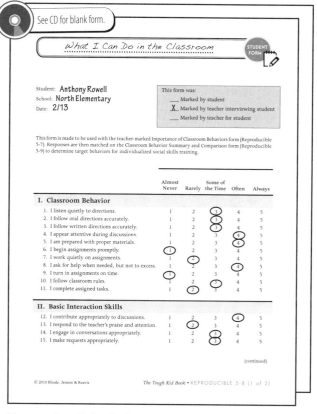

Reproducible 5-8 • What I Can Do
in the Classroom (*2 pages*)

Assessing a teacher's behavioral expectations is easy. Just ask. We have provided the Importance of Classroom Behaviors form (Reproducible 5-7) on the CD included with this book. It also appears in *The Tough Kid Tool Box*. Adapted from the *Social and Behavior Standards and Expectations Inventory* (Walker & Rankin, 1983), this form lists the 30 most common expectations of U.S. teachers in a checklist form. These are the expectations listed in Box 5-3. Reproducible 5-7 is also discussed in **Chapter 4**, with an example.

About three months before the Tough Kid is to be placed back in a general education classroom, ask the general education teacher to use this form to rate the most important behaviors she expects from her students. The form includes a

Likert-type rating scale to rate expectations from 1 (Not Important) to 5 (Extremely Important). Also ask the teacher to highlight the five behaviors she considers most important.

Once a teacher's rankings have been obtained, the Tough Kid and his current teacher can fill out a similar form (What I Can Do in the Classroom, Reproducible 5-8) to rate his current ability to perform the expected behaviors. A Tough Kid usually needs help in filling out the form and identifying his strengths and weaknesses. The Tough Kid and his teacher should address each item and answer honestly about whether the Tough Kid is capable of meeting each expectation. Each expectation is rated on a scale from 1 (Almost Never) to 5 (Always) to indicate the Tough Kid's ability to meet it.

See CD for blank form.

Classroom Behavior Summary and Comparison

The Tough Kid®

Student: **Anthony Rowell**
Date: **2/16**

General Education Teacher: **Mr. Sanchez**
Form Completed by: **Ms. Kaspar**

For each numbered expectation on the completed Importance of Classroom Behavior Plan (Reproducible 5-7), enter the ranking in the Teacher Rating column. For each numbered expectation on the completed What I Can Do in the Classroom form (Reproducible 5-8), enter the ranking in the corresponding Student Rating column. Subtract the number in the Student Rating column from the number in the Teacher Rating column to determine the Target Behavior score.

Expectation	Teacher Rating	− Student Rating	= Target Behavior Score
I. Classroom Skills			
1. Listens quietly to directions	4	3	1
2. Follows oral directions accurately	4	3	1
3. Follows written directions accurately	3	3	0
4. Appears attentive during discussions	3	4	−1
5. Is prepared with proper materials	5	4	1
6. Begins assignments promptly	4	1	3
7. Works quietly on assignments	5	2	3
8. Asks for help when needed, but not to excess	4	4	0
9. Turns in assignments on time	5	1	4
10. Follows classroom rules	5	3	2
11. Completes assigned tasks	4	2	2
II. Basic Interaction Skills			
12. Contributes appropriately to discussions	3	4	−1
13. Responds to the teacher's praise and attention	3	2	1
14. Engages in conversations appropriately	4	3	1
15. Makes requests appropriately	4	3	1

(continued)

© 2010 Rhode, Jenson & Reavis

The Tough Kid Book • REPRODUCIBLE 5-9 (1 of 2)

Reproducible 5-9 • Classroom Behavior Summary and Comparison (2 pages)

Enter the teacher's ratings and the Tough Kid's ratings on the Classroom Behavior Summary and Comparison Form (Reproducible 5-9 on the next page). Then for each expectation, subtract the Tough Kid's rating from the teacher's rating. Whenever there is a discrepancy of two or more points between the Tough Kid's rating and the receiving teacher's rating, there is a potential problem.

For example, if the receiving teacher rates item number 29 (Accepts "No" for an answer) as 5 and the Tough Kid and his current teacher rate his ability to meet that expectation as 3 (5 − 3 = 2), a problem exists. This rating difference indicates the Tough Kid has difficulty meeting an important expectation of his new teacher. The Tough Kid is going to need help.

TECHNIQUE TIP

The file Appendix_A.pdf provided on the CD contains everything you need to implement the Meeting Individual Teacher's Expectations Program: all of the reproducible forms, two versions of the skill cards, and detailed directions.

Note: Differences in the negative direction should not be considered problems. They indicate expectations that the student can meet but that the teacher does not value highly.

Also, check to see how the Tough Kid responded to the expectations that the general education teacher marked as those she believes are most important for success in her class. If the Tough Kid has difficulty meeting these expectations (rated them as below a 4), he will have difficulty in the new classroom. Consider teaching the Tough Kid the skills needed to meet these expectations.

Each of the 30 expectations listed in Box 5-3 has been broken down into three to five steps that can be taught as a mini-social skills program (see **Appendix A**). Before the Tough Kid returns to a general education classroom, he is taught the steps to the five most important behavioral expectations that were identified on the Classroom Behavior Summary and Comparison Form. The Tough Kid should be taught to define the skill, demonstrate the required steps to perform the skill, and know when the skill is needed (see Reproducible 5-10, Social Skills Lesson Plan, which is provided on the CD).

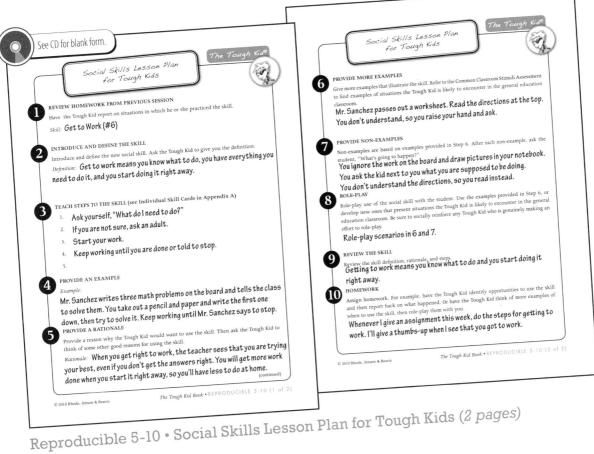

See CD for blank form.

Social Skills Lesson Plan for Tough Kids

The Tough Kid®

1 REVIEW HOMEWORK FROM PREVIOUS SESSION
Have the Tough Kid report on situations in which he or she practiced the skill.
Skill: Get to Work (#6)

2 INTRODUCE AND DEFINE THE SKILL
Introduce and define the new social skill. Ask the Tough Kid to give you the definition.
Definition: Get to work means you know what to do, you have everything you need to do it, and you start doing it right away.

3 TEACH STEPS TO THE SKILL (see Individual Skill Cards in Appendix A)
1. Ask yourself, "What do I need to do?"
2. If you are not sure, ask an adult.
3. Start your work.
4. Keep working until you are done or told to stop.
5.

4 PROVIDE AN EXAMPLE
Example:
Mr. Sanchez writes three math problems on the board and tells the class to solve them. You take out a pencil and paper and write the first one down, then try to solve it. Keep working until Mr. Sanchez says to stop.

5 PROVIDE A RATIONALE
Provide a reason why the Tough Kid would want to use the skill. Then ask the Tough Kid to think of some other good reasons for using the skill.
Rationale: When you get right to work, the teacher sees that you are trying your best, even if you don't get the answers right. You will get more work done when you start it right away, so you'll have less to do at home.
(continued)

© 2010 Rhode, Jenson & Reavis   *The Tough Kid Book* • REPRODUCIBLE 5-10 (1 of 2)

6 PROVIDE MORE EXAMPLES
Give more examples that illustrate the skill. Refer to the Common Classroom Stimuli Assessment to find examples of situations the Tough Kid is likely to encounter in the general education classroom.
Mr. Sanchez passes out a worksheet. Read the directions at the top. You don't understand, so you raise your hand and ask.

7 PROVIDE NON-EXAMPLES
Non-examples are based on examples provided in Step 6. After each non-example, ask the student, "What's going to happen?"
You ignore the work on the board and draw pictures in your notebook.
You ask the kid next to you what you are supposed to be doing.
You don't understand the directions, so you read instead.

8 ROLE-PLAY
Role-play use of the social skill with the student. Use the examples provided in Step 6, or develop new ones that present situations the Tough Kid is likely to encounter in the general education classroom. Be sure to socially reinforce any Tough Kid who is genuinely making an effort to role-play.
Role-play scenarios in 6 and 7.

9 REVIEW THE SKILL
Review the skill definition, rationale, and steps.
Getting to work means you know what to do and you start doing it right away.

10 HOMEWORK
Assign homework. For example, have the Tough Kid identify opportunities to use the skill and then report back on what happened. Or have the Tough Kid think of more examples of when to use the skill, then role-play them with you.
Whenever I give an assignment this week, do the steps for getting to work. I'll give a thumbs-up when I see that you got to work.

© 2010 Rhode, Jenson & Reavis   *The Tough Kid Book* • REPRODUCIBLE 5-10 (2 of 2)

Reproducible 5-10 • Social Skills Lesson Plan for Tough Kids *(2 pages)*

The teacher must also reward the student both with a tangible reinforcer and with social praise when he demonstrates the skill at the appropriate time. Simply teaching the skill once is not enough. The skill needs to be taught and practiced numerous times across the school day. Generalization strategies discussed in **Chapter 4** must also be incorporated.

Each of the 30 skills is accompanied by a cartoon icon of a student performing the skill. These icons will be used later in the program when the Tough Kid is taught to self-monitor his performance in his current special placement. They will also be used back in the general education classroom to prompt the student to use the skills. When incorporated into the student's self-monitoring form, the icons motivate and help the Tough Kid remember the steps through a cartoon-like picture. We will discuss self-monitoring forms in more detail later in this chapter.

Component 4:
Top 5 to Survive—The Teacher Pleaser Social Skills Program

Learning the new teacher's five most important behavioral expectations is not enough to ensure success in the general education classroom. The Tough Kid needs additional social skills, skills that are almost universally valued by teachers and are very helpful during the first few weeks the Tough Kid is back in the general education classroom. At a time when the receiving general education teacher may be expecting difficulties from the Tough Kid, our goal for him is to give the teacher unexpected Teacher Pleasers instead.

The Teacher Pleaser Social Skills Program is designed to teach the Tough Kid five universally valued social skills that put him in a favorable light with his new teacher. We call the skills the "Top 5 to Survive" because they are the most potent social skills for making an initial good impression on most teachers. These five Teacher Pleasers are skills listed in Box 5-4 on the next page. Some of these skills may seem to be common behaviors that simply involve helpfulness and common courtesy. However, it is a mistake to assume Tough Kids have these skills in their repertoires and know when to use them.

There sometimes can be overlap between the Teacher Pleasers and the individualized skills taught to the Tough Kid in Component 3. When this happens, simply teach the overlapping skill as part of the Teacher Pleaser Social Skills Program.

The Teacher Pleaser Social Skills Program is included in **Appendix B**. It features five social skills lessons designed to be taught to small groups of Tough Kids in the special education setting. We suggest the group meet three times per week. Also provide opportunities to practice the skills outside the group setting. The Tough Kid should master all lessons before returning to the general education classroom.

In each of the five social skills lessons, the skill is introduced and defined. Then the rules or steps to the skill are taught. Generally, each skill has three to four simple steps. An example and non-example of each of the skills is presented. Then the Tough Kid is given a rationale as to why it is important to know and use the skill, and finally, a role-play of the skill is conducted. Each lesson also includes a variant behavior (i.e., a similar but different form of the behavior). For example, for Not Interrupting there is a classroom variant of Not Talking Out. Similarly, for Making a Request the variant is Asking for Help.

After the skills have been taught and re-taught, they must be consistently rewarded throughout the day. To pull Tough Kids out for a group, train

---

BOX 5-4

"Top 5 to Survive": _Teacher Pleaser_ Skills and Variants

TEACHER PLEASER	SKILL VARIANT
Taking "No" for an Answer	Not Arguing
Following Directions	"Sure I Will" Program
Not Interrupting	Not Talking Out in Class
Making a Request	Asking for Help
Saying "Thank You"	Giving the Teacher a Compliment

Detailed lesson plans for teaching these Top 5 social skills appear in Appendix B.

them, and then hope that they will demonstrate the Teacher Pleaser skill will not be effective. The skill must be probed (e.g., ask the Tough Kid the steps to the skill), demonstrated, and rewarded (both tangibly and socially). See **Chapter 4** for additional generalization strategies to increase the likelihood that taught skills stick.

Teacher Pleaser skills are designed to dispel any preconceived negative expectations the general education teacher may have about the newly re-turned Tough Kid. It is hard for a teacher to dislike a student who smiles at her, thanks her, and asks for help appropriately. One lesson even teaches the sensitive skill of how to give a teacher a genuine compliment. The idea behind the Teacher Pleasers Social Skills Program is to make a good first impres-sion as well as recruit natural reinforcement from the general education teacher. This reinforcement will help the Tough Kid maintain appropriate so-cial behavior in the new setting.

In our experience, some receiving general edu-cation teachers think that teaching these types of skills to Tough Kids is disingenuous. They believe students should demonstrate the skills without specifically being taught or prompted to use them. However, Tough Kids usually have not learned these skills at home and certainly have not been successful in exhibiting them in school. We think it is important to give the Tough Kid every possible tool to succeed in the general classroom.

Component 5: Lucky Charms

As we mentioned earlier, in this book Lucky Charms is not a breakfast cereal but a general-ization technique. The Lucky Charms technique works on the principle of familiarity with a safe and successful environment. Part of the suc-cessful environment is imported back to the new unfamiliar environment. This helps the Tough Kid associate her new environment with safety and success. For example, when traveling have you ever taken something familiar from home, such as a clock or a picture of your family, and put it by your bedside in an unfamiliar hotel room? In essence, you are importing something familiar from your home environment into your unfamiliar environment. Doing so makes you feel a little more comfortable. Your family picture or the clock is your Lucky Charm.

Ayllon, Kulman, and Warzak (1983) coined the term *Lucky Charm* and used it with resource spe-cial education students returning to a regular classroom. This strategy was used to improve their academic performance in reading and math. In the study, the resource students were told to bring something from home, such as a picture, toy, or trinket, to school. The students then worked with their Lucky Charms on their desks. When they were ready to return to the general education classroom, they were allowed to put their objects on their desks. The students were told their Lucky Charms would help remind them to work when they were back in the general education classroom. This is a simple technique with dramatic results. The resource students' overall math productivity increased from 41% (without the Lucky Charms) to 94% with them. Similarly, reading performance increased from 46% to 94%. Allyon et al. (1983) concluded that the transfer of academic skills in the general education classroom was enhanced by the Lucky Charms because they had been associated with reinforcement and success in the resource classroom.

Jenson et al. (1991) used the Lucky Charms technique to help Tough Kids as they returned from a specialized school for students with emotional disturbances into general education environments. Lucky Charms in the form of pictures of their special education teachers were placed on the inside page of the notebooks they took back to their new general education placements. Junior high students used stickers from radio stations or sports stores as Lucky Charms on their notebooks (Figure 5-1). They were told that the pictures of their teachers or the stickers were in their notebooks to help remind them to work and behave appropriately.

Again, the results were dramatic. After one year, 16 Tough Kids were returned to their general education settings. Their on-task rates were the same as those of their nondisabled peers (approximately 80% on task), and their behavior was rated by the general education teachers as successful (3.5 on a 5-point success scale). Only one Tough Kid required a change of his original generalization placement.

Allowing Tough Kids to import part of their successful environment back into a new and unfamiliar general education setting can be a powerful generalization technique.

Component 6: Self-Management Skills

In the last two decades, research has focused on the use of various forms of self-management to facilitate and maintain gains made in special placements. Gains made in special placements

Figure 5-1 • Examples of Lucky Charms

regulated by self-management procedures have been reported to be more resistant to extinction than those established by teacher-controlled procedures alone (Briesch & Chafouleas, 2009; Rhode, Morgan, & Young, 1983).

Because we have covered self-management already in **Chapter 4**, we will not cover the same information here. However, we will discuss self-management information that is specifically for use with a comprehensive level system. In using self-management with a level system, students' appropriate classroom behavior must first be gradually increased (shaped) to acceptable levels. Accomplishing this will involve the use of a token economy (point system) that we will describe later. A successful outcome in the special placement is prerequisite for using the self-monitoring procedures in students' subsequent placements in general education settings. Thus, the first levels in a classroom system serve to bring Tough Kids under basic instructional control. After this has been accomplished and as they progress through the level system, they are ready to be taught increasingly complex academic and behavioral skills. As their behavior becomes more and more stable under the teacher's external control, they reach a point of readiness to take on increasing responsibility for their own behavior. This is the point at which self-management training begins.

In a five-level system, self-monitoring training normally begins at level 3 (the Green level in our system). By the time a Tough Kid has earned her way off level 5 (Purple), it is expected that she no longer needs to rely on a classroom point system controlled by the teacher. Self-monitoring within a level system is instituted through the use of the same matching procedure described in **Chapter 4**. In this case, the student is initially taught to evaluate her own classroom behavior using the

> **THINK ABOUT IT**
> *The first levels in a classroom system serve to bring Tough Kids under basic instructional control.*

same system her teacher has been using. The student carries her own self-monitoring card, which is a smaller version of the teacher's record-keeping sheet for points and timeouts. See the example on p. 206.

To begin with, the teacher and Tough Kid compare ratings at the end of each work or activity period for which the student has previously been earning points. As the student becomes more and more accurate, point matches are required less frequently. The student continues to award her own ratings for each work or activity period. Eventually, by the time a student has earned her way through the final level, the primary responsibility for monitoring her behavior rests with the student herself.

PUTTING IT ALL TOGETHER: THE TOUGH KID GENERALIZATION MODEL

The question that has to be asked is, "Is it worth going through all these generalization steps when placing a Tough Kid back in general education environment?" The answer is definitely "Yes!" for a number of reasons. First, it costs thousands of dollars to place Tough Kids in specialized settings for treatment and education. To rely on a "train and hope" method of placement puts all this investment at risk. Second, the

Tough Kid is likely to fail if placed without preparation and follow-up. If the Tough Kid fails, he will likely be placed in another program, be put on a home-school placement, or worse, just drop out of school. A little generalization insurance buys a lot of protection for your investment and the Tough Kid's success.

The Tough Kid Generalization Model is a multistep model that uses all of the techniques described earlier in this chapter. It is a systematic model for preparation and follow-up, and it requires some investment.

The first investment is a person who is familiar with the generalization model and is assigned to track and perform a six-week follow-up with the Tough Kid. For example, generalization visits to the Tough Kid's placement should take place two to three times in the first two weeks (the most dangerous time for placement failure). It helps when one or two of these visits in the first two weeks are scheduled and at least one visit occurs randomly (a "pop in" visit). After the first two weeks, the visits can be faded to once per week for the next four weeks. During this period, it is important to call or e-mail the general education teacher at least once a week. After the six-week follow-up period, periodic phone calls and e-mails are useful to answer questions and head off problems.

A second investment is a notebook that the Tough Kid takes with him back to the general education classroom. The notebook is used like a generalization tool and will hold the Tough Kid's Lucky Charm and self-management materials.

The steps to the Tough Kid Generalization Model are as follows.

STEP 1 **Establish a program level system.** A level system is an essential element of the specialized program for the Tough Kid. The Tough Kid should be placed in the level system at the beginning of his special placement. This level system can be similar to the five-step level system described earlier in this chapter, or it can be a simpler version such as a three-step level system. The level system should be designed as a shaping and fading system that teaches social skills, rewards academic performance, teaches self-monitoring skills, and uses self-evaluation techniques. As the Tough Kid progresses through the level system, he should be acquiring more and more appropriate behaviors, social skills, and academic skills.

The level system's initial steps should be designed simply to manage disruptive behavioral excesses such as noncompliance, aggression, and arguing. The middle section of the level system should teach and reward social and academic skills in order to remedy deficits in these areas. The later steps should be used to teach the Tough Kid how to self-monitor his own behavior and match it to an adult's evaluation. The last step is really not a step at all. In essence, the Tough Kid is off the level system and its privileges but is still self-monitoring and self-evaluating. At this top level, the Tough Kid has free access to all program privileges. Practice in self-monitoring and

THINK ABOUT IT

A level system is an essential element of the specialized program for the Tough Kid.

self-evaluation is essential because these are the skills the Tough Kid will use when he is on his own in the new classroom. It's also helpful at this level for the Tough Kids to make practice visits to their new classrooms.

The level system can be used with a token or point system, as described earlier in this chapter. This point system should lead to more and more privileges as the Tough Kid progresses through the level system. The success of earning points for appropriate behavior, demonstrating social skills, and performing academically is a good source of program progress data. Missed or lost points are also good sources of data to show where the Tough Kid is having problems and needs to improve. It is important that when a Tough Kid earns a point, it is paired with descriptive social praise from the program staff—for example, "Thanks for following my directions. It's a big help to me." Similarly, when points are lost, the loss is always accompanied by a reason—"I'm sorry, that's a missed point for being out of your seat without permission." If a Tough Kid consistently loses points for a particular behavior, it may be necessary to conduct an ABC Functional Behavior Assessment (as described in **Chapter 1**) to assess its antecedents and motivational consequences.

It is important for the Tough Kid to receive consistent feedback about his progress in the program and on the level system. Post the different

levels and their focus behaviors on the classroom wall so they are easily visible. If possible, write students' names above their step on the level system. Feedback can also come from the Tough Kids' point cards. Different cards correspond to the different steps in the level system, as described earlier in this chapter. At least once a week, each Tough Kid should meet individually with a staff member to receive feedback about his progress in the program and level system. Again, the point cards and points earned for the week can be reviewed, highlighting progress and areas that need more effort. During this time, the Tough Kid can exchange earned points for reinforcers from the classroom store. **Chapter 2** lists several reinforcers that can be used with Tough Kids.

Level systems should be the backbone of a good Tough Kid program, but problems can occur. The most common problem with level systems occurs when they are used as a response cost system, which can destroy the Tough Kid's motivation. As mentioned earlier in this chapter, level drops should occur only after a week's worth of data is reviewed. If a Tough Kid is dropped a level for an impulsive and egregious behavior, he should have some method or recourse to regain that level. To lose a whole level for one foolish behavior is a motivation killer. Level drops should be the result of several behaviors and should be decided on after the data has been reviewed.

Verbal threats from staff to "drop" a Tough Kid a level for a behavior are always counterproductive and ineffective. Tough Kids rapidly become immune to these threats, resulting in little or no effect on their behavior. Frequent threats can also quickly destroy a program's ratio of positive to negative interactions. Earlier in this book we recommended a ratio of at least 4 to 1 positives to negatives in a program. Threats quickly tilt this ratio to the negative side.

Another problem can occur when a Tough Kid gets stuck on a level and does not make reasonable progress. If a Tough Kid spends more than two or three weeks on a level, his progress should be reviewed. Sometimes behaviors required on a particular level need to be broken down into smaller steps and taught individually. For example, the Tough Kid may need more instruction and practice with a particular social skill. Or the Tough Kid may not have an essential skill that is needed to accomplish his academic work. Again, it may be necessary to conduct an ABC Functional Behavior Assessment on problematic behaviors or a curriculum-based academic probe (see **Chapter 1**).

> THINK ABOUT IT
>
> **THINK**
>
> " *Sometimes behaviors required on a level need to be broken down into smaller steps and taught individually.* "

Another level system problem is when the Tough Kid has made excellent progress through the lower and middle steps of the level system but has continuous problems on the upper levels. This is generally an indication that the Tough Kid does not want to return to the general education classroom because he fears he will fail. This can be especially true if the Tough Kid has been successful in a positive special program but has had a history of failures in the general education environment. There are several solutions to this problem.

First, familiarize the Tough Kid with the expectations of the receiving teacher and common stimuli in the classroom and school (to be discussed next).

Second, emphasize to the Tough Kid that his progress will be monitored and staff will help him succeed in the general classroom.

Third, if possible, have the Tough Kid spend more and more time in the general education environment using the self-management and self-evaluation skills.

Fourth, if the Tough Kid repeatedly fails at the upper levels, conduct an ABC Functional Behavior Assessment to make sure he is capable of meeting these behavioral requirements.

Finally, if the Tough Kid still has problems, let him know that you believe he is engineering these failures on purpose and that he will still be returning to the general education environment on a specific date in spite of these problems.

STEP 2 **Assess the common classroom stimuli.** As we mentioned earlier in this chapter, most people are uneasy about the unknown. This can be especially true of Tough Kids who have been out of the general education environment for a long time. The assessing common classroom stimuli approach is designed to alleviate some of this uneasiness by familiarizing a Tough Kid with what to expect in his new classroom and what it will look like.

The Common Classroom Stimuli Assessment form (Reproducible 5-6, p. 191) is generally completed when the follow-up staff member visits the new classroom. The form is easily filled out by observing the classroom and asking the new teacher a few questions:

- How is the classroom configured (i.e., type and arrangement of desks and where the teacher's desk is located)?
- What classroom materials are needed (e.g., notebook, textbooks, pencils)?
- What are the classroom rules?
- How will the student be graded, and how are citizenship behaviors rated?

Once this information is gathered, the Tough Kid's current classroom can be designed to include some of these common stimuli. For example, the Tough Kid can use some of the same academic materials and textbooks that he will find in his new class. The rules from the new classroom can be introduced and expectations for following these rules can be combined with the Teacher Pleaser Social Skills Program described in Step 3.

The Tough Kid's current classroom environment does not have to mimic the new classroom perfectly. But including some elements found in the new classroom should certainly help the Tough Kid adjust and feel at ease in his new environment.

STEP 3 **Teach the Teacher Pleaser Social Skills along with skills needed to meet the expectations of the general education teacher.** Social skills instruction should start at least three months prior to the return of the Tough Kid to the general education classroom. The Teacher Pleaser Program is actually a survival social skills program designed to overcome and dispel the prejudices and pre-judgments educators make about the Tough Kid. The program teaches five universally

valued social skills, such as saying "thank you," following directions, asking for help, and giving a teacher a compliment. The five skills are listed in Box 5-4 on p. 196, and lessons for teaching them appear in Appendix B.

The Tough Kid Teacher Pleaser Social Skills Program includes the steps to the skill, rules for deciding when to use the skill, a rationale why the skill should be used, examples and non-examples of the skill, role-play scenarios, a review, and a homework assignment. The Teacher Pleaser Social Skills Program can be used in conjunction with other social skills programs that a teacher might be using.

The Teacher Pleaser Program should be taught in a group format with other students at least three times per week. It is important that the skills taught in this program extend beyond the social teaching group to help ensure generalization. Probe the skills across the day —staff should ask the Tough Kid to explain the steps to the skill, its rationale for use, and when they should use the skill. Also have the Tough Kid demonstrate the skill.

For example, a probe from a staff during recess might be "Rocky, tell me how to give a compliment and why it is important." After the explanation from Rocky, the staff can solicit a compliment: "Great! Now think of a good compliment and give it to me." It is also important that the Tough Kid be socially and tangibly rewarded (points) for this probe. For a homework assignment, the Tough Kid can be asked to give at least three compliments that day to staff and other students and self-record the compliments. After mastering all five Teacher Pleaser skills, the Tough Kid is better prepared to survive in the general education environment.

We also recommend targeting the individual expectations of the Tough Kid's new general education teacher with the Meeting Individual Teacher's Expectations Program. At least three months prior to the Tough Kid's return to general education, a staff member interviews the new teacher and asks him to rate the 30 top behavioral expectations on the Importance of Classroom Behaviors form (Reproducible 5-7, p. 193). The new teacher should also highlight his five top behavioral expectations.

Next, the Tough Kid and his teacher fill out the student version of the form (Reproducible 5-8, What I Can Do in the Classroom, p. 193). Use the Classroom Behavior Summary and Comparison form (Reproducible 5-9, p. 194) to compare the teacher's and the Tough Kid's ratings. A 2-point or more difference between the new teacher's rating and the Tough Kid's rating on any particular expectation indicates a potential problem.

To remedy these problems, you will present the Tough Kid with individualized social skills lessons. Appendix A breaks each of the 30 expectations from the Importance of Classroom Behaviors form into the three to five steps needed to meet the expectation. A cartoon icon is associated with each expectation. The icons can be used to facilitate self-monitoring by the Tough Kid across the day when he is placed in his new classroom.

Teach one expectation at a time. You might work with the Tough Kid one-on-one, or conduct the specific training in a group in conjunction with the Teacher Pleaser Social Skills Program described above. The Tough Kid should also self-monitor the newly taught expectation across the day. This expectation and icon can be printed on a piece of paper for self-monitoring and rating purposes. Again, across the day the staff can probe the Tough Kid on the expectations and have him rate his ability to meet them. For example, the Tough Kid can self-monitor his on-task behavior when he is working independently at his desk. At the end of the day, a staff member can review the self-monitoring data and give the Tough Kid feedback about how well he has done.

With this training approach, the Tough Kid should start with one of the teacher's Top 5 expectations. After he has successfully met this expectation (generally after 1 to 3 days of training), another one can be added. The ability to self-monitor expectations and accurately rate behavior is an essential component of success in his new placement. Our experience has shown that some of the most difficult expectations for Tough Kids to meet are:

- Following directions
- Accepting "No" for an answer
- Following classroom rules
- Accepting criticism
- Paying attention

 **Follow up when the Tough Kid is back in the new classroom.** When the Tough Kid returns to the general education environment, he should be prepared to meet its challenges thanks to completing the special program's level system, the Teacher Pleaser Social Skills Program, and the Meeting Individual Teacher's Expectations program. He should also have a good idea about his new classroom and school through the Common Classroom Stimuli Assessment. But he also needs to return with the knowledge that a staff member will follow through and work with him in his new environment. He needs one more thing—a notebook.

Give the notebook to the Tough Kid as a generalization tool approximately three months before he returns to general education. In it will be his choice of a Lucky Charm, such as a photo of his teacher and staff, a picture of the classroom, or a sticker from a radio station or sports shop. The Lucky Charm is generally taped or pasted on the inside cover of the notebook so when the Tough Kid opens it, he sees the Lucky Charm. The notebook will also contain the classroom materials necessary for him to enter the classroom and be successful. It will contain the five behavioral expectations that his new teacher wants and the steps to meet these expectations. The notebook will also contain the self-monitoring materials the Tough Kid will use to evaluate his

behavior. An example of a Self-Monitoring Form (Reproducible 5-11A) is shown on the next page. This sample shows how a reminder of the Lucky Charm and the social skill steps can be incorporated on the Self-Monitoring Form for easy reference. The CD contains copies of Reproducible 5-11A and 5-11B, which is a version of the form for the teacher to use in rating the Tough Kid's performance.

On this form, the Tough Kid self-monitors his own behavior and the progress he is making in meeting the top 5 expectations of his general education teacher. These will generally be the individualized expectations identified and taught during his special education placement. At the end of the day, the Tough Kid rates his performance on the five expectations. If he thinks he has done well with a particular expectation, he draws a diagonal line in its box. If he has not done well, he writes the word *No* in the box. He takes the form to his teacher, who reviews the self-monitoring form and also rates his performance. If she agrees that he has done well on an expectation, she draws an opposite diagonal line in the box to create an X for that expectation for the day. If

Reproducible 5-11A • Self-Monitoring Form

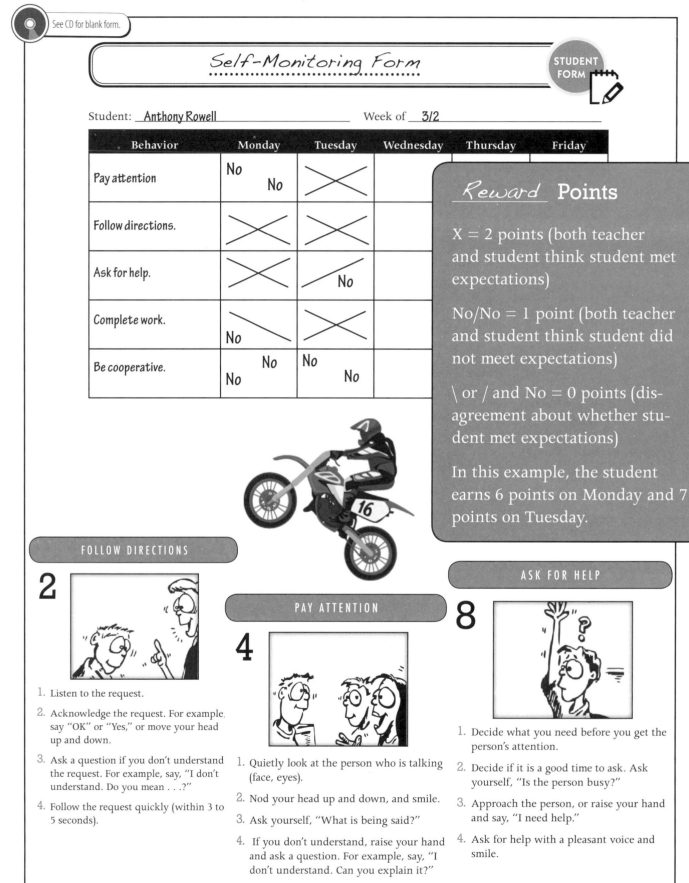

See CD for blank form.

Self-Monitoring Form

STUDENT FORM

Student: __Anthony Rowell__   Week of __3/2__

Behavior	Monday	Tuesday	Wednesday	Thursday	Friday
Pay attention	No No	✕			
Follow directions.	✕	✕			
Ask for help.	✕	No			
Complete work.	✕ No	✕			
Be cooperative.	No No	No No			

Reward Points

X = 2 points (both teacher and student think student met expectations)

No/No = 1 point (both teacher and student think student did not meet expectations)

\ or / and No = 0 points (disagreement about whether student met expectations)

In this example, the student earns 6 points on Monday and 7 points on Tuesday.

FOLLOW DIRECTIONS

2

1. Listen to the request.
2. Acknowledge the request. For example, say "OK" or "Yes," or move your head up and down.
3. Ask a question if you don't understand the request. For example, say, "I don't understand. Do you mean . . .?"
4. Follow the request quickly (within 3 to 5 seconds).

PAY ATTENTION

4

1. Quietly look at the person who is talking (face, eyes).
2. Nod your head up and down, and smile.
3. Ask yourself, "What is being said?"
4. If you don't understand, raise your hand and ask a question. For example, say, "I don't understand. Can you explain it?"

ASK FOR HELP

8

1. Decide what you need before you get the person's attention.
2. Decide if it is a good time to ask. Ask yourself, "Is the person busy?"
3. Approach the person, or raise your hand and say, "I need help."
4. Ask for help with a pleasant voice and smile.

she disagrees, she writes the word *No* in the box. The goal of this self-monitoring intervention is to reward both appropriate behavior and a match (rating agreements) with the teacher.

For example, if the box has two diagonal lines (an X), it is worth two points (e.g. both Tough Kid and teacher agree he has done well with that expectation that day). If the box has two *Nos* in it, it is worth one point (e.g., both Tough Kid and teacher agree he has done poorly with that expectation that day). If the box contains a diagonal line and a *No*, it is worth zero points (the Tough Kid and teacher disagree because one believes he met the expectation and one thinks he did poorly). If the Tough Kid is working on five teacher expectations, he can earn a maximum total of 50 points in one week.

The teacher keeps the Self-Monitoring Form for the follow-up staff member's visit. On that visit, the staff member should first check in with the teacher and ask about the Tough Kid's progress. The staff member then meets individually with the Tough Kid and goes over the Self-Monitoring forms and teacher's evaluation. It is important that this meeting be encouraging for the Tough Kid, even if he has had some problems. The emphasis should be on success. There should also be a reinforcement contract between the follow-up staff member and the Tough Kid for his performance and matching the new teacher's ratings. The payoff for appropriate behaviors and matches (agreements) with the teacher can take a variety of forms. A Mystery Motivator or a Grab Bag of reinforcers can be used. For example, if the Tough Kid has earned 25 points in the first week of follow-up, he is asked to reach into the Grab Bag and randomly select a reinforcer. Box 5-5 lists reinforcers we have used for rewarding Tough Kids for appropriate progress.

BOX 5-5

List of *Reinforcers* (Elementary)

- Fluorescent shoe laces
- Fluorescent highlighter pens
- Fluorescent friendship bracelets
- Key chains
- Erasers, pencil toppers
- "Junk" candy, pop rocks, gum, bubble gum, tape gum, sourballs
- Costume jewelry
- Small note pads
- Matchbox-type cars
- Micro-Machine-like vehicles
- Jumbo pencils
- Magnets
- Stickers
- Finger skateboards
- Super balls
- Rings
- Scented stickers
- Scented markers
- Office supples—pens, pencils, mini staplers, sticky notes
- Tape
- Mechanical pencils (disposable)
- Soda pop
- Twix candy bars
- Small bags of peanuts
- Pixie Stix
- Folders, binders
- Glitter
- Decorative and seasonal pins

The second week, the requirement to earn the reinforcer can be increased to 30 points, and over the next four weeks it can be slowly increased to a maximum of 40 points. Research has shown Tough Kids to be amazingly accurate (90% on average) in evaluating and meeting a new teacher's expectations (Jenson et al., 1991). They know when they have done well and when they have done poorly. The follow-up visits should be slowly faded out over a six-week period of time.

THE PLACEMENT CRISIS

A placement crisis for the Tough Kid will occasionally occur. What we mean by placement crisis is that the new school wants the Tough Kid to be removed or the placement changed because of problem behaviors. It is best to be prepared for this crisis. The overall guiding rule during a placement crisis is that the Tough Kid remains in the school unless he is a danger to himself or others. Once he is removed or sent home, it is much more difficult to resolve the crisis and get him back into school.

Placement crises for Tough Kids are generally precipitated by a common set of inappropriate behaviors. These inappropriate behaviors include being defiant to an adult, severe noncompliance, aggression toward an adult or peer, destruction of property, and belligerent or foul language. These inappropriate behaviors generally occur rapidly and unexpectedly, and the school generally has no contingency plan to manage them. When a crisis occurs, it is best to use an ABC Functional Behavior Assessment model (see **Chapter 1**) and ask the following questions.

ANTECEDENTS

- Who was the target of the inappropriate behavior?
- Where did the problem behavior occur?
- What adults or peers were present?
- What time or in what class period did this occur?
- Were there any other precipitating events that might have set off this behavior?

BEHAVIORS

- What specifically was the problem behavior or behavior(s)?
- Was the problem behavior a result of not learning a critical social skill?
- Was the problem behavior a result of not learning a critical teacher expectation?
- Was the Tough Kid a danger to himself or others?

CONSEQUENCES

- Was this behavior motivated by frustration or anger?
- Was the behavior rewarded by peer attention?
- Was this behavior an attempt to extort something from another student?
- Was this behavior an escape behavior (e.g., to avoid academics or a social situation)?

Once the ABC Functional Behavior Assessment data has been collected, a reasonable plan of action can be designed. It is best to get a commitment from the school administrator, teacher, or both to keep the Tough Kid in school while the problem is solved. The Tough Kid might have to be removed from the classroom and placed in some other supervised setting in the school (e.g., another teacher's classroom, the school psychologist's or counselor's office, principal's office, in-school suspension room) while the crisis is resolved.

One big advantage in defusing a crisis situation is time—that is, time before demands or decisions are made on the Tough Kid following the crisis. The longer the time interval, the more likely everyone will settle down and be able to work on the problem. It has been demonstrated that a Tough Kid is more compliant when a crisis is followed immediately by a 5- to 10-minute period during which he is simply supervised and nothing happens (Colvin, 2009). The worst outcomes occur when strident demands are made in the middle of a crisis episode with a Tough Kid. Everyone is upset (including the adults) and adrenaline is flowing. To force the situation will make it worse. To buy a little time will make it easier. During this time, the Tough Kid can wait in the supervised environment while the follow-up staff collects the ABC Functional Behavior Assessment information.

After the ABC information is collected, several solutions can be considered. More supervision may be needed if the behavior occurred when no adults were present. The Check-in/Check-out Program is a good solution (see **Chapter 3**, pp. 110–111). If peers were present and their attention appears to have motivated the Tough Kid, he needs to be separated from these peers. If the behavior occurred at a specific time or during a particular academic time and the Tough Kid appeared frustrated and noncompliant, he might be trying to escape this situation. It is not uncommon for a Tough Kid to become disruptive because he cannot meet the academic requirements of the classroom. Academic accommodations may have to be provided. If a specific adult is present when the problem behavior occurs, providing additional support or training with this adult might be necessary. For example, the adult may be using ineffective requests to try and get the Tough Kid to comply. That adult may need training on how to give Precision Requests. The Administrative Intervention (see **Chapter 4**) is also a very useful technique to use if the Tough Kid has had a blow-up with a particular adult, such as a teacher. After a cooling-down period where the Tough Kid is separated from the adult, he can be shaped into using his social skills and even giving an apology. Then he can ask to be readmitted to the classroom. The Administrative Intervention with social skills that leads to an apology has been shown to be a very effective intervention (see **Chapter 4**).

When the Tough Kid appears to be a danger to himself or to others, it should be treated as a serious crisis.

Many times Tough Kids are suspended for a Safe School Violation such as drug abuse, weapons, or severe aggression. Sometimes these incidents are serious, but sometimes the consequences can be absurd because the school has a zero-tolerance policy. For an example, two Tough Kids in Texas decided impulsively to swap their stimulant medications before class. They were caught and expelled for 180 school days because the school had a Zero-Tolerance Drug Abuse Policy and claimed they were dealing drugs. Though swapping medications is an impulsive, foolish

> THINK ABOUT IT
>
> **THINK** " The worst outcomes occur when strident demands are made in the middle of a crisis episode. "

behavior, expelling the Tough Kids for 180 days is even more foolish. It is important to know the federal safeguards both for the school and the Tough Kid in these situations.

Federal legislation—IDEA 1997 (20 U.S.C. §1412(a)(1)(A); 34 *CFR* 300.519-300.529)—provides several safeguards for any student with a disability (that is, a student who has been evaluated, qualifies, and has an Individual Education Plan [IEP]). For example, students with disabilities can be suspended for no more than ten days. After ten days of suspension, the student can be placed in an alternative placement (not his home) for 45 days for a Safe Schools Violation. During this time, a Functional Behavior Assessment must be conducted and a Behavior Intervention Plan (BIP) implemented if the problem behavior was a manifestation of his disability. Generally a manifestation determination is made on a number of variables, including whether the student could control his behavior or understand the consequences of his behavior. Many Tough Kids are impulsive, have trouble controlling their behavior, and do not understand the seriousness of the consequences. For example, the two Tough Kids who impulsively swapped their stimulant medications did not understand that they would be expelled for 180 school days. In this example, impulsively swapping medication was probably a manifestation of their disabilities.

After the 45-day period in an alternative setting, the student with a disability can return to his neighborhood school, where a Behavior Intervention Plan is implemented. The BIP should be based on the Functional Behavior Assessment that was conducted. In addition, ongoing data should be collected to ensure the BIP's success.

TECHNIQUE TIP

If the Tough Kid does not qualify for a special education disability and have an Individual Education Plan (IEP), he does not have the protections provided under federal law to students with disabilities.

Keeping Tough Kids in school is important. When they are suspended for long periods of time, they will be left unsupervised at home or on the streets. This only makes the situation worse for the educational community, the Tough Kid, and his family.

In a nutshell

Tough Kids often have bad reputations. Their behaviors such as aggression, noncompliance, and disruption have very negative effects on the adults and peers around them. Because of this, educators frequently want Tough Kids out of their schools. As a result, Tough Kids may end up in special placements and treatment programs. Good programs can often make significant positive differences in Tough Kids, both academically and socially. However, these special programs do not permanently "fix" Tough Kids. They can help change behaviors in positive ways and teach new skills. Once a Tough Kid is sent back to a general education environment, these behaviors have to be consistently managed or the gains will be lost. Too often, educators use the "train and hope" method of returning Tough Kids to general education settings. They train and change their behavior in a special program and then hope these new behaviors continue in general education. Unless specific generalization strategies are an integral part of the special placement program and the receiving general education classroom, they will not.

Successful placements back into the general classroom are based on careful planning, preparation, and follow-up. The Tough Kid Generalization Model treats the placement of Tough Kids back into their neighborhood schools as a systematic generalization process. By systematic generalization we mean the extension of newly trained or learned behaviors to new environments in which these behaviors have not been trained or learned (Wahler, Berland, & Coe, 1979). The newly trained or learned behaviors occur in the special program, while the new environment is the new general education placement. This type of generalization requires preparation of the Tough Kid before re-entering general education and self-management with follow-up once he gets there.

The preparation methods we have suggested include several components. We recommend a positive classroom level system to shape new behaviors and teach self-management skills. To prepare the Tough Kid for the general education environment, assess the common classroom stimuli in the new placement and familiarize the Tough Kid with those stimuli. We also suggest using the Teacher Pleaser Social Skills Program to teach the Tough Kid the five social skills most valued by teachers. In addition, it is helpful to assess and teach the five most important skills the Tough Kid will need to meet the individual expectations of the new general education teacher. To further link the special placement with the general education setting, we recommend letting

(Continued)

In a nutshell *(Continued)*

Tough Kids select Lucky Charms to carry back to their general education classrooms to remind them of the new behaviors they have learned. Once the Tough Kid is placed back in the general education setting, the model emphasizes self-monitoring to determine how well the Tough Kid is meeting the new teacher's expectations. The model includes a six-week follow-up period with visits from the program staff. During these visits, the Tough Kid's progress is reviewed and his appropriate behavior reinforced. Slowly the visits are faded out. With planned generalization, the Tough Kid has an excellent chance of succeeding in his new school placement.

References

Ayllon, T., Kuhlman, C., & Warzak, W. J. (1983). Programming resource room generalization using lucky charms. *Child and Family Therapy, 4,* 61–67.

Briesch, A. M. & Chafouleas, S. M. (2009). Defining behavioral self-management: A review and analysis of the literature. 1988-2008. *School Psychology Quarterly, 24,* 106–108.

Colvin, G. (2009). *Managing the cycle of acting-out behavior in the classroom.* Eugene, OR: Pacific Northwest Publishing.

Crone, D. A., Horner, R. H. & Hawken, L. S. (2004). *Responding to problem behavior in schools: The behavior education program.* New York: Guilford Press.

Epps, S., Thomas, B. J., & Lane, M. P. (1985). *Procedures for incorporating generalization and maintenance programming into interventions for special education students.* Des Moines, IA: Iowa Department of Education.

Jenson, W. R., Christopolus, K., Zimmerman, M., Nicholas, P., Reavis, H. K., & Rhode, G. (1991). *A much-needed link with regular education: The generalization of behaviorally disordered students.* Eugene, OR: University of Oregon, College of Education.

Lane, K. L., Givner, C. C., & Pierson, M. R. (2004). Teacher expectations of student behavior: Social skills necessary for success in elementary school classrooms. *Journal of Special Education, 38,* 104–110.

Maughan, D. R., Christiansen, E., Jenson, W. R., Olympia, D., & Clark, E. (2005). Behavioral parent training as a treatment for externalizing behaviors and disruptive behavior disorders: A meta-analysis. *School Psychology Review, 34,* 267–286.

Morgan, D., & Jenson, W. R. (1988). *Teaching behaviorally disordered children: Preferred strategies.* Columbus, OH: Merrill Publisher.

Nicholas, P. (1998). *Teacher's and school psychologist's selection and used of classroom interventions for reducing behavioral excesses.* Unpublished doctoral dissertation, University of Utah, Salt Lake City.

Rhode, G., Morgan, D. P., & Young, R. K., (1983). Generalization and maintenance of treatment gains of behaviorally handicapped students from resource rooms to regular classrooms using self-evaluation procedures. *Journal of Applied Behavior Analysis, 16,* 171–188.

Walker, H. M., & Buckley, N. K. (1972). Programming generalization and maintenance of treatment effects across time and across settings. *Journal of Applied Behavior Analysis, 5,* 209–224.

Walker, H. M. & Rankin, R. (1983). Assessing the behavioral expectations and demands of less restrictive environments. *School Psychology Review, 12,* 274–284.

Evidence Base

The CD contains a file (Evidence_Base.pdf) that lists additional references to studies that demonstrate the effectiveness of the various strategies and techniques discussed in this book.

Individual Skill Cards

This appendix contains a set of 30 skill cards for use in implementing the Meeting Individual Teacher's Expectations component of the Tough Kid Generalization Model. See Chapter 5 for more details on how to implement this generalization component. Also note that the file Appendix_A.PDF found on the CD contains all materials needed to implement this program.

LISTEN

1

1. Look at the person who is talking (face, eyes).

2. Ask yourself, "What is being said?"

3. Nod your head up and down, and smile.

4. If you understand, say something like "I get it" or "I understand."

5. If you don't understand, raise your hand and ask a question. For example, say, "I don't understand. Could you explain it again?"

FOLLOW DIRECTIONS

2

1. Listen to the request.

2. Acknowledge the request. For example, say "OK" or "Yes," or move your head up and down.

3. Ask a question if you don't understand the request. For example, say, "I don't understand. Do you mean . . .?"

4. Follow the request quickly (within 3 to 5 seconds).

FOLLOW WRITTEN DIRECTIONS

3

1. Read the directions.

2. Ask yourself, "What do they mean?"

3. Read them again.

4. If you understand the directions, follow them.

5. If you don't understand, raise your hand and ask a question. For example, say, "I don't understand. Could you explain?"

PAY ATTENTION

4

1. Quietly look at the person who is talking (face, eyes).

2. Nod your head up and down, and smile.

3. Ask yourself, "What is being said?"

4. If you don't understand, raise your hand and ask a question. For example, say, "I don't understand. Can you explain it?"

BE PREPARED

5

1. Ask yourself, "What do I need?"

2. If you are unsure, ask an adult.

3. If you have trouble remembering, make a list (on paper or in your head).

4. Make sure everything is together in one place (in your notebook or backpack).

5. Ask yourself, "What have I forgotten?"

GET TO WORK

6

1. Ask yourself, "What do I need to do?"

2. If you are not sure, ask an adult.

3. Start your work.

4. Keep working until you are done or told to stop.

WORK QUIETLY

7

1. Ask yourself, "What do I need to do?"

2. If you are not sure, raise your hand and ask an adult.

3. Start your work without talking or making noises.

4. Keep still and do your work silently.

5. When you finish, wait quietly.

ASK FOR HELP

8

1. Decide what you need before you get the person's attention.

2. Decide if it is a good time to ask. Ask yourself, "Is the person busy?"

3. Approach the person, or raise your hand and say, "I need help."

4. Ask for help with a pleasant voice and smile.

    The Tough Kid Book • INDIVIDUAL SKILL CARDS

COMPLETE WORK ON TIME

9

1. Ask yourself, "When can I finish this work?"

2. Ask yourself, "When will it be due?"

3. If you are not sure, ask an adult.

4. Do your work quietly until it is done, and hand it in on time.

FOLLOW CLASSROOM RULES

10

1. Listen carefully when the rules are explained.

2. If you don't understand the rules, ask a question.

3. If the teacher says you broke a rule and you don't understand, ask the teacher, "What is the rule, and what did I do?"

4. Repeat the rules to yourself.

5. Follow the rules.

COMPLETE WORK

11

1. Ask yourself, "When will my work be done?"

2. Ask yourself, "How much work do I have to do?"

3. If you are not sure, ask an adult.

4. Do your work quietly until it is done, and hand it in on time.

PARTICIPATE IN A DISCUSSION

12

1. Ask yourself, "Should I join this discussion?"

2. If yes, listen to what others are saying.

3. Pick something to say.

4. Raise your hand and wait to be called on.

5. When called on, say what you want to say.

The Tough Kid Book • INDIVIDUAL SKILL CARDS

ACCEPT PRAISE

13

1. Decide if you have been praised.

2. Use a friendly voice and smile.

3. Say something like "Thank You" or "I appreciate that."

TALK WITH OTHERS

14

1. Pick someone to talk to.

2. Pick something to say (usually something the other person is interested in).

3. Smile and look the person in the face.

4. Start talking in a friendly voice.

MAKE A REQUEST

15

1. Decide what you want to ask before you get the person's attention.

2. Decide if it is a good time to ask. Ask yourself, "Is this person busy?"

3. Approach the person and say, "Can I ask you something?"

4. If the person says "Yes," make your request in a nice and friendly voice.

5. If the person says "No," say something like "OK, maybe later." Think of something else to do instead.

PARTICIPATE IN A GROUP

16

1. Understand the group rules. (If you don't understand, ask an adult.)

2. Listen to what others in the group are saying.

3. Look at people while they are talking and don't interrupt.

4. When it is your chance, say something in a friendly voice.

FOLLOW RULES ON THE SCHOOL PLAYGROUND

17

1. Ask what the playground rules are.

2. If you don't understand the rules, ask a question.

3. If an adult says you broke a rule and you don't understand, ask, "What is the rule, and what did I do?"

4. Repeat the school playground rules to yourself.

5. Follow the rules.

FOLLOW RULES IN THE HALLS AND BATHROOM

18

1. Ask what the hall and bathroom rules are.

2. If you don't understand the rules, ask a question.

3. If an adult says you broke a rule and you don't understand, ask, "What is the rule, and what did I do?"

4. Repeat the hall and bathroom rules to yourself.

5. Follow the rules.

BE POSITIVE AND FRIENDLY

19

1. Do the "Friendly Test" on yourself. Ask yourself, "Am I smiling and talking in a nice voice?"

2. Ask yourself, "Does the rest of my body look friendly?" (hands, feet, etc.)

3. Think of something positive and nice to say to the person. You might say, "Nice to see you," "You look cool," or "Let's hang out."

4. Say the positive and friendly thing to the person.

BE COOPERATIVE

20

1. Ask yourself, "What is being asked of me?"

2. If you don't understand, ask for an explanation.

3. Do it in a cheerful and friendly way.

GET AN ADULT'S ATTENTION

21

1. Decide what you want to tell or ask the adult.

2. Ask yourself, "Is the adult busy?"

3. If the adult is busy, wait until she stops for a moment.

4. Ask the adult, "Can I tell (ask) you something?"

5. If she says "Yes," go ahead. If she says "No," wait for a better time.

GET A PEER'S ATTENTION

22

1. Pick who you want to talk to.

2. Decide what you want to say or do.

3. Wait until the person is not busy or talking.

4. Look at the person and start talking in a friendly way.

GET ALONG ON THE PLAYGROUND

23

1. Ask yourself, "Do I understand the rules on the playground?"

2. If not, ask an adult about the rules and the expectations for getting along.

3. Find a buddy to hang out or play a game with.

4. Be cooperative with the other students. (Play games, share, take your turns.)

5. If there is a problem with another student, relax, ignore, and walk away. Find an adult and report the problem.

EXPRESS ANGER APPROPRIATELY

24

1. Don't react—relax first. Take a deep breath and count to ten.

2. Wait at least one second and tell the person why you are angry.

3. Try to not have an angry face and voice.

4. If the problem persists, ignore and walk away.

5. As a choice, you may want to talk with an adult about why you were angry and what happened.

The Tough Kid Book • INDIVIDUAL SKILL CARDS

USE APPROPRIATE LANGUAGE (NO SWEARING)

25

1. Ask yourself, "Do my words upset others?"

2. Ask yourself, "Is this a word I can use in school and with adults?"

3. If the language you use upsets others and should not be used in school, pick new words.

4. If you don't understand why the words you use upset others, ask an adult.

COMPETE IN THE CLASSROOM AND IN GROUPS

26

1. Ask yourself, "Is this a competitive activity?"

2. Ask yourself, "What are the rules?"

3. If you don't understand the activity or its rules, ask an adult.

4. Realize that someone will win and someone will lose. You can't always win.

5. Be a good sport. Don't complain, and compliment the winner.

RESIST PEER PRESSURE

27

1. Listen to what the other kid or kids want to do.

2. Decide if it will upset adults or hurt yourself or other kids.

3. Ask yourself, "What are the consequences? Do I really want to do this?"

4. If you decide not to go along, say "I can't do this because . . ."

5. Suggest something else to do. If this doesn't work, ignore and walk away.

DISAGREE

28

1. Ask yourself, "Do I disagree with this person?"

2. If yes, ask in a nice voice if you can tell your side.

3. Ask how or why the other person feels that way.

4. Listen to the other person with a positive face.

5. See if you can compromise or work out a deal that both of you feel good about.

ACCEPT "NO" FOR AN ANSWER

29

1. Ask yourself, "Why am I being told 'No'?"

2. Figure out some other choices. Ask yourself, "What else can I do?"

3. Pick the best choice and do it.

4. Don't argue.

ACCEPT CRITICISM OR A CONSEQUENCE

30

1. Ask yourself, "Was I wrong?"

2. If yes, say you were wrong and that you will try harder.

3. If you don't understand, say, "What else can I do?"

4. Accept the consequences or criticism with a neutral face and voice. Don't be angry, and don't argue.

5. Apologize in a sincere way.

APPENDIX B

The Tough Kid Teacher Pleaser Social Skills Program

" The Top 5 to Survive"

Social skills are words and actions that help you pass as normal when you are interacting with other people. The Tough Kid Teacher Pleaser Social Skills Program is a mini-program with just five skills. But these five skills are critical for making a good impression on adults. That is why we call them the "Top 5 to Survive." Without them, the Tough Kid will have a difficult time surviving and interacting with adults. When Tough Kids first return to a general education classroom in their neighborhood school, they generally go back with reputations for being noncompliant, argumentative, intrusive, and not very socially skilled. This program is designed to focus on these five essential social survival skills:

- Accepting "No" for an answer without arguing
- Following directions
- Not interrupting
- Making requests
- Thanking an adult

Tough Kids can learn the steps for each of these skills so that they can use them effectively when they return to the general education setting and when they interact with adults.

Instructions for Implementing the Group

It is a good idea to review a general social skills curriculum such as *The Tough Kid Social Skills Book* by Susan Sheridan (1996, 2010; available from Pacific Northwest Publishing) and use that program for these subcomponents:

- Behavior management interventions
- Motivational interventions
- Group procedures
- Progress-monitoring procedures
- Generalization procedures

FREQUENCY OF THE GROUP

Each skill in the Teacher Pleaser Program should be taught in a group session that runs approximately 45 minutes. Schedule a minimum of one session per week.

STEPS FOR RUNNING THE GROUP

 Review the group's homework assignment from the previous week.

 Introduce and define the new social skill. Go around the group and ask students to give you the definition.

STEP 3 Teach the steps to the skill.

STEP 4 Give an example of the skill. Ask the group to give you other examples.

STEP 5 Give a rationale for the skill. Ask the group to give other good reasons for using the skill.

 Give more examples of the skill. To illustrate the examples, use teachers, teacher aides, parents, siblings, peers, lunch staff, school office personnel, bus drivers, custodians, and others.

STEP 7 Give non-examples of the skill based on the previous skill examples.

STEP 8 Teach a behavioral variant of the social skill.

STEP 9 Do the teacher-directed role-plays with the students in the group or the group facilitators.

STEP 10 Review the definition of the skill, the rationale for using the skill, and the steps to the skill.

STEP 11 Assign homework that will be reviewed at the start of the next group session.

Accepting "No" for an Answer

Objective

Students will learn actions that promote positive social interactions with adults and learns skills for accepting "No" for an answer.

Note: This skill overlaps **Skill 29: Accept "No" for an Answer** in Meeting Individual Teacher's Expectations (Appendix A).

1 INTRODUCE THE GROUP
(5 minutes)

If students are not familiar with you or with each other, begin the session with introductions. Give your name and say one interesting thing about yourself. Go around the group and have students provide:

- Name
- Grade
- School (if different for all students)
- One thing to remember about them or one thing they are good at

2 INTRODUCE AND DEFINE THE SKILL
(2 minutes)

Define the skill **Accepting "No" for an Answer**:

Accepting "No" for an answer means that when you ask an adult (a teacher, for example) for something and that person says "No," you accept the "No" without arguing or getting upset.

Ask students to give you the definition.

(Continued)

3 TEACH STEPS TO THE SKILL
(2 minutes)

1. Ask yourself, "Why am I being told 'No'?"

2. Figure out some other choices. ("What else can I do?")

3. Pick the best choice and do it.

4. Don't argue.

4 PROVIDE AN EXAMPLE
(5 minutes)

Give the following example of the skill:

You want to play a video game on the computer during free time. Your teacher says "No."

You decide she told you "No" because someone else is using the computer. You decide to read your favorite magazine instead.

A good choice is to wait until the computer is free, then ask your teacher if you can use it. If she stills says "No," don't argue and continue your reading.

Ask the group to give you other examples.

5 PROVIDE A RATIONALE
(5 minutes)

Provide a rationale for the skill:

If you accept "No" for an answer, the person who said "No" is more likely to say "Yes" the next time you ask for something. If you argue about the "No," the person may become upset and deny your request the next time you ask for something.

Ask the group to give other good reasons for using the skill.

6 PROVIDE MORE EXAMPLES
(2 minutes)

Give more examples that illustrate the skill. Use a variety of adults in these examples—teachers, teacher aides, parents, siblings, peers, school office personnel, lunch staff, bus drivers, custodians, and others.

• You ask to get a drink at the hall water fountain. The teacher says, "No, not right now." You say, "OK. Maybe later?"

• You want to sit next to your friend in class. The teacher says "No." You say, "OK," and then ask, "Is this a privilege I could earn?"

• You want to be the teacher's aide, but your teacher says, "No, it is not your turn." You say, "OK. When will it be my turn?"

- At the start of class, you want to show your friends your favorite toy (rubber vomit). The teacher takes it away from you and says, "No, you can't have this in class." You ask, "Can I have it back after class to show my friends on the way home?"

7 PROVIDE NON-EXAMPLES
(2 minutes)

Non-examples are based on examples provided in Step 6 above. After each non-example, ask, "What's going to happen?"

- You tell the teacher you need a drink and can't wait. He says "No." You ignore him and go to the water fountain.

- You tell the teacher that you never get to sit with your friends and it's not fair. She still says "No." You begin to argue with her and tell her she's not fair with you.

- You say to the teacher, "It's never my turn. You like the other kids better than me!" Then you insist that you should be the aide.

- You get mad and tell the teacher that the toy (rubber vomit) is yours and he can't take it away. He says "No" and asks you to hand it to him. You refuse and walk away with the toy.

8 BEHAVIORAL VARIANT: NOT ARGUING AFTER BEING TOLD "NO"
(5 minutes)

Discuss how arguing after being told "No" only makes the situation worse

Discuss the different types of arguing:

- Saying it's not fair

- Repeatedly asking for reasons for "No"

- Getting mad and telling the teacher that you are going to do it anyway

- Ignoring the teacher's "No" and doing it anyway

(Continued)

9 TEACHER-DIRECTED ROLE-PLAY
(10 minutes)

CAUTION: If the students joke or become silly during the role-plays of **Accepting "No" for an Answer**, it undermines the lesson.

Have students in the group or the group facilitators role-play scenarios such as:

- Your teacher says, "No, you can't have free time. You have to finish your work first."

- You ask if you can be first in line. Your teacher says, "No, not right now."

- During math period, the teacher tells you, "No, stop drawing and finish your assignment."

- You want to ask your friend a question during the reading assignment. The teacher says, "No, there is no talking during silent reading."

10 REVIEW ACCEPTING "NO" FOR AN ANSWER
(5 minutes)

Review the skill definition, rationale, and steps.

DEFINITION: Accepting "No" for an answer means that when you ask an adult (e.g., a teacher) for something and he says "No," you accept the "No" without arguing or getting upset.

RATIONALE: The teacher is more likely to say "Yes" the next time you ask for something. If you argue about the "No," the teacher may become upset and deny your request the next time you ask for something.

STEPS for this skill are:

1. Ask yourself, "Why am I being told 'No'?"

2. Figure out some other choices. ("What else can I do?")

3. Pick the best choice and do it.

4. Don't argue

11 HOMEWORK
(2 minutes)

Have the students practice the skill during the week when they are told "No" by an adult. Tell them to remember what happens and how they handle it. At the beginning of the next social skills group, have all of the students report on their situation and how they handled it.

Following Directions

....

Objective

Students will learn actions that promote positive social interactions with adults and learn skills for following directions.

Note: This skill overlaps **Skill 2: Follow Directions** in Meeting Individual Teacher's Expectations (Appendix A).

1 REVIEW HOMEWORK FROM PREVIOUS SESSION
  (5 minutes)

Have all of the students report on the situation in which they practiced the skill for **Accepting "No" for an Answer** and how they handled it.

2 INTRODUCE AND DEFINE THE SKILL
(2 minutes)

Define the skill **Following Directions**:

Following directions means that when an adult gives you a request, you acknowledge the request and do it within a short period of time.

Ask students to give you the definition.

(Continued)

3 TEACH STEPS TO THE SKILL
(2 minutes)

1. Listen to the request

2. Acknowledge the request. (For example, say "OK" or "Yes," or move your head up and down.

3. Ask a question if you don't understand the request. For example, say, "I don't understand. Do you mean . . .?"

4. Follow the request quickly (within 3 to 5 seconds).

4 PROVIDE AN EXAMPLE
(5 minutes)

Give the following example of the skill:

Your teacher asks you to go sit down at your desk when you are talking with your friends. You listen and look at her as she is giving you the request. Then you say "OK" and go and sit down at your desk without delaying or wasting time.

Ask the group to give you other examples.

5 PROVIDE A RATIONALE
(5 minutes)

Provide a rationale for the skill:

If you follow someone's request the first time it is given, the person will be pleased with you and your

behavior. In the future when you ask for something, that person will be more likely to say "Yes."

Ask the group to give other good reasons for using the skill.

6 PROVIDE MORE EXAMPLES
(2 minutes)

Give more examples that illustrate the skill. Use a variety of adults in these examples—teachers, teacher aides, parents, siblings, peers, school office personnel, lunch staff, bus drivers, custodians, and others.

• Your teacher asks you to come in from recess, but you are having fun with your friends. You stop what you are doing and say, "I'm coming." Then you come in from recess.

• You are running down the hall in your school. An unknown adult says to you, "The school rule is to walk in the hallway. Please walk." You say, "OK, I'm walking now" and you start to walk down the hall.

• You are getting on the bus and the bus driver says to you, "Please take your seat so we can get going." You say, "OK, I'm finding one now." You find an empty seat and sit down.

• You are in the lunch line. The lunch lady says to you, "Please take what you need and move on so others can get something to eat." You say, "Yup, I'm getting it right now." You take what you want and move down the line.

7 PROVIDE NON-EXAMPLES
(2 minutes)

Non-examples are based on examples provided in Step 6 above. After each non-example, ask "What's going to happen?"

- You tell the teacher, "Wait a minute, I'm not finished," and go on playing with your friends.

- You tell the adult who asked you to walk, "You're not my boss." You keep running down the hall.

- You say to the bus driver, "Don't rush me." Then you ignore the driver while you look for a seat near your friends.

- You say to the lunch lady, "I can't decide, so don't tell me to hurry." You take your time selecting your next lunch item.

8 BEHAVIORAL VARIANT: USE "SURE I WILL"
(5 minutes)

The "Sure I Will" program (see **Chapter 3**) is used with Precision Requests.

When an adult makes a request of you, respond with "Sure I Will" and follow the request.

Vary the "Sure I Will" response with "Okee, dokee," "No problema," or "Happy to—just for you."

9 TEACHER-DIRECTED ROLE-PLAY
(10 minutes)

Be sure to socially reinforce students who are genuinely making an effort to role-play. Have students in the group or the group facilitators role-play scenarios such as:

- The teacher tells you to sit down and take your seat while you are telling your friends about a cool new video game.

- The custodian asks you to pick up some trash on the playground, even though you didn't do the littering.

- Your mom says you have to clean your room and hang up your clothes before you can go outside. But it's Saturday morning and your friends are waiting for you.

(Continued)

- Your teacher asks you to stop talking to your friends and finish your arithmetic assignment. But you weren't talking—it was the kid next to you.

10 REVIEW FOLLOWING DIRECTIONS
(5 minutes)

Review the skill definition, rationale, and steps.

DEFINITION: Following directions means that when an adult gives you a request, you acknowledge the request and follow it within a short period of time.

RATIONALE: If you follow an adult's request the first time it is made, that person will be pleased with you and your behavior. In the future when you ask for something, that person will be more likely to say "Yes."

STEPS for this skill are:

1. Listen to the request.

2. Acknowledge the request. (Say "OK" or "Yes," or move your head up and down.)

3. Ask questions if you don't understand the request. ("I don't understand. Do you want me to . . .?")

4. Follow the request quickly (within 3 to 5 seconds).

11 HOMEWORK
(2 minutes)

Ask the students to try the "Sure I Will" response to an adult request during the next week and remember how the adult reacts. At the beginning of the next social skills group, have all of the students report on their experiences.

Not Interrupting an Adult

....

Objective

Students will learn actions that promote positive social interactions with adults and learn skills for not interrupting.

Note: This skill overlaps **Skill 21: Get an Adult's Attention** in Meeting Individual Teacher's Expectations (Appendix A).

1 REVIEW HOMEWORK FROM PREVIOUS SESSION
 (5 minutes)

Have all of the students report on the situation in which they practiced the skill for **Following Directions** and how they handled it.

2 INTRODUCE AND DEFINE THE SKILL
(2 minutes)

Define the skill **Not Interrupting an Adult:**

Not interrupting happens when you want to tell an adult something or ask permission from an adult who is engaged or busy.

Instead of interrupting, you wait quietly until the adult is not busy and then speak to the adult.

Ask students to give you the definition.

(Continued)

 **TEACH STEPS TO THE SKILL**
(2 minutes)

1. Decide what you want to tell or ask the adult.

2. Ask yourself, "Is the adult busy doing something?"

3. If the adult is busy, wait until he stops for a moment.

4. Ask the adult, "Can I tell (ask) you something?"

5. If he says "Yes," go ahead. If he says "No," wait for a better time.

 **PROVIDE AN EXAMPLE**
(5 minutes)

Give the following example of the skill:

You want to ask permission to play a video game on the computer during free time.

Your teacher is talking with another adult who has come into the classroom. You ask yourself, "Is she busy?" The answer is "Yes." So, you wait until the teacher stops talking to the adult. When the teacher doesn't seem to be busy, you ask, "Can I ask you a question?" She says "Yes." Then you go ahead and ask if you can play the video game.

Ask the group to give you other examples.

 **PROVIDE A RATIONALE**
(5 minutes)

Provide a rationale for the skill:

If you interrupt adults when they are busy, they are likely to be annoyed with you. When you ask them something, they are likely to say "No." If you don't interrupt and instead wait until they are not busy to ask if you can ask them something, they will be more likely to say "Yes."

Ask the group to give other good reasons for using the skill.

6 PROVIDE MORE EXAMPLES
(2 minutes)

Give more examples that illustrate the skill. Use a variety of adults in these examples—teachers, teacher aides, parents, siblings, peers, school office personnel, lunch staff, bus drivers, custodians, and others.

• You have to tell the teacher that you forgot your lunch money and need to be put on the credit list. The teacher is busy lining up the class to go to lunch. Instead of interrupting him, you get in line and raise your hand. When he finishes lining everyone up, he calls on you. You ask to be put on the credit list.

• You really need to go to the restroom, but your teacher is talking to an adult in the classroom. You go up to the teacher and adult and wait. If they keep on talking to each other, raise your hand. If they still don't pay attention to you (and you really have to go), you say, "I'm sorry. I have an emergency and need to go to the restroom really fast."

- Your teacher sent you to the central office with a note for the secretary. The note says that you need to be released early to meet your mom and go to a doctor's appointment. When you get to the office, the secretary is behind the counter talking on the telephone. You stand close to the counter, smile, and make eye contact with the secretary. Wait until she is finished, and then ask permission to tell her something. When she says "Yes," give her the note and tell her you will be leaving school early that day.

- You are on the playground at recess. You need to tell the adult recess monitor that you have permission from your teacher to have a ball to play kickball. But the recess monitor is talking to another group of kids. You walk up to the recess monitor, wait until she stops talking, and ask if you can tell her something. Then ask for the ball to play the game.

7 PROVIDE NON-EXAMPLES
(5 minutes)

Non-examples are based on examples provided in Step 6 above. After each non-example, ask, "What's going to happen?"

- When the teacher is trying to line the class up to go to lunch, you get out of line without permission, go up to the teacher, and tell him you need to be put on the credit list.

- You say to your teacher, who is talking with the adult, "I've got an emergency and I'm going to the restroom." Without waiting for permission, you walk out of the classroom and go to the restroom.

- When you get to the office, you interrupt the secretary and tell her you have something important to tell her and it can't wait.

- You walk up to the recess monitor who is talking to other students and blurt out, "I have permission from my teacher to have a ball."

8 BEHAVIORAL VARIANT: NOT TALKING OUT IN CLASS WITHOUT PERMISSION
(5 minutes)

Discuss how talking out in class is like interrupting an adult, but instead you are interrupting the whole class.

Discuss the different types of talk-outs in class:

- Blurting out something without following classroom rules such as raise your hand and ask permission to speak

- Leaning on your desk and raising your hand, but wiggling or waving your hand in a disruptive way

- Getting out of your seat without permission while the teacher is teaching, going up to her, and interrupting the whole lesson

(Continued)

- Saying over and over, "Teacher, teacher, I have something to say," while the teacher is trying to teach a lesson

9 TEACHER-DIRECTED ROLE-PLAY
(10 minutes)

Make sure you reward students in the role-play who accurately follow all of the steps for **Not Interrupting an Adult**. Have students in the group or the group facilitators role-play scenarios such as:

- The teacher is busy grading papers at his desk. You need permission to work on the computer.

- Your teacher has sent you to tell the principal that you are the Office Aide for the week. You see the principal in the hall—she is taking a group of adults around your school for a tour.

- Your dad is trying to fix the kitchen sink. He seems busy and irritated that the pipes will not fit. You need to ask him permission to go to your friend's house and play.

- The teacher's aide is helping another student with an in-seat math assignment. You need help with your assignment, too.

10 REVIEW NOT INTERRUPTING AN ADULT
(5 minutes)

Review the skill definition, rationale, and steps.

DEFINITION: Not interrupting happens when you want to tell an adult something or ask permission from an adult when the adult is engaged or busy.

Instead of interrupting, you wait quietly until the adult is not busy, then speak to the adult.

RATIONALE: If you interrupt adults when they are busy, they are likely to be annoyed with you. When you ask them something, they are likely to say "No." If you wait until they are not busy and ask if you can ask them something, they are more likely to say "Yes."

STEPS for this skill are:

NOT INTERRUPTING AN ADULT • CONTINUED

1. Decide what you want to tell or ask the adult.

2. Ask yourself, "Is the adult busy doing something?"

3. If the adult is busy, wait until she stops for a moment.

4. Ask the adult, "Can I tell (ask) you something?"

5. If she says "Yes," go ahead. If she says "No," wait for a better time.

11 HOMEWORK
(5 minutes)

Have the students remember a time during the week when they need to tell or ask a busy adult something, but they don't interrupt. At the beginning of the next social skills group, have all of the students report on their experience and how they handled it.

Making a Request of an Adult

Objective

Students will learn actions that promote positive social interactions with adults and learn skills for making requests.

Note: This skill overlaps **Skill 15: Make a Request** in Meeting Individual Teacher's Expectations (Appendix A). The Behavioral Variant overlaps **Skill 8: Ask for Help**.

1 REVIEW HOMEWORK FROM PREVIOUS SESSION
(5 minutes)

Have all of the students report on the situation in which they practiced the skill for **Not Interrupting an Adult** and how they handled it.

2 INTRODUCE AND DEFINE THE SKILL
(2 minutes)

Define the skill **Making a Request of an Adult:**

Making a request of an adult means asking for something or for help in a polite and friendly voice.

Ask students to give you the definition.

3 TEACH STEPS TO THE SKILL
(2 minutes)

1. Decide what you want to ask before you get the adult's attention.

2. Decide if it is a good time to ask. Ask yourself, "Is this person busy?"

3. Approach the adult and say, "Can I ask you something?"

4. If the adult says "Yes," make your request in a nice and friendly voice.

5. If the adult says "No," say something like, "OK, maybe later." Then think of something else to do instead.

4 PROVIDE AN EXAMPLE
(5 minutes)

Give the following example of the skill:

You need help with your assignment because you don't understand the instructions.

When the teacher is not busy, you raise your hand (or approach his desk) and ask, "Can I get some help with this?" When he says "Yes," you say that you don't understand the instructions and ask him to explain it again.

Ask the group to give you other examples.

5 PROVIDE A RATIONALE
(5 minutes)

Provide a rationale for the skill:

If you make a request in a polite and friendly voice, the adult is more likely to say "Yes" or to help you. If you interrupt or ask in an unfriendly and unpleasant voice, the adult is more likely to say "No" or not help you.

Ask the group to give other good reasons for using the skill.

6 PROVIDE MORE EXAMPLES
(2 minutes)

Give more examples that illustrate the skill. Use a variety of adults in these examples—teachers, teacher aides, parents, siblings, peers, school office personnel, lunch staff, bus drivers, custodians, and others.

- You need to sharpen your pencil. The Class Rules say you have to ask permission to leave your seat. Your teacher is busy helping another student with an assignment. You wait until she is finished and she scans the classroom. You raise your hand. When she comes over to your desk, you smile and in a nice voice explain that your pencil has broken. You ask, "May I please go to the pencil sharpener?" She says "Yes."

(Continued)

- You are sitting at your desk in the classroom. The student behind you keeps pulling your hair and poking you in the back. You have asked him to stop, but he continues. You raise your hand. The classroom aide comes over to your desk and says, "What's wrong?" You tell the aide that the student behind you is bothering you so you can't work. The aide says to that student, "Stop bothering people or you will have to go to Think Time."

- You and your friends want to go to the mall and hang out, but you don't have permission or money. You ask your mom, "Can I go to the mall with my friends, and can I have five dollars? I'll mow the lawn when I get back." Your mom says "Sure" and gives you five dollars.

- You did your homework last night, but this morning you were so rushed that you left it on the kitchen table. You approach the teacher before class when he isn't busy and ask if you can tell him something. He says "Sure." You tell him you forgot your homework this morning because things were so busy. You ask if you can hand it in tomorrow. The teacher says, "You can hand it in tomorrow, but please don't forget again."

7 PROVIDE NON-EXAMPLES
(2 minutes)

Non-examples are based on examples provided in Step 6 above. After each non-example, ask "What's going to happen?"

- Your pencil broke and it's not your fault. The teacher is busy. You decide to get out of your seat without permission and go to the pencil sharpener.

- You tell the student behind you to stop bothering you, but he continues. You turn around in your seat and say in a very loud voice, "Leave me alone!"

- Without permission or telling your mom, you go to the mall. You have no money, so you try to borrow some from your friends.

- You decide not to tell the teacher and just hand in your homework tomorrow.

8 BEHAVIORAL VARIANT: ASKING AN ADULT FOR HELP
(5 minutes)

Most requests you make to adults are to either ask permission for something or ask for help. A request for help is very important because it means you don't understand something and need instruction or clarification to continue.

There are several variations for asking for help:

- Start the request with: "I don't understand. Can you help me?"

- Start the request with: "I'm not sure. Can you help me?"

- You dropped your tray in the lunch line and everyone is laughing at you. You are not sure what to do. How do you request help from the lunch lady?

- You just don't get how to do your math problem. You have already asked the classroom aide for help, but you still don't get it. How do you ask the aide again for help?

- Start the request with: "I didn't get it. Can you tell me again?"

- Start the request with: "I need help to . . ."

10 REVIEW MAKING A REQUEST OF AN ADULT
(5 minutes)

Review the skill definition, rationale, and steps.

DEFINITION: Making a request of an adult means to ask for something or for help in a polite and friendly voice.

RATIONALE: If you make a request with a polite and friendly voice, the adult is more likely to say "Yes" or help you. If you interrupt or ask in an unfriendly and unpleasant voice, the adult is more likely to say "No" or not help you.

STEPS for this skill are:

1. Decide what you want to ask before you get the adult's attention.

2. Decide if it is a good time to ask. (Is the adult busy?)

9 TEACHER-DIRECTED ROLE-PLAY
(10 minutes)

Be sure to socially reinforce students who use polite and friendly voices for their requests. Have students in the group or the group facilitators role-play scenarios such as:

- You didn't get the assignment that is being passed out in class. How do you get the teacher's attention and ask for the assignment?

- You are lost and don't know how to get home. You know your address, but are not sure how to get there. Then you see a mail carrier. How do you ask for help?

(Continued)

3. Approach the adult and say, "Can I ask you something?"

4. If the adult says "Yes," make your request in a nice and friendly voice

5. If the adult says "No," say something like, "OK, maybe later." Then think of something else to do instead.

11 HOMEWORK
(5 minutes)

Ask the students to think of one thing they would like to ask an adult in the coming week. List the requests and then assign each student the task of making his or her request. You can even role-play or practice the requests in the group. When they come back next week, have students tell what happened when they made their requests.

Saying "Thank You" to an Adult

....

Objective

Students will learn actions that promote positive social interactions with adults and learn skills for saying "Thank you."

1 REVIEW HOMEWORK FROM PREVIOUS SESSION
(5 minutes)

Have all of the students report on the situation in which they practiced the skill for **Making a Request of an Adult** and how they handled it.

2 INTRODUCE AND DEFINE THE SKILL
(2 minutes)

Define the skill **Saying "Thank You" to an Adult:**

When an adult says or does something for you that makes you feel good or helps you, then you say "Thank You" to the adult.

Ask students to give you the definition.

(Continued)

3 TEACH STEPS TO THE SKILL
(5 minutes)

1. Make the decision to thank someone.

2. Think about how you are going to say it. (It should be sincere, friendly, and genuine.)

3. Decide if it's a good time or if the person is busy.

4. Thank the person with a pleasant face and friendly voice.

4 PROVIDE AN EXAMPLE
(5 minutes)

Give the following example of the skill:

You are having trouble with the assignment the teacher has given you. You didn't get all the steps for solving the problems from her lecture. As you are sitting there, the classroom aide comes over to your desk and says, "I'll help you get through the first couple of problems. Let me show you the steps." When she finishes and is ready to leave your desk, you say, "Thank you so much. You were a big help."

Ask the group to give you other examples.

5 PROVIDE A RATIONALE
(5 minutes)

Provide a rationale for the skill.

If you give a friendly and genuine "Thank you" to an adult, that person is more likely to help you or give you permission in the future. If you don't say "Thank you," people might think that you didn't appreciate their help or permission and they might not give it in the future.

Ask the group to give other good reasons for using the skill.

6 PROVIDE MORE EXAMPLES
(2 minutes)

Give more examples that illustrate the skill. Use a variety of adults in these examples—teachers, teacher aides, parents, siblings, peers, school office personnel, lunch staff, bus drivers, custodians, and others.

• You ask your teacher if you can have extra free time if you finish your assignment early. She says you can. You say to her, "Thanks! This makes me want to get my work done."

• At the vending machine, you get a soda and open it. It fizzes and squirts all over the floor. The custodian comes over with a mop and rags and both of you clean up the mess. When you finish, you say to the custodian, "Thank you! It was a big mess and I didn't know how to clean it up."

SAYING "THANK YOU" TO AN ADULT • CONTINUED

- You can't seem to get your home computer to start up. Your older brother comes over and shows you the steps to get it to work. You say, "Thanks, bro—that's a big help."

- You drop your notebook. Papers spill all over the classroom floor. Your teacher helps you pick up your papers and organize them back into your notebook. You say to the teacher, "Thank you so much for helping me."

- After you finish cleaning up the mess with the custodian's help, you say, "Wow, that was a big mess," and walk back to the classroom.

- Your big brother helps you get the computer running. You say to him jokingly, "And now would you do my homework?"

- You take your notebook, ignore the teacher and her help, and just go back to your desk.

7 PROVIDE NON-EXAMPLES
(2 minutes)

Non-examples are based on examples provided in Step 6 above. After each non-example, ask, "What's going to happen?"

- You get permission for the free time and rush over to the activity center without saying anything to your teacher.

8 BEHAVIORAL VARIANT: GIVING A COMPLIMENT TO AN ADULT
(5 minutes)

Compliments and saying "Thank you" to adults are similar because you want to say something that makes them feel good and lets them know you appreciate them.

Sometimes compliments and a "Thank you" go together because when you finish saying "Thank you," you add a compliment at the end. Examples are:

- "Thank you. You really know how to do this!"

- "Thank you! You have this down to a science."

- "Thank you! How did you get so good at this?"

- "Thank you! I could never have done this without your help. You are great!"

(Continued)

9 TEACHER-DIRECTED ROLE-PLAY
(10 minutes)

Make sure you reward students in the role play who accurately follow all of the steps for **Saying "Thank You" to an Adult**. Have students in the group or the group facilitators role-play scenarios such as:

- You are in the school library and need information for an assignment. You ask the librarian to help, and he goes out of his way to help you get the information you need. How do you thank him with a compliment?

- You are lost in the school. An older student you don't know asks if he can help you find your classroom. How do you thank the older student?

- You are way behind in getting your homework done at home. Your mom sits down with you and helps you get it done. How do you thank her?

- You don't know the rules of a game. The recess monitor helps you learn the rules and play the game. How do you thank her with a compliment?

10 REVIEW SAYING "THANK YOU" TO AN ADULT
(5 minutes)

Review the skill definition, rationale, and steps.

DEFINITION: When an adult says or does something for you that makes you feel good or helps you, you say, "Thank you."

RATIONALE: If you give a friendly and genuine "Thank you" to an adult, the adult is more likely to help you or give you permission in the future. If you don't say "Thank you," the adult might think that you didn't appreciate the permission or help and might not give it in the future.

STEPS for this skill are:

1. Make the decision to thank someone.

2. Think about how you are going to say it. (It should be sincere, friendly, and genuine.)

3. Decide if it's a good time or if the person is busy.

4. Thank the person, using a pleasant face and friendly voice.

11 HOMEWORK
(2 minutes)

Ask the students to think of one person they would like to thank with a compliment during the coming week. List the people the students identify and then assign them the task of thanking that person. You can even role-play or practice the "Thank you" in the group. When students come back next week, have them tell about their experiences.

Additional Resources

The Tough Kid Bully Blockers Book: 15-Minute Lessons for Preventing and Reducing Bullying

Julie Bowen, Ph.D., Paula Ashcraft, Ph.D., William R. Jenson, Ph.D., and Ginger Rhode, Ph.D.

Tough Kids can be bullies, and they can also be victims of bullying. This positive and proactive program guides you through implementing a bully-blocking program in your school or classroom. A field-tested set of 15-minute lessons is designed to equip students—whether bullies, victims, or bystanders—with six skills to reverse bullying behavior. A companion CD includes reproducible posters, forms, homework assignments, and worksheets.

Bully Blocker Shorts

This compelling set of fast-hands videos demonstrates the six skills for preventing and reducing bullying presented in *The Tough Kid Bully Blocker Book*. *The Bully Blocker Shorts* stand alone, but are a perfect resource for previewing and reviewing skills taught in *The Tough Kid Bully Blocker Book*. You and your students will want to watch the Shorts over and over.

The Tough Kid Social Skills Book

Susan M. Sheridan

When students don't know how to resolve conflict, express frustration, or interact with others, they have difficulty with schoolwork and in their personal lives. This Tough Kid volume addresses ten specific social skills, including dealing with teasing, using self-control, solving arguments, and joining in. Improve the quality of your classroom and a student's chance to succeed in life. *The Tough Kid Social Skills Book* is a great place to start! Includes a CD of reproducible forms.